Budgerigars

Budgerigars

THE COLOUR REVOLUTION

Don Burke

Contents

Dedication

My wife Marea was the driving force behind me and she assisted me in creating a digestible book.

Bob Pitt, president of the Australian Heritage Budgerigar Association, provided constant support and access to his birds for photos.

I am very grateful to Roger van Delft and Benjamin Seyed, the major developers of Black Winged and Black Faced crosses.

Nigam Pandya in India has given much of his time and enlightened about the thousands of Budgerigar breeders in his country.

And lastly, I wish to pay homage to Steve Jobs for developing the iPhone, without which I would never have been able to get so many photos of varieties, breeding methods, illnesses, and all of the subtleties needed for readers to become a master breeder of Budgies.

Quote from Neville Cayley, from the introduction to *Budgerigars in Bush and Aviary* (1933):

"One of the chief charms of the Budgerigar is its small size. This places it in a class apart from other parrots. And being an Australian species it is the duty of Australians to combat and condemn any attempt that may be made to alter its size and so spoil one of the world's most beautiful parrots."

Why did I write this book?

"I am a pilgrim of the future on my way back from a journey made entirely in the past."
Pierre Teilhard de Chardin, palaeontologist and theologian, 1962

I have worked hard to try to write a readable book on Budgerigars. Usually, Budgerigar books are reference books for looking up specific things. Budgerigar books are not the sort of books that you can curl up in bed with.

My hope is that this collection of my life's experiences with Budgies will be fun reading (at least in parts) as well as a useful reference work for many Budgie breeders.

The Budgie world is changing, and smaller more colourful birds are deservedly taking over. There are ever better Rainbows, White Caps, Black Faced and Black Winged with stripes, and other combinations, plus Pastels and so many other new combinations. I have tried hard to collect a representative collection of photos of them.

Inside the front cover is a fold-out flap/bookmark which includes a glossary of many of the key technical words that you may encounter. This provides word meanings at hand as you move through the book. There is also a diagram of the parts of the budgerigar for easier reference. Hopefully as you meander through the pages, this will help rescue you from intimidating words along the way, particularly genetic 'monsterpieces'. For way too long a minority of people have used confusing genetic language to bluff poor readers into thinking that they are experts. I have tried to use as few confusing words as possible and to explain the meaning of the rest.

Most chapters have an 'At a Glimpse' box to begin with. If some information is a bit too nerdy, I have confined it to the chapters titled 'Master Class' at the back of the book, 'where the nerds meet'.

There is much new science in this book. Again, I have tried to make it accessible. Forgive me if I either fail, or if this is just self-indulgence.

I have also looked into the future to try to see where the Exhibition Budgie is heading. I fear that the large Modern Exhibition Budgie needs finessing quite a bit. It is in danger of becoming the French or English bulldog of the bird world. You may remember the BBC TV documentary titled *Pedigree Dogs Exposed* some years ago which led to a government inquiry and strict rules applied to dog clubs. Do we Budgie breeders want to risk that happening to us? Perhaps we should review the Modern Show Budgie to see if it is too big and wide and carries too much feathering. Its vision is impaired by directional feathers – a curious name in that this feathering in front of its eyes impairs its ability to know which **direction** it is actually heading in. These issues are expanded upon it this book as there is a clear need to modernise certain aspects of the Budgerigar world.

This is the first Budgie genetics book that I know of since *Genetics for Budgerigar Breeders* in 1961. I love that book, but I have chosen to examine it to see what errors are now evident. Its biggest errors are the absence of any references to hereditary modifiers, plus the understandable absence of the very new discovery of the electrome's role in gene control.

The hereditary modifier research that I have done over 40 years was frustrating and glacially slow to come together. Yet the brilliant Nobel Prize winning geneticist Barbara McClintock was into this in the year of my birth, 1947. Her fellow scientists forced her to abandon her non-gene heredity research because they thought that it was nonsense. Now there is abundant recent science to back it up, even if it hasn't filtered down to the Budgie world yet.

I have been lucky in that I had Australian Heritage Exhibition Budgies and Bush Budgies to cross with Modern Showbirds to find out the arcane hereditary mechanisms. Working out how long flight and tail feathers were created and transmitted was a frustrating 20 years of my life. Even discovering wing pattern types 1 and 2 was bewildering and confusing. Genes are obvious and consistent, but modifiers are disappearingly erratic and almost never constant, unless you can do advanced DNA laboratory research – which I am not in a position to do.

Hence the Teilhard de Chardin quote above.

Don Burke

Introduction

Budgerigars: the Colour Revolution

The Budgerigar is the world's most popular pet bird, and deservedly so.
- It makes a wonderful pet when hand-raised from a baby, quickly becoming one of the family.
- It can mimic the human voice.
- It is robust and very easy to care for.
- It is a very cheap pet to buy.
- It breeds easily in large numbers.
- It is available in a vast number of beautiful colours.
- It is a superb competitive exhibition bird.
- It is a perfect fast-breeding bird for learning the science of genetics.
- And it is a breeder's dream for creating ever newer and more artistic colour combinations.

Left: Dog, cat, fish and Budgie are the world's most popular pets. Arguably, the Budgerigar is the prettiest of the lot. They are cheery, inquisitive and very intelligent. This is a new variety: a baby Golden Top Rainbow.

This book looks at the Budgerigar in the era of the smartphone: the social media world and beyond. The Modern Budgerigar competes for family time and love with the new fashionable pets such as 'designer dogs' which are a brilliant advance on pedigree dogs of the past. The Cavoodle (Cavalier King Charles Spaniel x Poodle) is a living teddy bear that loves a cuddle and is always happy. It helped so many people through the Covid pandemic. But then, so did the cheery Budgie. They are inquisitive and always putting on a show: the perfect low-maintenance companion for life in the modern world. We will also look at what we have done with and to this tiny miracle. Have we been good or bad masters.

The Budgerigar too is changing. They have gone from tiny wild-type Budgie pets, to colourful companions so loved by HRH Queen Elizabeth II, to exhibition trophy winners, and now to the spectacularly colourful modern acrobats of the Asian era. Asian breeders have long been among the world's best animal and plant breeders. They have turned to breeding colourful Budgerigars in the new millennium and the results are magnificent. Their Rainbow Budgerigars have transfixed millions of people all over the world. Breeders in India, Pakistan, China, Japan, Bangladesh, and on into Iraq, Iran and the Arab counties of North Africa such as Algeria, as well as Mexico, are deeply committed to their precious little friends.

Vast numbers of Wild Budgies swarm above our red desert sands. These murmurations often extend from horizon to horizon. Photo: Science Photo Library.

Wild Budgies swarming past a termite nest. Photo: Joshua Brunner.

From a Wild Budgie (below) to a giant Modern Showbird today (right). We should never forget the charm and beauty of the tiny Wild Budgie.

Of course, the Budgerigar began its conquering of the world in its native Australia. In murmurations of millions of Budgies, Australia's harsh red deserts are their homes. The sight of perhaps a million Budgies soaring overhead, covering the sky from horizon to horizon is a joyous and astonishing realisation that not all of our Earth's precious animals are dying out. Having said that, Budgies live a boom-and-bust life in the wild:

they breed in millions in good (i.e. wet) years and die in millions in bad years. Farmers have been known to shovel truck loads of dead Budgies from farm sheds where the poor birds were trying to escape from the dry, 50°C desert heat. Life is cheap for Wild Budgies.

Nonetheless, human interference in Budgerigar habitat has created a paradise for Australia's tiny treasure. Each and every farm dam across the deserts of Australia's arid interior represents a precious pit-stop for this long-distance nomad which used to streak as much as a hundred kilometres for a drink. Budgies are aerial acrobats that have the need for speed and also the need for seed.

The beautifully coloured Budgerigar has evolved into a placid pet that loves being in a cage. This is an Amethyst.

Many of my Budgies that were not hand-raised come to me to play when I enter their aviaries. They preen my hair and perch all over me. Like dogs, many Budgies seem to prefer people to members of their own species.

I can never forget the day at Dubbo (in inland New South Wales) when Marea and I quietly eased our car in among a flock of Wild Budgies cavorting along a local creek lined with River Red Gums. There were hollow branches full of young Budgies and there were plenty of grass seeds to eat. Still the Budgies had time to wander over for a peek at us. They landed on the car and curiously stared in at us through open windows. This was a mesmerising moment for us.

Of the 800 or so Aboriginal languages and dialects across Australia, the word Budgerigar was one that was remembered – maybe derived from Betcherrygah or similar. And it meant 'good eating'. Living in a Death Valley-like environment, knowing what could be eaten meant survival. Aboriginal kids used to climb trees with a stick to rake out young Budgies, then scorch the feathers off them in the fire. Manna from red gums.

With fat bellies from too much fast food, it is hard for us today to understand eating such intelligent and friendly little cuties. But needs must. Remember the explorers Burke and Wills starved to death in the desert because they couldn't survive on what the Aboriginal people could – despite the Aboriginals giving them food. Budgies have gone from a source of food to special friends and companions.

Today, enthusiasts all over the world are breeding ever more colourful new varieties of Budgies. Modern breeders can dream up a colour combination and produce it in Budgies in a short period. There are even Hagoromo Budgies that look like twin-rotor helicopters.

These are some of my Clearwing Budgies. Happy and ready to breed.

From my experience, Budgies like living in captivity. When a 20m tall gum tree fell on my ten by eight metre aviary full of approximately 100 captive-raised wild Budgies, about 50 remained in the aviary even though two enormous walls were gone. I opened the door into an adjoining aviary, leaving them the options to either go bush or stay. All of the 50 roared into the next aviary, but the other 50 had made the dash for freedom before I had arrived. They returned the following morning!

There are so many varieties of Budgies yet to develop, such as the Ultraviolet Budgies below. Photographed under black UV lighting.

Glow in the dark Budgies!

These two new mutation Budgies are White Caps put under black ultraviolet lighting. In daylight, they look nothing like this. See pages 139–145.

The front bird has an amazing amount of yellow UV facial fluorescence, and on its forehead it is white rather than yellow.

One day we will have UV classes at Budgerigar exhibitions. Just imagine how much fun the kids would have with that!

There is so much more fun to be had with our tiny Budgie friends. Please join us.

Budgerigar varieties

Clearbodies

Darkwings: the world's first Clearbodies

Australia produced the world's first Clearbody Budgerigars way back in 1930. Not only that, but around 1962 a Black Winged Yellow (then incorrectly known as a Greywing Yellow) won Champion of the NSW State Show at Sydney Town Hall. The winning bird had a dazzling

> **At a Glance**
>
> The Darkwing is the world's first Clearbody. It is a Black Eyed Yellow or Black Eyed White with a semi-dominant mutation that re-darkens the wings.

pure yellow body with an inky-black wing colour and I believe that it belonged to Frank Amos. This is arguably the greatest Budgerigar breeding triumph in Australia's history. Today, these birds are known as Darkwings. Genetically they are Black Eyed Yellows or Black Eyed Whites with **dark wings**. I fell in love with them at first sight and began breeding them in 1959. It is a variety seen only in Australia.

The Texas Clearbody turned up in 1950, and later on in 1955 the Easley Clearbody also came along. Our Australian Darkwing mutation was around in 1930! All this became clearer when my wife Marea gave me a copy of Neville Cayley's *Budgerigars in Bush and Aviary* for Christmas. It was the 1935 second edition of this book, which was first published in 1933. This book is dazzlingly insightful for its time.

Cayley refers to Black Winged Yellows, Black Winged Whites, Greywing Yellows and Greywing Whites as "in

Left is one of my early Heritage 'Greywing' Yellows. It actually is a Black Winged Yellow Darkwing. When I first began breeding them, they were, in effect, very pretty Bush Budgies.

existence, and probably will be established in the near future." That is, too rare to be seen as an established variety in 1933 (it's curious to note that the variety is still on the verge of extinction today). Cinnamonwing Yellows and Whites are mentioned as established varieties. This was due to the fact that almost all Black Eyed Yellows were Cinnamonwings since Cinnamonwing Dilutes the wing and body colour even more (i.e. it makes the Black Eyed Yellows even yellower). The Cinnamonwing Yellows were developed around 1930. It astounded me that way back then Cayley noted that: "some recognised authorities (stated) that yellow or white cannot carry the Greywing factor." That is, that even in 1933, genetics experts correctly denied that a Greywing Yellow or White could exist. Those experts were proven correct by Ken Yorke in 1997. Ken discovered that the Darkwing is a Black Eyed Yellow or White with an added dominant gene for re-darkening the wings to create a Clearbody. It occurs in Cinnamonwing and Normal (i.e. Black Winged) forms. The Black Winged form of the Darkwing looks a bit greyish, hence the name 'Greywing Yellow'.

Left: One of my early Heritage so-called 'Greywing' Whites: in reality it is a Black Winged White Darkwing. It is quite easy to intensify the wing markings to an inky black colour.

Today, the Darkwing is slowly being bred up again. It is hardly a common bird, but it does have some dedicated supporters. Darkwings, Black Eyed Yellows and Black Eyed Whites form a precious and interlinked group; all are Australian, very beautiful and well worth saving. To breed Darkwings, you must base your breeding on a really good strain of Black Eyed Yellows or Whites. That is, most matings are Darkwing to Black Eyed Yellow or White.

Left: This is a six-month-old male Darkwing Cinnamon (Sky) White. He too is a large bird. Most of his wing is not moulted out. Only the scapulars are adult colour. The (Grey) White Darkwing above is his aunt.

Right: This is one of my Modern Cinnamonwing (Grey) White Darkwings. She is very much the size of winning Modern Exhibition Normals.

Black Eyed Whites are also starting to be bred with Modern Exhibition qualities. This has been a difficult variety to develop, but good birds are around now. Black Eyed Whites and Yellows are the essential base variety for producing Darkwings.

We have come a long, long way with the Darkwing. Below are examples of my original, primitive Darkwings.

Right: This large female Modern Black Eyed White is one of my best birds.

Below: an old-fashioned Black Eyed Yellow with three Cinnamonwing White Darkwings. These three female Darkwings that I bred are the birds that I used as the foundation stock that led to the production of my Modern Darkwings, such as the female Modern Cinnamonwing White Darkwing and the male Modern Cinnamonwing White Darkwing shown in this section. This has been a long, hard labour of love.

A prediction from the past … The illustration on the left is from M. Armour's 1951 book, *Exhibition Budgerigars*. He says in the caption:

"The highly attractive cock portrayed, a Laced Yellow, is a possible bird of the future."

Clearly, he was unaware that 'Greywing Yellows', which can have black wings and a yellow body colour, had existed in Australia since 1933, a full 18 years before his book was published! Note that his 'Laced Yellow' appears to be an Opaline.

Darkwing breeding expectations

Darkwings are a **modifier-based** variety like Black Eyed Yellows and Whites, Clearwings and Banded Pieds, thus Normal breeding charts are largely unhelpful.

All Darkwings are, at base, either Black Eyed Yellows or Black Eyed Whites. That is, they are a compound variety. The Darkwing mutation re-darkens the wings on Black Eyed Whites and Yellows, Greywings, Clearwings and Dilutes. So far as we know, it does not affect any other variety. When combined with Black Eyed Yellows and Whites, the result is the Darkwing variety that we see on the showbench. Darkwing is a semi-dominant variety, with the Single Factor birds being of a lighter wing colour than the Double Factor Darkwings. A genuine Darkwing **Black Winged** Yellow or White must be a Double Factor bird.

Almost all Darkwings are Single Factor birds, so if you cross a Single Factor Darkwing to a Single Factor Darkwing you get 50% Single Factor Darkwings, 25% Double Factor Darkwings and 25% Black Eyed Yellows or Black Eyed Whites.

Single Factor mated to Double Factor produces 50% of each type in the progeny.

Double Factor mated to Double Factor produces 100% Double Factor young.

Single Factor Darkwing mated to Black Eyed Whites and Yellows produces 50% of each in the progeny.

Double Factor Darkwing mated to Black Eyed Whites and Yellows produces 100% Single Factor Darkwings.

Single Factor Darkwing mated to Normal produces 100% Normals split for Black Eyed Whites and Yellows, of which 50% are also split for Darkwing.

Double Factor Darkwing mated to Normal produces 100% Normals split for **both** Darkwing and Black Eyed Whites and Yellows.

The devil in the detail

The real challenge in Darkwings is the Black Eyed Whites and Yellows issue: that is, that Black Eyed Whites and Yellows are not a mutation as such. Dilute is the mutation which can be modified into pure white or yellow, which we then call a Black Eyed White or a Black Eyed Yellow. The modifiers are innately complex and unstable – they do not act in a simple dominant or recessive mode; instead you get blending inheritance. Put another way, outcrossing Darkwings or Black Eyed Whites and Yellows to Normals does enormous damage to their colour. Black Eyed Whites and Yellows suffer both wing and body colour darkening (i.e. suffusion), but Darkwings mostly just suffer body colour darkening. This damage takes a talented breeder about five generations to largely conquer, if you don't outcross again.

For the purists

Strictly speaking, Darkwing is not dominant to Black Eyed. These two mutations act independently of each other, that is, all Darkwings are Double Factor Black Eyed

Whites and Yellows regardless of whether they carry one or two Darkwing genes. Put technically, the Darkwing gene is not a multiple allele of Dilute, Greywing or Clearwing. For that matter, Clearwing is not a mutation at all: it is just a heavily modified Greywing. The mistaken belief that Clearwing is a separate mutation is the root cause of the poor colour in Modern Clearwings worldwide.

Easley Clearbodies

At a Glance

Easley Clearbodies must be the easiest and by far the best Clearbody to breed. In a Normal, the body is ideally white or yellow and the wing black. It can occur in most varieties including Cinnamonwings, Opalines, etc. It is a simple dominant mutation, with the Double Factor bird having slightly better colour all over: i.e. a lighter body colour and a darker wing colour. Below left is a Hagoromo Easley Clearbody, possibly a Greygreen.

Easley Clearbody Hagoromo.
Photo: Shaykh Abeed Hasan.

Easley Clearbody Opaline Cinnamon
Sky Blue. Photo: Kevin Eatwell.

Texas Clearbodies

You could argue that the Texas Clearbody has the greatest potential for spectacular yet subtle colour development of all Budgie varieties. Sometimes, the name of a variety restricts the imagination of breeders. This Clearbody has the potential for breathtakingly soft violet body colour and much more. The body could perhaps be a soft, glowing palette of new colours rather than just being totally clear of colour.

This is a recessive sex-linked mutation, but somehow its unexpected popping up from dads that are split for Texas Clearbody is always a welcome moment. To selectively breed for a totally white or yellow body with black wings would be a tragedy.

Texas Clearbodies have black, brown or grey coloured wing markings with pale body colour. They come in green or blue colours plus all Golden Faced and Yellow Faced varieties, and White Caps as well. The wing markings are an irregular mix of black and grey colours. The flight feathers are an irregular streaky pale grey.

As a recessive sex-linked variety, females can never be split for Texas Clearbody, they are either visual Texas Clearbodies or non-Texas Clearbodies. But the males can be a Texas Clearbody, or split for Texas Clearbody, or a non-Texas Clearbody. Thus you can mate two visual Normals together and around half of the young females will be Texas Clearbodies because dad is split for Texas Clearbody.

Some countries just call them 'Clearbodies' but this leads to confusion because there are Easley Clearbodies as well.

See Sex linkage on page 185 for more information.

Left: a Normal Violet Texas Clearbody.
Below: a Sky Normal Texas Clearbody.

Crested Budgerigars

Crested Budgerigars – a new whorled view

When I started to breed Crested Budgerigars in 1958 I was 11 years old. The only other person who was keen to breed them was Cec Fulton, who lived about 2km from me. He had collected some but, from memory, had not produced much in the way of birds with crests.

I managed to breed a lot of them, mostly Clearwings, that were top show birds, although not eligible for any major awards due to their status as an 'Any Other Variety' type of Budgerigar. I produced them in Normal and Australian Yellow Faced Blues as well.

In 1963 I published a preliminary article on the genetic basis of the variety (BSA journal *Budgerigar*, August 1963). The article had been rejected for two years as being of no interest, but finally a very abbreviated and jumbled version was published. The reason I wrote it was that not enough crests were being produced by my birds. I kept careful records which indicated that one gene at least seemed to be involved, but it didn't work as genes should. So I tried to develop a theory that explained the poor penetrance of the crest gene (i.e. the low numbers of Crested young). All that I could think of was a gene for crest and another gene that collaborated in crest formation. I invited others to help with 'comparing notes', but no one ever replied. No one wanted Crested Budgies, so when I married in 1969, they were sold as a curiosity to a few pet bird keepers. I did offer them all, free, to exhibition breeders, but at the time new varieties, especially Cresteds, weren't wanted. Then, as now, if breeders can't win a trophy, they won't breed it.

In 1960 I had sent my provisional theory, based on my experimental results, to the Crested Budgerigar keepers of the day in the UK.

My original theory, published when I was 16 years of age, needs major revision: it was not correct as first published. Many new genetic discoveries have been made since 1963 but no really new or useful theory on crest inheritance has arisen since 1963, so I thought that it was time to look at the subject matter, 50 years later.

To start with what we knew in 1963:

Crest inheritance is problematic; you just don't get the sort of numbers of crests that any single-gene theory would predict.

This sort of confusing result is sometimes left in the 'too hard' basket, labelled with vague terms like 'incomplete penetrance' of the gene involved. What this means is, we don't know how it works. That is, a precise theory to explain the strange behaviours of the gene or genes involved is yet to come.

The new discovery of the **ELECTROME** shaping the development of all animals finally solves all of these problems. We now are reasonably confident that the electrome controls both placement and the shape of crests, including Hagoromos.

The big advance

Over the last 50 years, statistics on the numbers of Crested progeny vs. non-Crested (crest-bred) progeny have been developed. Useful statistics exist on percentages of Full Circular, Half Circular, Tufted and Crested bred progeny from crest matings.

Thanks to those who recorded these statistics, including Ken Yorke, Rob Hugo, the Crested Budgerigar Club of Australia, Jackie Jansen, the Crested Budgerigar Club UK and A.F. Fullilove. Thanks also go to George Clarke, who collated the figures.

Let's start again

Firstly, it is clear to me now that what we call Crested Budgies aren't crested at all.

They exhibit feather whorls, which are common all over mammals (hair whorls) and on the heads of some (if not all) wild bird species. Whorls are mechanisms to radiate the angles of feather or hair growth to allow for changes in shape or angles of the animal itself. We all have a whorl on the back of our heads. This permits the hair to grow forward, backward and to both sides. If you didn't have the whorl, the hair on the back of your head and neck would grow upwards! Humans also have hair whorls on their backs, chests, etc – these are more visible in hairy males.

In mammals, hair whorls force the coat to lay flat on the animal and also to shed water when the coat is wet. In birds, feather whorls exist overwhelmingly for streamlining so that the bird can fly fast. Whorls also act to shed rainwater.

I am now confident that all birds have a huge whorl in the centre of their faces, centred under the cere. Even though this central 'dot' is invisible, it directs all facial feathers to grow radially outwards and backwards from the dot, hugging the face.

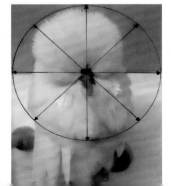

Left: This diagram shows the centre of the whorl underneath the cere. Notice how all feathers grow radially outwards and backwards from the central dot, covering the forehead right around to the mask.

This creates the perfect aerodynamic shape when in flight, like the front of an aeroplane.

Duplications of this facial whorl produce conventional crests as well as Hagoromos as we know them.

Left: If you look carefully at this pin-feather stage young Albino Budgie on the left, you can see that all the facial feathering appears to grow outwards radially from a spot in the central notch in the top of the cere.

To prove my theory, I thought that if it is correct, some parrots might have the central dot of their facial whorl visible. So I searched through hundreds of photos of parrots to see if a central dot was visible on any. It took me many hours, but sure enough, I found that wild Monk Parakeets do have the central dot showing. AND, the final proof was that the feathers below the dot grow downwards over the cere as any crest (whorl) would do.

Monk or Quaker Parakeets. Photo: Christopher DeNatale.

Whorls exist in 100% of normal wild parrots of certain species (if not of all wild bird species). That is, what we call a crest can be 100% penetrant. Had crest breeders looked up 'genetic whorls' in books or on Google, they would have had the answers many years ago.

All birds also have a whorl on the point of each scapular (wing butt) to get the wing feathers to mould around this complex moving shape. The pin feathers on this baby show this very well.

A true crest, as on a Sulphur-crested Cockatoo (and most other cockatoo species), features much longer feathers on the head which are erectile and which face

backwards. They can erect them at will. These feathers are never whorls – due to the aerodynamic problems associated with whorls. At speed, Budgie whorls would buffet the birds' heads around considerably. The erectile crest on a Sulphur-crested Cockatoo, however, can be pulled down to prevent aerodynamic problems.

Left: Sulphur-Crested Cockatoo.

Right: If you think about it, the 'blow' (i.e. the erect feathers) on a modern Budgie's forehead is an erectile structure with elongated feathers. That is, it perfectly fits the definition of a true crest. What we call crests are correctly called whorls.

What about the electrome? This discovery is absolutely amazing. Every cell in all animals and plants is a battery. The initial blueprint immediately after fertilisation is an electronic structure which lays out everything, where eyes, legs, hands, everything, goes. Then it creates bones, muscles, etc, on the framework.

Clearly the electrome has a locking mechanism to prevent whorls appearing in the wrong areas. That is, a genetic system to prevent whorls that occur in areas which would upset the basic aerodynamics of a bird. A genetic insurance policy if you like. See Sally Adee's article 'You are electric' in *New Scientist* magazine on 25 February 2023.

An area mechanism is essential. That is, a hereditary system which locates and pins down exactly where the central 'dot' of whorls occur is always needed. This system controls where all whorls, including complex ones like Hagoromos develop. It also explains why some Hagoromos are 'Star Gazers'. That is, they have severe neurological disorders. The formation of the head or neck crest in some Hagoromos damages the

brain during early development. This has largely been gotten rid of by the skilled breeders (see Hagoromos, page 26).

Left: Japanese Helicopter Crest, a.k.a. Hagoromo. Note the full-circular head crest too. These are all caused by the same mechanism.

The electrome controls many genes that produce the details in animals and plants.

So, with Tandem Repeats and many other modifiers also in control, genes are playing an ever-shrinking role in evolution and the domestication of plants and animals. And Mendel's neat mathematics may not apply. That is, crests may never comply with the ratios of Crested young that we expect.

Since genes are not major players in the game of whorls, strange things happen. For instance, the position of whorls on the facial areas of horses and cattle is a reliable indicator of temperament and intelligence.

Right: Cattle with facial hair whorls high on the forehead are more likely to panic when restrained compared to those with lower facial hair whorls.

What can we put forward as the 2024 theoretical basis for whorls?

Whorls of hair or feathers occur during the embryological development of babies. They are largely controlled by the electrome which organises the genes. Thus we can't expect precise results from whorl matings. For instance, when scientists raised 15 or 20 'identical' cloned Friesian cows, the white markings were different on all of them. Even though they were all genetically identical! Equally, identical human twins often have different hair whorls on their heads. Sometimes the whorls are clockwise in one twin and anticlockwise in the other. But there are still the statistics which are helpful. So here we go:

FC = Full Crest.

HC = Half Crest.

T = Tufted.

M = Multi Crested.

N = Normal with no known crest predecessors.

CB = Crest Bred (but not visually crested.

Mating	Percentage of progeny					
	Visual	CB	T	HC	FC	M
FC x FC	63%	38%	19%	13%	31%	0%
FC x HC	54%	46%	19%	17%	17%	0%
HC x HC	63%	37%	22%	15%	26%	0%
FC x T	66%	34%	28%	12%	26%	0.5%
HC x T	62%	38%	23%	15%	20%	5%
T x T	48%	52%	31%	7%	9%	0.6%
FC x CB	45%	55%	23%	9%	11%	2.3%
HC x CB	35%	65%	20%	8%	7%	0%
T x CB	28%	72%	19%	4.6%	4.3%	0.6%
CB x CB	13%	87%	11%	0%	1.9%	0%
FC x N	23%	77%	20%	1.2%	2.4%	0%
HC x N	11%	89%	10%	0.9%	0%	0%
T x N	15%	85%	13%	2%	0.2%	0%
CB x N	1%	99%	1%	0%	0%	0%

Thanks to the late Rob Hugo and the Budgerigar Club of Western Australia for access to their assistance. Also to Nola Bradford for the use of her photos.

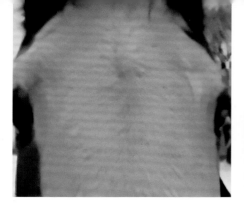

Higher whorls also meant slightly higher intelligence. Similar results were found in scientific tests with horses. Whorls also were linked to many other bodily processes including sperm production, left handedness, etc.

The nature of the whorls on a dog's chest indicate greater or lesser intelligence or trainability. A lot of research exists now to relate whorls to IQ, mental disorders, sperm production, left or right handedness, homosexuality, size at maturity, etc.

Hagoromos

There are mechanisms in almost all animals that create two of many parts: two eyes, two wings, two feet, two ears and so on. It is called bilateral symmetry. So as the group of crests encountered the shoulders, they are forced to divide into two to form the rotors. All of this is almost certainly controlled by the electrome (for more on the electrome, see pages 19 to 28).

Early Hagoromos had messy rotors and there were major neurological problems as well. Very skilled breeders in the Middle East through to India, Pakistan and surrounding areas mostly bred these characteristics out. The neurological disorders occur when the brain and skull are interfered with by the whorl developments nearby. The

Right: Yellow Lutino Hagoromo.
Photo: Shaykh Abeed Hasan.

Hagoromos are a group of crests, a.k.a whorls. Hagoromos are the most elaborate form of crest/whorl since they are a series of crests starting at the front of the head and forming a ridge all the way down the back of the neck to the wings. When the crests reach the wings, they form a duo of crests much as the wings are also twin structures. As we have seen in the crests/whorls section, there is also a pair of whorls on the tip of the shoulders of the wings of all birds as well to create a three dimensional aerodynamic shape.

Above: Black Winged Grey Hagoromo.
Photo: Osama Gomaa.

affected birds are sometimes called 'star gazers' because their heads twirl around, and the bird seems to be looking to the heavens. It is essential that all breeders continue to cull such birds to avoid breeding dysfunctional Budgies.

Because the multiple whorls are controlled by the electrome, they form one extended unit. That is, all of those whorls (head to wings) form one entity. Thus the genetic statistics on full circle crest/whorl production on page 25 loosely apply to Hagoromos. Maybe treat Hagoromos as Full Crests genetically. Breeding them is NOW much easier: all that you need to do is to select for symmetrical rotors and whorls plus freedom from neurological problems or unbalanced behaviour.

Obviously you just keep mating

Right: Violet Rainbow Hagoromo.
Photo: Osama Gomaa.

Hagoromos to Hagoromos, or Hagoromos to Hagoromo-bred birds until you produce perfect Hagoromos. The electrome is very efficient at aligning and regulating animal bodies since that is its basic function in life, so much of your work in breeding perfect Hagoromos is done for you automatically.

Genes play almost no part in whorls or crests of any type. If a gene is involved, it is controlled by the electrome.

Above: Perhaps a Spangle Greygreen Black Winged Hagoromo. Photo: Shaykh Abeed Hasan.

Right: Texas Clearbody Hagoromo.

Dilutes, Clearwings and Greywings

Black Eyed Whites and Black Eyed Yellows

Which variety of Budgie do you think is the hardest to breed? Certainly, Fallows are hard to breed – super-modern Fallows are very rare indeed. Clearwings are hard to breed with super contrasting colour between wings and body, PLUS modern feather and type. But in my experience, it is the Black Eyed White that wins the prize for the all-time nightmare to perfect. While it is dead easy to breed a stunning Dilute, it is impossible to breed a really modern Black Eyed White with pure white colour. It is clear to me that both the white body colour and the clear white wing colour have been linked to poor feather quality for more than 70 years.

In particular poor head feathering, including short mask feathering and poor directional feathering, seems to have been tightly bound to pure white colouring. This is true to a lesser degree with Black Eyed Yellows, so while difficult, Black Eyed Yellows are much easier to breed than the Black Eyed Whites. So much so that, to the best of my knowledge, there has never been a truly great Black Eyed White. No Black Eyed White has ever won Champion of Show so far as I know.

For the record, I bred and exhibited Black Eyed Yellows in the late 1950s and into the 1960s and as a teenager won a number of major Open awards with them, including Best Opposite Sex in show, etc. They were easy to breed then. Yellows were bred to a high quality from the 1940s onwards: **but** there were **never** any even halfway decent Black Eyed Whites. None of the quality Black Eyed Yellows that I know of ever produced any Whites, since they were all homozygous Yellows – never split for White. The reason for this is simple – homozygous Yellows are a much deeper, brilliant shade of yellow. This deep yellow conveniently hides the wing and body colour suffusion, making the homozygous birds look pure yellow. Yellows split for White are an insipid yellow colour, which allows the underlying wing markings and pale green body colour to show through – so judges put these birds down the order at shows. Thus unconsciously, Black Eyed Yellow breeders always selected for homozygous yellows … and most still do. Judges also came down much harder on poor colour in Whites than they did on the equivalent poor colour in Yellows.

I began breeding my miserable little Whites in 1957. They were small, ugly, misshapen, and not very white at all. I worked so hard on them for miserable results. On and off I have bred them until today. I always hoped to win champion of show with a Black Eyed White one day.

Loyal friends have often said that my Black Eyed Whites are the best around (by then they were at least very white). This is like saying that my collection of toenail clippings is better than anyone else's. I suppose that my friends felt sorry for me: "Poor Don and his wretched Whites … still, he loves them so much!"

About six years ago Peter Dodd loaned me a stylish White male and I purchased a buff White female from Ernie Wise. I crossed them to my strain of homely, but beautifully coloured Whites and started to make progress. Peter Dodd was one of the greatest Black Eyed Yellow breeders ever, and his words still haunted my mind: "Black Eyed Whites are just too bloody difficult."

Nonetheless, three years ago I bred about 70 really nice Black Eyed Whites. They were a long way from 'Best in Show', however. The best of them was a stylish Modern White male (see photo). Still, one stylish male doesn't necessarily make a winning strain. Early the following year I hatched six young Black Eyed Whites from my top pair.

As they grew, all were very good indeed, BUT one stood out as something special: a snowy white young female with all of the bells and whistles, see photo above. She had excellent directional feathering, a long mask and a huge head. Plus all the other bits – wide shoulders, large overall size, and so on. By six months of age she was everything that I ever wanted. The best news is that I have about 40 of these 'improved' Whites now.

My hope in showing you these photos is to say that every variety can be perfected, so never give up on your dream (and never forget Ian Hannington and his best in the world Fallows, see page 54). My main aim is to find one or more serious breeders who will take my Black Eyed Whites forward into the future and make them even better birds. It would break my heart if these agonisingly difficult Whites fizzled out because no-one can be bothered with them. We never really own elite Budgies – we just hold them in trust for future breeders.

My Whites are now a stable strain of elite Exhibition Budgerigars that will reliably produce good young. But had I known how heartbreakingly difficult it would be and how long it would take to get there (60 years), I would have probably ... done it anyway.

One last thing. The survival of the Black Eyed Whites is largely up to the judges now. I am happy for the judges to come down hard on Whites that are not white enough. But the judges must then train their eyes to pick the suffusion semi-hidden under the intense yellow of Black Eyed Yellows, and come down hard on that too.

At the moment, only the very best judges are doing this well.

Above is my first stylish male Black Eyed White. What look like pale wing markings are in fact the shadows of the leading edges each wing feather. If you look at his body feathers that overhang the top of his wing, the same shadows are visible, proving that they are not wing markings. This bird is 100% clear on his wings and body.

Above right: This is a Modern Black Eyed Yellow that I photographed at a show. This is the sibling variety to Black Eyed Whites. All the breeding methods in this section apply equally to Black Eyed Yellows. Black Eyed Yellows are much easier to breed than Black Eyed Whites. Black Eyed Yellows split for White are an insipid yellow colour, but Double

Factor Yellows are a rich golden yellow.

Left: This is my best Black Eyed White ever. At nearly seven months of age in this photo, she is pure white and is very large with good shoulders and directional feather. She is as good as the best Normals and Spangles around.

Left: This is a recent promising young Black Eyed White on his first day out of the nest. He is enormous, and has great shoulders and feather. I dreamed for many decades of having Whites with decent conformation and feathering – now they finally exist. To all really dedicated Budgie breeders, let me assure you that the enormous pleasure that you get from producing excellence in that agonisingly difficult variety or colour is worth all of the pain along the way and then some.

Right: This is a five- or six-month-old male Black Eyed White. I can't wait to pair him up. It never occurred to me that it was possible to get them so white! Remember that this is a white of amazingly light suffusion.

Left: This is the best Black Eyed White that I was ever lucky enough to breed.

Below: This is the same five- or six-month-old male Black Eyed White (his mask feathers are still moulting out) with his full brother a Darkwing Cinnamonwing (Sky) White. The Australian Darkwing mutation creates a dark Cinnamonwing or Normal (i.e. black) wing colour on a Yellow or White Budgerigar. The Darkwing was the world's first Clearbody, created in 1930.

My aviary full of Black Eyed Whites.

Clearwings are the Rubik's Cube of genetics

Have you ever played with a Rubik's Cube? You look at it and think: "That can't be too difficult to master!" So you **twist** it ... and you never get it back to how it was originally ever again – i.e. all of one different colour on each side. Clearwings are exactly like that. You think: "Surely they are quite simple to breed. I can outcross (AKA **Twist**) them to **improve** them." Like Albinos and Cinnamonwings, if I outcross them

At a Glance

I have bred Clearwings for most of my life. To me they are the most beautiful Budgerigar variety of all. I have spent decades researching them to get perfect body colour and perfectly clear wings. If you follow my breeding methods, you too can have spectacular Clearwings in your own aviaries. But first, some advice and insights (To save time, maybe go directly to 'The Recipe for Perfect Clearwings' on page 40).

to Normals they will reappear in a generation or two unaffected by the outcross at all. But this just does not happen with Clearwings. If you outcross your Clearwings you will never breed a correctly-coloured Clearwing again.

Eighty-five years after they were first exported to England, no-one in the entire world, including

Australia, has ever bred a line of 'Modern' Clearwings with the original perfect colour. Why? They can succeed with most other varieties.

The eerie similarities

Let us look into the similarities. Both the Rubik's Cube and Clearwings were created by an individual genius. The cube was created by Professor Ernő Rubik of Hungary, and Clearwing Budgerigars were created by Harold Peir of Peakhurst in Sydney, Australia.

- Both creations are almost impossible to play with successfully.
- It takes a very talented person to restore both to their original condition.
- Once you get one, they tend to become an addiction.

Examples of perfect colour in Clearwings. Left is a Dark Green and right is a Light Green.

What went wrong with Clearwings?

Harold Peir was a humble market gardener in Sydney who also bred Budgies. He did not use the principles of genetics to create Clearwings, nor did he discover a Clearwing mutation, because there is no Clearwing mutation. Harold was aware of general genetics of Budgies, but he used the time-honoured principle of bit-by-bit selection instead. That is, in each generation, he selected those individuals which most met the intended outcome: a Budgerigar with a dark body colour and white or yellow wings.

This creation process that Harold used was well documented in the 1935 edition of Neville Cayley's book, *Budgerigars in Bush and Aviary*, as well as in other Budgerigar books of the era.

Mix of Heritage Exhibition Clearwings.

A male Heritage Light Green Clearwing and female Violet Clearwing.

What went wrong was that Budgie breeders completely muddled up the hereditary basis of the Clearwing. They believed that all hereditary aspects of animals and plants were controlled by genes. This we now know is wrong. Genes are minority players in both the domestication and evolution of animals. Curiously, all Exhibition Budgerigar breeders use the bit-by-bit method for most improvements in Budgie breeding. They ceaselessly select for a bit longer mask, a bit wider shoulders, a bit bigger head ... and on it goes. Yet no-one notices that this is not the usual genetic method! That is, genes are not in control of any of these processes.

Using the wrong theory of the hereditary basis of the Clearwing meant that all those who outcrossed Clearwings had virtually no hope of producing well-coloured

Clearwings again. The only bit that is clearly controlled by a gene mutation is the Full Body Colour dominant gene. Thus, breeders had some success in breeding good body colour in their Clearwings.

What about myself?

I listened to Harold Peir's instructions from 1935. The great Budgie breeder Harley Yardley perfected the Harold Peir Clearwing during the 1950s, and all of my Clearwings are descended from his birds. While I experimented with modernising Clearwings from the 1950s onwards, I always held onto a large number of 100% pure Harold Peir Clearwings. Over the years, I was able to decode the nature of Clearwing heredity and to realise what a Genius Harold Peir was. So, today I maintain a huge flock of pure Heritage Clearwings from circa 1930. I can't claim that these birds were created by myself, but I have finessed them to a level that I am sure Harold Peir would cry tears of joy over. He would be so happy that someone carried on his work.

The greatest dangers for Clearwings now are those who still use the wrong theory to breed them. But worse than them are those who fail to support the preservation of the best-coloured Budgerigars ever bred: Australian Heritage Exhibition Clearwings. Without these elite Exhibition Budgies, we can never again perfect the Clearwing.

It still amazes me that the British, and the rest of the world, didn't keep a pure line of Australia's exquisitely coloured Clearwings that we sent them, as a back-up. They just immediately outcrossed them all to 'improve them', and ruined them forever. The perfectly coloured Royal Blue Australian Heritage Exhibition Clearwings were right there in Windsor Castle, being looked after by the future Queen Elizabeth after being sent as a gift from Australia.

Left and right above are Violet Clearwings – the middle one is a Red Violet.

Above: Left is a Red Violet Heritage Clearwing, right is a plain Violet Clearwing.

Above: Left is a Heritage Exhibition Violet Clearwing, right is a Red Violet Clearwing.

Above: Left is a Red Violet Dark Green Heritage Exhibition Clearwing, right is a Red Violet Olive Clearwing.

What about you?

The ironic thing is that Clearwings are dead easy to breed given that the genius Harold Peir and Harley Yardley have done the heavy lifting. Using Peir's and Yardley's methods, I have been able to make major improvements as well. Forget genes, and just select for the characteristics that you want: i.e. very clear wings and very dark body colour. Give these aspects priority over size, head, feather, etc. To accomplish this in Australia, we created the Australian Heritage Exhibition Budgerigar Club. It is wedded to the 1962 Australian National Standard of Perfection, which, under our constitution, can never be changed, except for adding new varieties and colours, plus the correction of any errors.

The problem with the Modern Exhibition Budgie system is that they constantly change the Standard of Perfection which applies to all types of Budgies. When you do this, breeders must then outcross their birds to be competitive. If you constantly outcross Clearwings to Normals, you can never maintain acceptable colour and markings in them, or in any other variety of Budgerigar which is based on the bit-by-bit selection process. These other varieties are: Black Eyed Yellows and Black Eyed Whites (i.e. Dilutes bred for perfect colour), Darkwings (Australian Clearbodies), Rainbows, Hagoromos (Helicopter Budgerigars), Cresteds and Banded Pieds, This group needs its own protected section if they are to become a legitimate and popular part of today's shows. The AHBA is doing this, and it is working.

Thus, like Canaries, there need to be different types of Budgies with different standards. Canaries have so many types: Norwich, Gloster, Yorkshire, Red Factor, etc, all of which are shown in different classes at shows. This would help our hobby.

After spending much of my life struggling with Clearwing breeding, I have now developed a 20-step recipe that will, I hope, help my fellow breeders of this most beautiful of all Budgie varieties.

The recipe for perfect Clearwings

1. Contrast is the key objective, so always look at that first: the contrast between light wing colour and deep body colour. Contrast is KING. The priorities are, in order: contrast, followed by wing clarity, then body colour.

This female Red Violet Dark Green Heritage Clearwing has perfect contrast. She is the equal best-coloured Clearwing Budgie that I have ever bred or seen. This bird is the most important Budgie that I have ever bred. She is prepotent for wing clarity, intense body colour and swank. See her progeny in the section entitled 'Prepotency' on page 183. She is a Red Violet Dark Green Clearwing, and grandmother of my first Red Violet Clearwings.

2. Never mate two birds with dirty (i.e. heavily-marked) wings together, however, when necessary for other improvements, mating a really clear-winged bird to a dirty one is fine. Dirty wings are more or less dominant.
3. Understand that mating a very clear-winged bird to another very clear-winged bird is ideal, but even this mating will not produce 100% very clear young. Many bits of DNA modify wing colour, and they are not 100% reliable.
4. There are two different types of wing markings on Clearwings. Try to learn the differences between Type 1 and type 2 wing patterns. This is crucial for success. Type 1 wing markings create a large area of grey colouring on each wing covert feather, and the flights and tail are an even grey colour. The body colour is also a bit darker. Type 2 wing markings are one or two thin lines of grey on each wing covert feather, with much lighter-coloured flight and tail feathers. The body colour is slightly lighter as well in type 1 birds. The easiest way to tell the two wing patterns apart is to check the primary flight feathers: if these are grey, it is usually type 1.

These are two sibling Violet Heritage Clearwings. The Clearwing on the left has a type 2 wing pattern. The bird on the right has a type 1 wing pattern. Note the darker grey flight feathers and the darker body colour in the type 1 bird on the right. These brothers are classic examples of the differences between type 1 and type 2 wing patterns.

5. In general, mating type 1 to type 2 Clearwings yields poor results in terms of wing colour. Sometimes it must be done, but try to avoid it as your wing colour will go backwards for a time.

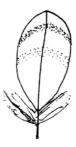

Type 1   Type 2   Type 2

Clearwing wing feathers showing the two distinct feather patterns. Note that type 2 can have one or two grey bars.

6. It is possible to get very clear wings in both type 1 and type 2 wing patterns, BUT it is far easier to get **perfect** wings with the type 2 pattern. In any case, if you look very closely, the type 1 birds tend to have faint grey primary flight colours and a just visible grey cast over their wings no matter how hard you try to perfect them.

Above: These are sibling English Yellow Faced Modern Clearwings. The male on the left has the type 2 wing pattern and his sister on the right has the type 1 wing pattern. The two patterns are not always this obviously different, but this shows the basics of the differences. Note the greater area of grey on the female's wings and her darker flight feathers. Her wings look much darker, but the grey markings are the same depth of colour on both birds. The male just has a greater area of cream-yellow on each wing.

7. Pale body colour, especially pale chest colour is best not used for breeding unless the bird has other outstanding qualities.

Left: These are two Dark Green Clearwings. Neither has good, deep body colour, although their wings are very clear. The Clearwing on the left has poor body colour which is even paler on the chest. She lacks contrast and should not be used for breeding, however, she is an excellent beginner's bird due to her perfect wing colour. After all, perfectly clear wings are the ultimate aim of Clearwing breeding.

8. Ignore cheek patch colour, even if the standard or judges make a fuss about it. Pale cheek patches indicate that the Budgie is split for Dilute (new observation from Ali M Hasan).

9. Develop a system for classifying all of your Clearwings for your records. Record type 1 or type 2 wings, plus a series of varying wing colour descriptions: very dirty, dirty, bit dirty, fairly clear, clear, very clear, perfectly clear (by 'dirty' I mean dirty, greyish wing markings). Write these down against all parent birds and classify their chicks as well in your breeding book or computer records.

10. If possible, photograph all parents and all really outstanding Clearwings for your records. Many years later, this can help you to recognise how your Clearwings breed and which parents are important.

11. Each year, have an overall breeding aim. One year select strongly for contrast, the next year for wing clarity, the next for contrast, the next for body colour, etc. This is my order of things, but, depending on what the strengths and weaknesses of your birds are, you might vary it a bit.

12. Every year do one or two matings that are creative and risky. Progress often comes from taking a risk.

13. Maybe keep two different groups of Clearwings if you are undertaking the risky process of trying to breed Modern Clearwings. Select some with superb colour contrast and those with Modern Exhibition qualities such as larger size, bigger heads, longer masks, more feather, etc.

14. If you wish to try breeding **Modern Clearwings**, the best outcross is a super-Modern Dilute that has come from a top strain of Exhibition Normals. This should produce 100% visual Clearwings split for Dilute if your Clearwing is a Double Factor Clearwing, and 50% Clearwings and 50% Dilutes if your Clearwing parent was split for Dilute. Any Dilutes from this sort of mating are also worth breeding from.

Above: This is the result of a creative mating. I was trying to produce a pinkish-lilac Heritage Clearwing by mixing Cinnamonwing, Clearwing and Red Violet all together in one bird. It worked, and now we call them Amethysts. These are among the prettiest of all Budgie colours.

15. Outcrosses to Normals or Dilutes will sometimes produce pale body colour in the Clearwing progeny, because the outcross lacks the dominant Full Body Colour gene. Backcrossing to Clearwings with dark body colour will fix it.

16. Outcrosses to Normals or Dilutes will also produce very dirty wings, but don't worry. Clearwings are only modified Greywings, so reversion of this type is not unexpected when you outcross. Just backcross for three or four generations to very clear-winged birds, and by then clearer wing colour should be re-established in the progeny. Broadly speaking, dirty wings are dominant to very clear wings. My research has proven that genes as such do not control the finer exhibition aspects of birds. Hereditary modifier elements in the DNA do this job but they are not genes and they aren't really dominant or recessive – they sort of blend with each other. Like mixing paint.

17. If very clear-winged Clearwings are not available in your area, then you should seek out some Black Eyed Yellows or Whites in Australia or some Light Yellows or Whites in the UK and Europe (if you can find any). The ideal Yellow or White bird for crossing to Clearwings has very clear wings but plenty of colour on the body, however, spangles are of no use at all. When mated to dirty-winged Clearwings, these Yellows or Whites might help clear the wings in the young. They were what was used way back in the 1920s and 1930s by Harold Peir to clear up the wing colour in early Clearwings. Maybe some breeders of pet shop Budgies in your area might have some Light Yellows with fairly clear wings?

18. Occasionally, Clearwings produce Dilute young with pale blue or green body colour. These Clearwing-bred Dilutes are very useful for crossing back to Clearwings **if** their wings are very clear. These Dilutes usually carry all of the DNA modifiers needed to produce beautifully coloured Clearwings. We will cover hereditary modifiers in the genetics chapter on page 163.

These are Clearwing-bred Sky Dilutes that appeared in a nest of Heritage Clearwings. Their wing colour is superb. They carry all of the DNA modifiers that you need to produce great body colour as well, so you should consider using them in your Clearwing breeding program if they turn up in your nests.

19. However, any Cinnamonwing Clearwings produced are only useful for producing Amethyst Clearwings (i.e. Cinnamon Clearwing Red Violets). Cinnamonwing Clearwings have pink feet, 50% body colour, light-coloured cheek patches, and often very pale cinnamon wing, head and neck markings. Cinnamonwing Clearwings are severely penalised at exhibitions.

20. Lastly, make up your mind – do you want to breed beautifully coloured Clearwings or do you want to breed large Modern Exhibition Clearwings? It is very, very difficult to breed birds with both exquisite colour AND Modern Exhibition qualities. The HUGE problem is that both Clearwing characteristics, and Modern Exhibition qualities like large heads and masks, etc, are all modifier controlled. So there are vast numbers of little modifiers fighting for different effects in each bird. A real mess. So, if perfect colour is your thing, stick to Heritage Clearwings. If you desire to know more about the beautifully coloured Clearwings, join the Australian Heritage Budgerigar Association via the Facebook page. The hope is that one day we can export them from Australia to the rest of the world again.

This is a male Australian Heritage Sky Clearwing. He is the equal-best Clearwing that I have ever bred. Australian Heritage Budgerigars are bred to conform to the 1962 Australian National Standard.

A young Australian Heritage Clearwing Red Violet, one week after leaving the nest. Note that he has a far deeper violet body colour than today's Normal Violets – plus pure white wings! Any artist can tell you that violet (a.k.a. purple) is a mixture of blue and red: this bird has heaps of red in his genuine violet colouring.

A young Yellow Faced Violet Heritage Clearwing.

This is an Amethyst Fallow – i.e. a Red Violet Heritage Clearwing Fallow. Note its glorious pinkish-lilac sheen. Curiously, sometimes Fallow darkens the wing markings.

Mix of Violet, Red Violet, Mauve and Cobalt Heritage Exhibition Clearwings. All have very clear wings.

These are a new variety: Australian Heritage White Cap Seafoam Clearwings.

Left: Very stylish Australian Heritage Clearwing Yellow Faced Violet.

Middle: Modern Golden Faced/Yellow Faced hybrid Violet Clearwing.

Right: A young White Cap Seafoam Rainbow – i.e. a White Cap Seafoam Opaline Clearwing. See more White Cap Rainbows in the Rainbow section on page 69.

Dilutes

Dilute is a recessive mutation which reduces both body and wing colour intensity by about 80–90%. It occurs in both green and blue series birds, and from a distance many people would call them yellow or white Budgies. When serious breeding began around 1900, breeders immediately tried to breed them to be the purest of whites or the purest yellow. It is a pity that they didn't breed both pure whites and yellows plus soft coloured pastel-coloured Budgies.

Left: This is a Dilute White, maybe Sky or a Grey Blue.

As pure yellows and whites were stabilised, the original whites and yellows (AKA Dilutes) were often called 'suffused'. Although suffused is a positive word meaning a spreading of something that produces an unusual colour or quality, breeders came to use 'suffused' to mean 'contaminated with the wrong colour'. More recently they came to call them Dilutes. Even so, to this day, the colour in Dilutes seems not to be valued. Budgie clubs have missed a wonderful opportunity to name and develop new and attractive colours.

In most countries colour is just not that important. Lately, this is starting to change.

A green series Dilute.

A Golden Top Rainbow Dilute.

Imagine the spectacularly coloured Budgies that we all could breed? These subtle and beautiful Budgies could attract new members in large numbers, and even more if the members were actively involved in creating the changes.

This Opaline Violet Clearwing-bred Dilute (i.e. a Violet Pastel) won Grand Champion Budgerigar at the Hawkesbury Show in Australia in 2023. This show put strong emphasis on colour based on the Standard of Perfection.

This is a Clearwing-bred Dilute; it has all the hereditary modifiers that Clearwings possess. The hereditary modifiers in this Dilute are what Harold Peir used to turn a Greywing into a Clearwing. There is no mutation for Clearwing.

Above: Comparison between a Black Eyed White (above) and a Dilute White (right). The female Black Eyed White is totally white, but her mutation is Dilute. Hereditary modifiers made the difference, not genes. The Dilute male below is typical of the dilute mutation in an unaltered state.

Greywings

Greywings were one of the first mutations in Budgies. They are also one of the most variable as well. Their wing colour can vary from very light to dark grey and there are many variations in body colour, of which the Full Body Colour dominant mutation is the best.

This is a pair of sublimely beautiful Full Body Coloured Greywing Violet Sky Blues. There is an as yet unidentified wing darkening mutation or modifier in there as well. Both have type 2 wing patterns (see Clearwings, page 41). I doubt that you will ever see a more beautifully coloured pair of Greywings than this Australian pair.

Surprisingly, the Clearwing **is** a Full Body Coloured Greywing with wing clarity modifiers. Clearwing is not a mutation, but it is a recognised variety. The same situation applies to Black Eyed Whites, Black Eyed Yellows, Banded Pieds and Darkwings – none of these varieties are based on mutations. There are mutations in them, but hereditary modifiers are the main players.

Worldwide, Clearwing genetics is a mess. This young bird is the result of crossing a 100% pure Australian Heritage Clearwing to a Modern European Normal, then crossing the resulting split Clearwings together. This bird, according to the European theory of breeding Clearwings, is a Clearwing. Yet it would be accepted into any Greywing class at any Budgie show worldwide.

At a Glance

The Greywing is a very beautiful variety of Budgerigar. However, because the Budgie breeders in Europe and the UK were given the wrong genetic model for breeding Greywings, Dilutes and Clearwings, they have struggled for more than 80 years to even tell the difference between the three. This section sets out to help the breeders of all three varieties to have more fun and to breed better varietal Budgies.

This Budgie is the 2013 European Champion Greywing, but it is clearly a Dilute. Its pale cheek patches prove that it is a Dilute. Compare its colour to the pair at the beginning of this section.

This bird is the 2013 European Champion Clearwing, but it is almost certainly a very poorly coloured Greywing. It is definitely not a Clearwing – all the magic modifiers are missing.

The confusion above was created when F.S. Elliott and E.W. Brooks published the book *Budgerigar Matings and Colour Expectations*, which was based the brilliant research of geneticist Dr Hans Duncker on Budgerigar genetics. Elliott and Brooks inserted their own incorrect theory that the Clearwing Budgerigar was a multiple allele of Greywing, Dilute and Normal. Duncker never said that Clearwing was a multiple allele of Greywings and Dilutes. In fact he never tested Clearwings genetically at all. The Clearwing was produced in Australia about three years after Dr Duncker had finished his research!

These are two Full Body Coloured Sky Dilutes, bred from Clearwings, which are similar in body colour to the European Champion 'Greywing' above.

From my research involving the breeding of more than 2,000 Clearwings, added to the details from Harold Peir via Neville Cayley's book *Budgerigars in Bush and Aviary*, which was written at the time, we now know that the Clearwing **IS** a Greywing. Greywings can be almost whatever you want them to be. Greywings vary enormously under the influence of hereditary modifiers.

So Budgie clubs need to work out what they want a Greywing to look like. I believe that the first photo in this chapter, of a pair of Violet Sky Greywings, is a great starting point.

Clearwings were produced from Full Body Coloured Greywings with type 2 wings. Their creator, Harold Peir, just selected from a group of Full Body Coloured Greywings in an aviary, until, little by little, by selection, they got lighter wing colour. Peir was adamant that no Clearwing mutation ever appeared. This was cited by Neville Cayley in his 1936 book *Budgerigars in Bush and Aviary* (and also by other leading UK experts at the time). I also tracked down Harold Peir's grandson, Richard Peir, who worked closely with his grandfather on the Budgies. Richard was deeply involved with the Budgies, especially with the Clearwings, and insisted that his grandad never found a mutation for Clearwing at all. He said that his grandad just had the idea of creating a Whitewing Blue Budgie and dedicated much of his life to changing his Full Body Coloured Blue Greywings into Whitewings. And he succeeded.

Left: This is a female Full Body Coloured Violet Greywing in Australia – a very nice bird indeed. She has a type 1 wing pattern (see Clearwings page 41). Harold Peir used birds with type 2 wing patterns to develop Clearwings.

Back to basics: Greywing is recessive to Normals, but dominant to Dilutes. Never cross a Greywing to a Clearwing as this will just destroy the hundreds of precious modifiers involved on creating the breathtakingly beautiful Clearwing. Maybe we should have a worldwide competition to produce the best line of tomorrow's beautiful Greywings. It is so sad to see a beautiful variety of Budgie like Greywings looking drab, with no magic.

Lastly, the pale-coloured Budgies often exhibited as Greywings do have their own beauty and magic. They should be placed in classes for Pastels.

In the Australian Heritage Budgerigar Association we have classes for Pastel Budgies. These are the softer coloured Budgies often, but not always, based on Dilute versions of other mutations. We even have a sub-group within the AHBA for Pastel Budgies headed by Naomi Watts. The aim here is to see which pastel shades are popular with our members. The most popular ones will be voted upon by the members to see if they are popular enough to become new varieties. In the AHBA, members have 100% control over new varieties.

This is a Pastel White Cap Seafoam Rainbow. It is one of the more harmonic Pastels, featuring colours that work very well together.

Another Pastel Budgie. Genetically it is a Pastel White Cap Mauve Rainbow.

Again, we think that these softer silvery colours work well together.

The Australian Heritage Budgerigar Association will support any other club anywhere in the world who wishes to create their own Pastel classes. If you do create these classes, please post photos on the AHBA Facebook page. We would also love to see any other new colour varieties of any sort.

Fallows

Australian and German Fallows – why it's almost impossible to improve them

Fallows are Budgies with dark red eyes with white iris rings, and brownish-black wing and other markings, combined with very pale body colour. The mutation, as with all Fallow mutations, is recessive to Normal.

This is one of Ian Hannington's amazing Fallows in 2008.

Ian Hannington produced Australia's (and possible the world's) best Fallows for their time. I interviewed Ian and recorded how he managed to break the very strong gene linkage between poor feathering and the Fallow gene. Here is his story…

Before we get to Ian's story, I need to mention my own experiences with Fallows. Back in the 1960s my Fallows were dreadful. Mercifully, since the competition also was dreadful, I did OK on the show bench. Eventually I thought these are awful birds and I don't like them. They were tiny birds with no feather bulk, tiny heads and short masks. Bush Budgies with pale colour and dark pink eyes.

When you cross a Fallow to a Normal, you get 100% Normals split for Fallow. When you back-cross a Fallow to one of the split Fallows you get 50% Fallows

At a Glance

Ian Hannington's techniques in re-inventing (Australian and maybe German) Fallows is arguably one of the greatest breeding achievements with Budgerigars: incessantly cross Fallows to great Normals, then breed split to split. Once you get ONE decent Fallow, keep it and sell off ALL the rest. Now base your Fallow breeding 100% on this one bird by crossing it to pure Normals to get new splits. Never cross any of your new Fallows to any other Fallows or splits… ever!

My studies from the 1960s onwards of the Australian Fallow and later on Ian Hannington's smart breeding, are the only meticulous studies of any type of Fallow breeding that I know of. Hence the longish story. I will lump the other Fallows in shorter sections.

and 50% Normals split for Fallow. If you mate split Fallow to split Fallow, you get 25% Fallows, 50% split Fallows and 25% Normals. The problem is that you can't visually pick the difference between the split Fallows and the Normals from this mating. What drove me nuts was the fact that the splits were vastly better birds than the visual Fallows. Time and time again my efforts to upgrade my Fallows failed – the little brutes! In the same nest, the splits were lovely but the visual (i.e. Double Factor Fallows) were awful.

Even at age 14, I became suspicious that the Fallow gene was linked to genes for small size and short and fine feather genes. And it is almost impossible to break them apart. Thus, they travel as a group – this is gene linkage at its very worst. What a disaster.

Then my friend Russ Dunn rang me saying that he had a Fallow for me. I replied, "You don't breed Fallows." He explained that it just popped up out of a line with no history of Fallows in it. I went out to see it and it was superb, as good as any winning Exhibition Normal of the day. A big female with coarse feather, a huge head and swank. I purchased the female and thought, "that's it, I'll burn all of my bridges."

I sold all of my Fallows and split Fallows and decided to base all of my Fallow breeding on this one female. I crossed her to good quality Normals and produced 100% splits. Agony – I couldn't wait for year two. As soon as the splits were mature, I crossed two of them together, while I mated mum to another good Normal. When the first young Fallow came from the brother to sister mating it was stunning. Big, bold and beautiful. This line of Fallows settled down to produce many lovely birds, all equal to the current Normals of the era. I sent photos to *Cage and Aviary Birds* in England with an article on my birds and received excellent reviews for these Fallows.

My original Fallow from Russ Dunn was a crop-out – an oddity that popped up from a line of Normals. Somehow along the many years that the Fallow gene lay hidden as an invisible, Single Factor recessive, the linkage to awful size and feather broke down. Or it was an identical new mutation of Fallow, linked to great feathering. Now, the Fallow was linked to modern size and feather. On the show bench in Australia, they were hard to beat. I mention this not to brag, but to point out that much the same happened with Ian Hannington.

Some years back, Ian became very disappointed in his Fallows. They kept "going backwards" to poor quality, small birds. Understandably, he decided to sell the lot, all 80 of them. The purchaser encountered awful problems and most of them died, leaving three splits. Ian decided to buy the three splits and they formed the basis of his new line of Fallows. He purchased no Fallows at all at that time. Out of every 15 Fallows that he produced from his splits, one was of good quality, and he crossed these each year to his best three Normals. And he produced the best Fallows that I have ever seen. He had broken the linkage to bad feathering and size. Maybe the only person after Russ Dunn to do so.

Breaking the linkage between Fallow and poor feathering is almost impossible.

Left: How is this for a Fallow? Ian Hannington bred this bird around 2007.

He did buy two Fallows more recently, but nothing came of it. Ian's system of burning bridges – moving away from older-style Fallows and constantly crossing his birds to new Normals is the way to go. This eventually breaks down the linkage.

But you must never back-cross to inferior old-style Fallows or split Fallows again … EVER! If you do, you will lose every gain that you have made, as the Fallow gene re-welds itself to junk.

What is the Fallow Formula?

The key to breeding Fallows is to get even just **one** Fallow that is a super show bird – Ian got four! Then sell all of your old Fallows and split Fallows, every one! Now, breed the Super Fallow only to good Normals to produce new splits. Don't cross this bird to your old unsatisfactory Fallows or any of your existing split Fallows. **Never** breed from Fallows that are poor show birds – you will almost always breed poor-quality Fallows this way.

My suggestion is that you follow Ian Hannington's advice on Fallows. Sell all your old Fallows and start anew. Upgrading poor-quality Fallows is not worth trying in my view.

Right: Ian Hannington's techniques for re-inventing Fallows have resulted in arguably one of the greatest breeding achievements with Budgies that I have heard of. Incessantly cross Fallows to great Normals, then breed split to split. Once you get ONE decent Fallow, keep it and get rid of ALL the rest. Now base your Fallow breeding 100% on this one bird by crossing it to pure Normals to get NEW splits. Never cross any of your new Fallows to any other Fallows or splits … EVER!

Below are the basics of Ian's two matings from which he produced the two split Fallows that, mated together, hatched four amazing Fallows that all had the linkage to bad size and feathering broken. The new linkage was to super feathering and size.

To quote Ian: "The Grey Spangle male and the Normal Grey female were the grandparents on both sides of the Sky Fallow male. Two of their offspring were paired to the best two Fallows I had at the time, then the best of the young split Fallows from each pairing were paired together the following year. Between them they produced the four best Fallows I ever bred, three males and one female, which were almost identical. One of the young males went on to win reserve open young bird at the BSA Annual."

It would be tempting to say that this was a really good mating. But to say this is to entirely miss the point. This group of matings destroyed the damaging linkage that has kept ALL FALLOWS as third-rate Exhibition Budgerigars. After Ian's brilliantly intuitive matings, his four great new Fallows were re-linked to the features of a totally Modern Showbird.

Above: These are two Australian Fallows which are linked to poor size and feathering. Note that the Opaline gene darkens wing markings.

Right: This is an Australian Fallow Violet Clearwing. Curiously, the body colour and wing markings are greatly intensified as both parents were 100% clear on their wings. Maybe the Violet gene affects Fallow colour. Or maybe it is part of the type 1 and type 2 wing patterns. I am experimenting with it to see what it breeds.

Dun or English Fallows, plus the other Fallow varieties worldwide

Dun Fallows have the reddest eyes of all Fallows, plus they have no white iris ring. There is a brightness of overall colour about the Dun Fallow that makes it very appealing. Their brownish wing colour varies a bit and the body colour varies from almost white to about 50% of Normal colour.

Like all Fallows, the Dun Fallow is recessive to Normal. It is said that all different varieties of Fallow, when mated together, produce non-Fallow young (i.e. they are not multiple alleles). This is unlikely to be true since some varieties such

This seems to be a Double Factor Golden Faced Sky Blue Dun Fallow.

as Australian and German Fallows seem to be the same mutation. This means that they will produce 100% Fallows when mated together. But there is evidence that certain varieties of Fallow DO produce non-Fallow young when crossed together.

The rest of the Fallows

All Fallows have brownish wing markings, very pale body colour and pinkish eyes. Both wing and body colours can vary enormously within each group. In terms of genetics, they are all recessive to Normal and there is no reason to cross any of the different Fallow mutations together.

In terms of points of difference, the eyes have it. Eye colour in Fallows is important in working out which Fallow you have. Below is a Fallow identification chart. It is not perfect since Fallows vary so much in body and wing colours.

The following grid sums up all Fallow differences:

	Eye colour:	Iris ring:	Body colour:
Australian Fallow	dark plum	white	pale to 50%
German Fallow	dark plum	white	pale to 50%
English Fallow	bright red	bright red	pale
Texas Fallow	red	red	around 50%
Scottish Fallow	pink	pink	pale
Californian #1 Fallow	red	white	pale
Californian #2 Fallow	red	red	pale

In this book, Australian Fallows have been given much more space due to the extensive research that I have done on them. The very important discovery here is that the Australian Fallow gene is strongly linked to poor exhibition qualities, i.e. the appearance of smaller size and smaller head, mostly due to poor feathering. In the section on Australian Fallows I have set out ways to break the linkage and, more importantly, how to ensure that the old damaging link never returns. It will return unless you follow my simple instructions.

The only other varieties I know of that shares linkages to poor-quality exhibition features, are the Recessive Pied and the Australian Golden Faced Blue. The Recessive Pied and its love child, the Dark Eyed Clear, were both linked to bad feathering but modern breeders have re-linked them to better feathering. The only essential is that you never breed from any of this group if it has bad feathering.

Right: These are two Dun (a.k.a. English) Fallows. The huge pink eyes below are close-ups of Dun Fallows' eyes to aid in identifying them.

Golden Faced Blues are the most stubborn of all linked genes – they hang on to dreadful size, poor feathering and small heads and will never let go. The Single Factor Golden Faced Blue split for White Faced Blue does not show bad linkage, but the Double Factor Golden Faced Blue does. The nasty point here is that the Double Factor Golden Faced Blue is the desirably coloured form with a rich golden face and very blue body colour. The Single Factor Golden Faced Blue has the less desirable greenish body colour, but it is a much better showbird. The bad news is that I have been working on this problem since 1960 and I have never been able to break the linkage. BUT, if you cross a Golden Faced Blue to a Yellow Faced Blue you will get some young that carry one gene for Golden Faced Blue and one for Yellow Faced Blue, and they look almost perfectly like a Double Factor Golden Faced Blue, except that they are excellent showbirds. Golden Faced Blue and Yellow Faced Blue are multiple alleles with Green and Blue. Only a brilliant judge could identify one of these hybrid Golden Faced Blue from a Double Factor Golden Faced Blue.

The only other linkage of a Budgerigar variety to show quality is the Spangle. To my eyes, the Spangle is always just that bit better than non-Spangles in swank, i.e. pizzazz. They stand up and show off. Note that Cinnamonwings have finer feathering which does no harm and Greys have coarser feathering which does no harm either (maybe some good?).

There is a belief among breeders that greys pass on the coarser feathering to their non-grey babies. Equally, many believe that Cinnamonwings pass on their finer feathering to their non-Cinnamonwing babies. Both of these beliefs are incorrect.

For more information on linkages see the chapter 'Gene linkage, huh?' on pages 163 & 340.

This is apparently a Blue Black Faced Dun Fallow. There are many wonderful hybrids occurring between Black Faced and Black Winged mutations with other Budgerigar varieties. Some wonderful times lie ahead with these new blackish varieties. All photos on pages 58–60: Louis van Zuilen Photography, Roger van Delft and Benjamin Seyed.

Pieds

Australian Banded Dominant Pieds

The above paintings are from *Budgerigars In Colour* by A. Rutgers (1958).

The world was so excited about Australian Banded Pieds from the 1940s to the 1980s. As with Clearwings, Australians used hereditary modifiers and modifying genes to shape the random Pied mutation into a desirable showbird.

Sadly, as with the Clearwing, European and UK Budgie breeders couldn't understand modifiers at all, and the Banded Pied became extinct worldwide by 1980. If it wasn't a simple mutation, no one could breed it.

To recap, the Aussie Dominant Pied mutation has no control over the pied pattern or extent, no matter whether it is in the single or Double Factor form. It just says: "you are a Pied". So what determines the various patterns and the amounts of white or yellow on an Australian Pied?

Surely, Double Factor Pieds are mostly white or yellow? No, the so-called Reverse Pieds are not necessarily Double Factor Pieds at all. No, no, no!

At a Glance

The Banded Pied can be brought back to life quite easily. There is a basic dominant mutation for the Australian Dominant Pied which produces Pieds, but it has no say over the pattern or extent of the Pied markings whether they are Single or Double Factor. In the book *Genetics for Budgerigar Breeders*, the authors said: "Homozygous and heterozygous individuals do not differ in appearance." This is spot on, but throughout the book they never could explain how the different pied and other patterns and variations in mutations are created, nor did they say: "We don't know how patterns work." Modifiers of any mutation simply didn't exist, FOR THEM. Yet the leading Nobel Prize winning Scientist Barbara McClintock had developed a theory that mobile elements regulated genes by inhibiting or modulating their actions, 12 years before *Genetics for Budgerigar Breeders* was published in 1961. As a scientific book, *Genetics for Budgerigar Breeders* leaves a lot to be desired. This section will explain my new discoveries of pied patterning which fill in the unforgiveable gaps left by T.G. Taylor PhD and Cyril Warner. Their mistakes in how the Clearwing variety is inherited were an amazing 27 years out of date at the time of publishing. They will be corrected in the Clearwing heredity section in this book.

Straight Line Pieds. In hereditary aspects they all just have very wide bands.

There is a major modifier gene, which I have called the Straight Line gene, that always tries to straighten any pattern on the bird, and another is the Banded gene. The Straight Line gene tries to create a straight line across the breast at the top of the band: think of the base of the purple on the breast of a Gouldian Finch. Then the Banded gene tries to create a band across the belly. But it can produce as many as three bands on one bird. There are perhaps another 100 hereditary modifiers that complete a perfect band.

All Australian Dominant Pieds that carry ONE gene for the band are Banded or Winged Pieds, even if the bands are a bit wiggly. All Pieds that are Double Factor for the **band gene** are Rumped or Reverse Pieds.

To repeat, these Rumped Pieds can be either Single Factor or Double Factor for the PIED GENE itself. The Pied gene never determines how much white or yellow is on the Budgie. It does not work like the Spangle gene where Double Factor birds are almost all yellow or white. Please repeat this every night for a week, just before you go to bed.

Rumped Pieds. These are Double Factor for the Band pattern gene, not the Pied gene itself. They can be either single or Double Factor Pieds.

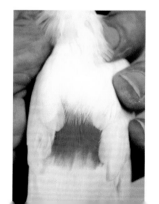

Can we simplify how it works? Yes! Any farm kid from 10,000 years ago could create Banded Budgies or Belted Galloway cattle (see page 323). It is that simple, it is only our rigid gene fixation that destroys our ability to breed perfection.

To breed a perfect Banded Pied is just a matter of constantly selecting for a straight band across the belly. Just select for a pleasing look that is straight. But you

A Violet Rumped Pied showing its typical rump colouration.

A 'v'-shaped or Chevron Banded Pied. Note the two violet horses' heads facing away from each other on its belly. The width and shape of the band can be shaped by any enthusiastic breeder.

need to forget about genes since they play a very small part in it. Belted Galloway cattle were created long before Mendel invented genetics. Yet, they are very similar in heredity to Banded Budgies.

The key bit is to train your eye to spot almost-bands. You need to train your imagination as to what is nearly a band. And then breed from that. It is that simple. FORGET GENETICS! I see almost-Banded Budgies among the Dominant Pied posts of so many lovely Budgies every day. So, it is quite easy to find your own living construction kit for building Banded Pieds in your aviaries.

The other key element is to understand that the Band, Straight Line, Winged and Rumped Pied mechanisms act entirely separately from the PIED gene itself. That is, any Normal, non-Pieds from Banded and Rumped Pied parents in particular are very useful for breeding Banded Pieds. I am now calling them Band-bred Normals.

For a much more detailed story about the Australian Dominant Pied go to the 'Master Class' section on page 321.

Dutch (a.k.a. Continental Clearflighted and Frosted) Pieds

The Dutch Pied is a Dominant Pied, but its pattern is very variable. It can be a Clearflighted Pied, right through to a Frosted Pied where white or yellow occur scattered all over the bird. Sometimes the pied area is restricted to a pink toe or toenail. These minimally marked Pieds (i.e. visually non-Pieds), usually females, still can produce well-marked Pieds even when mated to a non-Pied mate. As with all Pied mutations in Budgies, females usually have less extensive pied areas than males.

Left: A Dutch Pied showing the classic markings: white on the chest, scrambled scapular markings and mixed black and white flight feathers.

It appears that no one has studied the heritability of the various pied patterns in the Dutch Pied, but the frosted variant in particular does appear to have a hereditary basis.

The Dutch Pied combines with Recessive Pied to produce a Dark Eyed Clear. See Recessive Pieds on page 67. Basically, you need to backcross to Recessive Pied to get a Double Factor Recessive Pied combined with either a Single Factor or Double Factor Dutch Continental Pied.

Left: It is very difficult to describe the Dutch Pied mutation. Usually, you get some Pied primary flight feathers, often mixed in with non-Pied feathers, and maybe some Pied areas under the mask area on the chest. Dutch Pieds can also produce semi-Pied scrambled areas of wing markings on the scapulars. Some Dutch Pieds have a Frosted Pied pattern as well. This is probably done by a modifier gene changing the Dutch Pied pattern. There is a remote chance that Frosted Pieds might be Double Factor Dutch Pieds and maybe there are one or two similar Pied mutations that resemble Dutch Pieds.

The lower left bird is a Frosted Dutch Pied. Notice his blotchy white areas, plus the altered pattern with much more white between the black markings on the scapulars. Photo: Phillip Bosci.

Pieds are quite variable, and the modifier elements that control Pied patterns have not been rigorously studied apart from my research on Banded and Rumped Australian Dominant Pieds.

The biggest differences between the Australian Dominant Pied and the Dutch Pied are:

1. The Dutch Pied has pied areas on its upper chest whereas the Australian Pied has pied areas on its middle to lower stomach area.
2. The Dutch Pied primary flights tend to be a mix of pied and non-pied areas. The Australian Pied has uniformly pied primary flight feathers all together.
3. The Dutch Pied often has a messy mix of pied and non-pied feathers on its scapulars, but the Australian Pied has less pied areas on its scapulars.
4. You get Frosted Pieds in the Dutch Pied birds, but no frosted areas in the Australian Pied birds.

Above: This is a Greygreen Dutch or Continental Pied photographed from two different angles. Note the yellow breast and also the clear flight feathers and rather jumbled wing markings.

Left: This is a pink toenail Dutch Pied male. Note his white tail feather. Male Pieds in all pied mutations tend to have more white or yellow feathering (pied areas) than females.

The female equivalent of this male is often a visually Normal female with one pink pied toenail. These females still breed 50% Pied young when mated to a Normal male. Many of these young have significant pied areas on them.

Thus the unsuspecting breeder mates a pair of apparently Normal birds together and produces 50% Pied young. Strange behaviour for a Dominant Pied mutation!

Photo: Phillip Bosci.

Recessive Pieds and Dark Eyed Clears

The Recessive Pied is a beautiful Pied indeed. It is so popular that it is often referred to as just a Recessive. This name is to be avoided as there are so many recessive mutations in Budgies.

Pieds seem to love bending or breaking the rules of genetics. Recessive Pied males often have a visible pied spot on the back of their heads and Dutch (a.k.a. Clearflighted) Pieds, which are supposed to be Dominant Pieds, often produce 'Normal' young that have just a pink toe or toenail. These pink-toenail Budgies still breed as Dominant Dutch Pieds.

At a Glance

Recessive Pieds have come a long way in recent years. They used to have a linkage to poor feathering, but these days the linkage has been broken and most have good feathering. **Never purchase a Recessive Pied with poor head feathering as it is very hard to get rid of.**

Left: Recessive Pieds are easy to identify since they have fully black eyes as adults – i.e. no white iris ring. This bird has reasonable feathering, but don't buy any Recessive Pieds with poor feathering as it links to the Recessive Pied gene and is hard to eradicate.

Below: Two Recessive Pieds that appeared in a Bush Budgie nest (i.e. they are genetically Wild Budgies). Note that the Green female has much more body and wing colour than the Blue male. This is typical for all female Recessive Pieds.

Left: This is a 'split' Recessive Pied male. A significant percentage of Recessive Pied males have the pied spot on the back of their heads. Females almost never have these spots.

As with all Recessive varieties, when you cross a Recessive Pied to a non-Pied, you get 100% birds split for Recessive Pied. A Recessive Pied mated to a split Recessive Pied, produces 50% Recessive Pieds and 50% splits. Two splits mated together produce 25% pure Normals, 50% splits and 25% Recessive Pieds.

Recessive Pieds, when combined with Dutch (a.k.a. Clearflighted) Pieds, then backcrossed to another Recessive Pied, produce a percentage of Dark Eyed Clears. That is, pure white or yellow colour with jet black eyes with no iris ring. They often exhibit the linkage to poor feathering that Recessive Pieds suffer from.

All Dark-Eyed Clears are Double Factor Recessive Pied plus Single or Double Factor Dutch Pied.

Right: Dark Eyed Clear White. It is a nice bird, but it lacks good head feathering due to linkage to the hereditary bad feathering condition. Still a lovely bird though! Notice the all-black eyes.

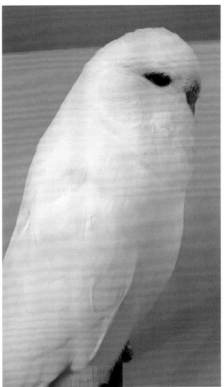

Rainbow Budgerigars

Rainbow Budgerigars

Left: This scrum of young birds includes Sky Blue, Cobalt and Violet Rainbows as well as Amethyst Rainbows (the pinkish-lavender birds at top left and lower centre). Amethysts are genetically Cinnamon Pinkish Violet Clearwings – in this case with Golden Faced Blue and Opaline added. There is also a Yellow Faced Clearwing near the centre. Photo: R. Elwell.

All Rainbows are Clearwing Opaline Golden Faced Blues or Yellow Faced Blues or, more recently, White Caps. With Golden Faced Blues, they can be Single Factor or Double Factor: Single Factor has a greenish-blue body colour at maturity and Double Factor has a rich blue body colour at maturity.

I still remember breathlessly purchasing my first Rainbow from a local pet shop, and hurrying home with the greatest treasure of my life. This section is for all those wishing to breed a little bit of magic – a **RAINBOW BUDGERIGAR**.

Rainbows are spectacular Budgies with a kaleidoscopic range of colours. No other Budgerigar variety or combination of varieties has so many colours on one bird. They have green, blue, yellow, white, purple, golden-bronze*, grey and other colours. Photo: R. Elwell.

---

* See the photo caption of a juvenile White Cap Teal Blue Rainbow on page 77.

Rainbows are actually fairly easy to breed if you have a recipe, so I am going to list a few of the ways to breed them.

The key thing to do is to seek out parent birds as listed below. The genetics here are messy, so selecting key parents that are already part of the way there is really essential – and you **MUST** keep detailed breeding records.

At a Glance

The Rainbow Budgerigar is perhaps the most beautiful of all Budgerigar varieties. This was the variety that won me over to keeping and breeding Budgies as a seven-year-old kid in 1954. Perhaps this is the variety that will win over today's cyber kids to our hobby. If we do it right! Kids have so many other things to do these days.

Method 1

Buy a pair of Rainbows and most of their young will be Rainbows. Male Rainbows are much more useful than female Rainbows, but do not pass up a chance to buy either sex.

Method 2

1. Create your own Rainbows, which are a combination of Clearwing, Opaline and Australian Golden Faced Sky Blues or Violets. If you can buy a male Opaline Blue Clearwing you are halfway there already. A male Opaline Australian Golden Faced Blue Normal is also good. A female Golden Faced (or Yellow Faced) Clearwing is really good too. If all else fails, buy a couple of pairs of Blue Clearwings and some Golden Faced Blue Normals, plus some male Opaline Normals (females are not as useful).

2. Pair up two pairs of a male Opaline Blue Clearwing to a female Golden Faced Blue Clearwing. Half of the young females should be Rainbows and the other half will be Opaline Blue Clearwings. Half of the young males will be Golden Faced Blue Clearwings carrying an (invisible) Opaline gene and the other half will be Blue Clearwings carrying the hidden Opaline gene. All young from this mating will be useful in later matings. The following year, mate a young male Golden Faced Blue Clearwing carrying the hidden Opaline gene, to a female Rainbow from the other mating. You can expect about half of all the young, both male and female, to be Rainbows.

3. Mate two pairs consisting of a male Opaline Golden Faced Blue Normal to a female Blue Clearwing. All of the young will carry one hidden gene for Clearwing. All males will carry a hidden gene for Clearwing and a hidden gene for Opaline – so they will visually look like Normals. All females will be visually Opaline Normals. Half of all young will be Golden Faced Blues. The following year, mate a visual Normal Golden Faced Blue male from the mating to a visual Opaline Normal Goldenface female from the other mating. 25% of the resulting young will be Clearwings, of which 75% of these will be Golden Faced Blues, and half will be Opalines. That is, roughly one in 10 young will be a Rainbow. Again, please remember that, from a breeding point of view, **MALE RAINBOWS** are the most important ones to keep.

Left: This is a very useful bird for breeding Rainbows. He is a nine-week-old Australian Golden Faced Blue x English Yellow Faced Blue (Hybrid) Double Factor Violet Sky Clearwing. All that you have to do now is to add Opaline. His patchy colour is because he is deeply into his first moult.

NB: You can cross Australian Golden Faced Blues to English Yellow Faced Blues to produce hybrid Golden Faced Blues/Yellow Faced Blues. These birds look almost exactly the same as Double Factor Golden Faced Blues and are perfect for use in breeding Rainbows. This young bird is my best-ever Golden Faced Blue Clearwing.

Working it out for yourself – i.e. the genetics of Rainbows

The genetics of Rainbows can seem a bit tricky, but if you work out each gene mutation separately, it is not too bad. So here we go!

Normal is dominant to Clearwing, so Normal mated to Clearwing produces 100% visual Normals 'split' for (i.e. carrying a hidden form of) Clearwing. Two of these 'splits' mated together will produce 25% Clearwing young and 75% Normal-looking young.

Australian Golden Faced Blue is semi-dominant to Normal White Faced Blue. Budgies carrying one Golden Faced Blue gene and one White Faced Blue gene have a golden face and blue body colour as a baby but they moult out to have a golden face with a greenish-blue body colour at maturity. Budgies carrying two Golden Faced Blue genes have a cream-coloured face as a baby, but a golden face and blue body at maturity. So a budgie carrying one Golden Faced Blue gene and one White Faced Blue gene mated to a White Faced Blue budgie will produce half White Faced Blue young and half young with one Golden Faced Blue gene and one White Faced Blue gene (i.e. a golden face and greenish-blue body colour at maturity.

Right: This is a female Single Factor Australian Golden Faced Red Violet Clearwing. Note the greenish suffusion on her body colour as well as a bluish sheen. The Double Factor Golden Faced Blues has a much bluer body colour. You get one of these in every four young by crossing two Single Factor Golden Faced Blues together.

Opaline is messy. It is a 'sex-linked' variety, which means that this mutation can only be carried on the Z sex chromosomes. Males have two Z chromosomes (ZZ) and females one Z and one W chromosomes (ZW). All visual male Opalines have two Opaline genes, one on each Z chromosome. If a male has only one Opaline gene on one of his Z chromosomes, he is 'split' for Opaline and looks like a Normal. Females can only carry either one Opaline gene **or** one Normal gene on their one Z chromosome. Females can therefore either be a pure Normal or a pure Opaline – they can never be split for Opaline – i.e. if they have an Opaline gene, they show it. So, from a mating of an Opaline male to a Normal female, all the young females will be Opalines, and all the young males will be Normals split for Opaline. An Opaline female mated to a Normal male produces Normal males split for Opaline and pure Normal females.

The good news is that we may have recently discovered a dominant, non sex-linked form of Opaline which should make breeding Rainbows much simpler in the future. See below.

The colours of Rainbows

All Rainbows are Clearwing Opaline Golden Faced Blues (or Yellow Faced Blues or White Caps or Golden Tops). But they can be Single Factor or Double Factor Golden Faced Blues: as we saw on the previous page, Single Factor has a greenish body colour at maturity and Double Factor has a rich blue body colour at maturity. **It is my view that Double Factor (true-blue) Golden Faced Blues are by far the prettier birds.** Both Single Factor and Double Factor Golden Faced Blues have golden-coloured faces. The body colour can be Sky Blue, Cobalt Blue, Violet or even Mauve.

This pair of Golden Top Rainbows is really quite useful for the production of very attractive Rainbows. They are Double Factor Golden Top Mauve Rainbows. Mated to Sky Opaline Clearwings, either one will produce Cobalt or Violet Rainbows. To some people, Violet Mauve Rainbows may not look as pretty as Violets (below left), but they sure can breed lovely Violets.

Violet

Violet-Sky

Baby Rainbows like this Violet & Violet-Sky look great as babies but turn green at maturity. Photo: R. Elwell.

Above is an English Yellow Faced Violet Clearwing. Notice that his face colour is more of a soft lemon yellow than the strong golden yellow of the Golden Faced Blues. This male was feeding a brood of seven young when photographed – hence his dirty face.

If you are serious about breeding Rainbows, it is almost essential to have some pure Clearwings like this Red Violet Clearwing. Violet Clearwings are always in demand.

If you use the English Yellow Faced Blue instead of Golden Faced Blue, the Rainbows will be a bit insipid, but this is a matter of taste.

Confusion

One of the confusing things about both Modern Show Budgies and pet-shop Budgies is that they usually carry a number of hidden, undesirable mutations. That is, they are not as purebred as they once were. For instance, a male may carry one hidden gene for Cinnamonwing which may pop up in his daughters, producing pale body colour. This sort of washes out the colour of Rainbows a bit. Some Budgies may carry the Dilute gene, which may also pop up in their young, producing overall Pastel colours. The Australian Heritage Budgerigar Association has included Dilute and Cinnamonwing* Rainbows in its Standard of Perfection. Many pet-shop 'Rainbows' may be Spangles which you might not notice at first, but Spangle can mess up an otherwise good Rainbow. For instance, if a Budgie carries two Spangle genes, it is usually yellowish or white all over.

All of these hidden surprises lurk within Modern Budgies – they are sort of hybridised. Sometimes these Budgies can produce lovely surprises which are most attractive. However, when you are trying to breed something as specific and complex as a Rainbow, these 'pop-up' babies are very confusing indeed. You will just have to learn to cope with confusion and disappointments. Hopefully you will have a mentor among your Budgie friends who can sort out issues of this kind. You need to be aware that, sometimes, very plain-looking young just might be very valuable breeding stock in the production of Rainbows. You might just be ONE cross away from breeding truly sublimely coloured Rainbows.

Rainbows have always posed real problems for the Budgie-club bureaucrats because they lie at the outer limits of combinations of simple mutations. For instance, until now (2024), the Australian Budgie clubs, with the exception of the Australian Heritage Budgerigar Association, have never even developed an Australian Standard of Perfection for Rainbows. That is, there are no legitimate classes for this beautiful variety at shows in Australia, their country of origin. Some progressive clubs provide Rainbow classes and perhaps they use an overseas standard to judge them by. Rainbows were developed in Australia around 1940. Kids loved them but the adult Budgie breeders were not supportive of either the kids or their precious Rainbows. This is such a pity. This chapter is dedicated to all young Budgie breeders.

Discussion

What if I can't find really nice Clearwings with CLEAR wings?

It really doesn't matter. In ordinary Clearwings, dirty wing markings are ugly and a fault. These same wing markings on Rainbows can be very beautiful and are usually

---

* Take care as Cinnamonwing and Opaline tend to stick to one another, i.e. they are loosely linked genetically.

This is a 'pop-up' Cinnamonwing Mauve Rainbow, i.e. a Clearwing Cinnamonwing Opaline Double Factor Golden Faced Mauve. Her pale lavender cheek patches, pink feet and pale body colour indicate the presence of the Cinnamonwing gene. Her lavender cheek patch also confirms that she is not a Grey. She is still a useful female for producing Rainbows when mated to the right male. Be very thorough when you are inspecting Budgies for purchasing from breeders or pet shops, as Cinnamonwing can glue (genetically link) to Opaline, which could mess up your breeding a bit. Look for Budgies that are Clearwing, Golden Faced and Opaline. Avoid Cinnamonwing unless you want to breed Pastel Rainbows. Photo: R. Elwell.

an essential part of their overall brilliant colour (see the photos on page 80 of golden-bronze-winged Rainbows from Ken Gray's book *Rainbow Budgerigars*). This beautiful gold-bronze colouring is caused by the type 1 Clearwing wing-pattern gene. Type 2 wing markings are faint and covered by the Opaline Blue wing colour.

How do I tell the difference between Australian Golden Faceds and English Yellow Faceds?

Australian Golden Faced Blues have a strong golden face colour. The Single Factor Golden Faced Blue has a greenish-blue body colour and the Double Factor Golden Faced Blue has a true-blue body colour. Single Factor English Yellow Faced Blues have a creamy yellow face colour and a blue body colour. Curiously, the Double Factor English Yellow Faced Blue is indistinguishable from an ordinary Blue Budgie. And, if all else fails, inspect the photos of the Yellow Faced Blues and the Golden Faced Blues Clearwings in this section.

Where can I find good Rainbow breeding stock?

Try searching online for 'Buy Rainbow Budgerigars'. There are many very good breeders of Rainbows who have been breeding exactly what consumers want for many years. You may need to inspect several breeders' birds over some months, but you should soon find some lovely birds. There are magnificent Rainbows throughout the Middle Eastern countries and in Asia, including in Thailand, India, Pakistan and Bangladesh. Turkey has good Rainbows too. Many of the world's most beautifully coloured Budgies are bred by amazingly talented people in these countries.

Mixed Rainbow babies.

Credit R. Elwell

On the left is a good example of a dazzling wing colour on a Violet Rainbow. This one is more silvery bronze than golden bronze.

Left: A beautiful Sky Rainbow with a kaleidoscope of colours. Photo: R. Elwell

Right: Golden Top Rainbow. This is a new mutation discovered in Port Macquarie in Australia. It has a richer golden face colour and better feathering in the Double Factor form than Golden Faced Blues. It is highly probable that Rainbow breeders all over the world are using this and similar mutations, without realising that they are new mutations.

Below left: A juvenile White Cap Teal Blue Rainbow. Note how well the bronze wing markings go with the other colours. In the Australian Heritage Budgerigar Association's Rainbow Standard of Perfection, judges have the freedom to decide on the artistic merit of birds like this one. Note that the Opaline mutation creates a uniform and pleasing body colour.

Below right: For comparison, this is a Violet Double Factor Golden Faced Clearwing. All young Double Factor Golden Faced Blues have soft cream-coloured faces and wings. Birds like this are the perfect outcross to Rainbows to add better wing colour and overall style.

Above: Two White Cap Rainbows. On the left is a young Mauve Single Factor White Cap Rainbow. On the right is a Seafoam Single Factor White Cap Rainbow.

Above: On the left above is a Seafoam (Sky) Double Factor White Cap Rainbow. Surprisingly, she has no Green genes in her at all. All Double Factor White Caps are green coloured with a white cap or forehead. On the right is a Seafoam White Cap Rainbow under black ultraviolet light.

Salvation?

This is a CURIO. It seems to be a young dominant, non sex-linked Opaline Clearwing Red Violet, so we have named this new variety 'Ocean Mist'. If, after more test matings, it turns out to be confirmed as a dominant Opaline, breeding Rainbows will become much easier in the future. For instance, females will be equally as good at producing Rainbows as males. Plus, this opalescent mutation appears to have a basic white wing colour. That is, it has white flight and other wing feathers with body colour over the top. This is exactly what most Rainbow breeders want – a non-sex-linked Rainbow with no grey on the wings. Sex-linked varieties are very confusing for most breeders.

It pays to maintain very accurate breeding records. This bird (above) would never have been discovered without accurate breeding records which proved that he was not a true Opaline. Mated to another related 'Opaline', he produced 15 ordinary, non-Opaline Violet Clearwings out of 28 young! About half of the young in both colours were male and female. This is not possible if both parents were true Opalines. The only possibility seems to be that this male is carrying a new dominant opalescent mutation. See the chapter 'Breeding without genetics' on page 154 for the breeding record form and advice on how to use it.

Left: A near-perfect juvenile Heritage Clearwing Golden Faced/Yellow Faced Violet hybrid male to breed to Rainbows. While it looks like a Double Factor Golden Faced Violet, it doesn't have the poor head and feathering linked to all Double Factor Golden Faceds.

The AHBA Rainbow Budgerigar Standard

The Rainbow Budgerigar is a Clearwing-based variety composed of Clearwing, Opaline and one of the Yellow Faced Blue varieties, including White Caps. The ideal is a bird of many rich, vibrant and **distinct** colours: blue, violet, amethyst, yellow, gold, blue-green and golden-bronze. As with all Clearwing varieties, really clear wings (i.e. wings devoid of all grey markings) are the basic ideal, except for bronze-winged birds or birds with grey or mauve body colour. With Rainbows, the wings should be coloured the same as the body colour with no markings visible. Nonetheless, yellow, cream or bronze wing markings are acceptable. Totally blue wings are ideal.

This Standard covers an entire group of Budgies, all correctly referred to as Rainbows. All Yellow Faced Blue varieties are acceptable, including Australian Golden Faced Blue, Australian Golden Top, English Yellow Faced Blue, English Yellow Faced Blue Mutant II and Australian White Cap. In the case of The Australian Golden Faced Blue and the English Yellow Faced Blue Mutant II, this Standard accepts the Double Factor birds with their bluer colour as preferable.

These photos above show Rainbow Budgerigars featured in Ken Gray's excellent book *Rainbow Budgerigars.* Notice the golden-bronze wing markings. The Australian Golden Faced Violet Rainbow female on the left has deeper body colour (indicating that she has a type 1 wing pattern) plus deeper golden-bronze wing markings. The male's wing markings are golden-bronze, but are also a bit muddy and grey, which is acceptable but less desirable. Ken describes this male as being an English Yellow Faced Blue.

- The Amethyst version of the Rainbow is acceptable, i.e. a Cinnamonwing Clearwing Opaline Yellow Faced Violet. There are two Amethyst Rainbows on the first page of this Standard (the pinkish-lavender birds at the top left and the lower centre).
- Rainbows with rich golden-bronze wing markings and mask spots are also acceptable, provided that these wing and mask markings are vibrant and golden (see photos below from Ken Gray's book). Muddy grey wing markings are a fault.

This is an example of a dazzling wing colour on a Violet Rainbow. This one is more silvery bronze than golden bronze. Golden bronze is preferable. An English Yellow Faced Cobalt Rainbow.

White Cap Rainbows have only recently appeared in Australia. Genetically they are White Cap Opaline Clearwings – i.e. the White Cap mutation has replaced the Golden Faced or Yellow Faced mutations. The White Cap gene creates two different forms of this mutation:

A Single Factor form which has a yellow mask and a whitish forehead (i.e. cap). The wings are creamy white with greenish-blue body colour and the body is also a greenish-blue.

A Double Factor form which is identical to a Green Budgerigar except that its forehead (i.e. cap) is a creamy white.

There is also a Bronze White Cap Rainbow which is the same as a White Cap Rainbow except that it has a golden-bronze wing markings.

This is a photo of a White Cap Seafoam Clearwing which forms the basis of White Cap Rainbows. Note that the wings are very clear with a creamy white colour. The mask is light yellow and the forehead is a creamish-white.

This Bronze White Cap Seafoam Rainbow has the same greenish-blue colour on its wings as it has on its body. Judges might expect blue on its wings, but this is not how this mutation works.

This is a White Cap Violet Mauve Rainbow. In this case judges could well opt to accept the almost matching grey wing markings as preferable to white markings.

This is a Violet White Cap Rainbow. Note its similar greenish-violet colour on its body, wings and mantle (the 'v'-shaped area between its wings at its shoulders).

This is a young Bronze White Cap Seafoam Rainbow. His overall colour and markings are near perfect.

Pastel Rainbows are also acceptable: i.e. (Clearwing-bred) Dilute Opaline Yellow Faced Blue, provided that the softer colours are distinct and attractive. Ideally these Dilutes should be Clearwing-bred to enhance their depth of the soft, bluish body colour. See the photo below of two Pastel Rainbows.

This Standard recognises that some of its terms like 'attractive', 'rich and vibrant colours' and 'bluer colour', and even 'muddy grey wing markings' are somewhat open to personal interpretation; this is very much in the spirit of this colourful and spectacular Budgerigar. Judges can use their own judgement to select the best-coloured, most attractive birds within the wording and spirit of this Rainbow Standard. Judges are invited to provide feedback on the workability or on other aspects of this Standard.

These are Pastel Rainbows, that is Clearwing-bred Double Factor Australian Golden Faced Blue Opaline Dilutes which carry the body colour intensifiers found in Clearwings.

This is a young Pastel White Cap Seafoam Rainbow. Genetically it is an Opaline Cinnamonwing Clearwing White Cap Sky Blue.

Left: This seems to be the first White Cap Green Rainbow that has been bred. It is genetically a Double Factor White Cap Opaline Clearwing Sky Blue. It is neither a Green nor a Blue Budgerigar genetically. There has been some discussion about whether or not it belongs in the Rainbow Standard, or in Rainbow classes at shows. At maturity, it will look like a Green Opaline Clearwing with a white forehead (i.e. cap). The AHBA notes that, bred to an Opaline Blue Clearwing, it will breed 100% White Cap Seafoam Rainbows. We note that this bird does not fit into any other classes at shows apart from Rainbows. So, for the time being, we believe it belongs in the Rainbow group.

Left: This young Violet Rainbow has very good, distinct colours and very clear wings, hence the yellow wing markings. This is an acceptable wing colour. Note that this bird does not have the golden-bronze wing markings, which are nonetheless, equally desirable. Photo: R. Elwell.

Rainbows are spectacular Budgies with a kaleidoscopic range of colours. No other Budgerigar variety or combination of varieties has so many colours on one bird. They have green, blue, yellow, white, purple, golden-bronze, grey and other colours.

Judges' notes

In an ideal Rainbow, the mask and head is yellow with barely visible head and neck striping (except in the golden-bronze type). The blue body colour extends up to the level of the scapulars on the back. Judges are permitted artistic freedom to allow splashes and sparkles of colour all over the birds. The cheek patches are purple to lavender as per the underlying variety of Clearwing or Amethyst or Dilute. Greenish

areas are permitted if they add to the dazzling colour of the individual bird, but don't overwhelm the blue areas. This Standard is very much in development at the time of writing, so judges have some flexibility in judging. Any feedback is welcome from breeders and judges alike.

For basic point scoring, please refer to the Scale of Points for the Opaline Clearwing on page 9 in the AHBA's 1962 Standard of Perfection.

Left: Australian Standard Type of Budgerigar male – adopted 1962.

Yellow Faced Blue (Parblue) Group

Australian Golden Faced Blues

For the last 80 years, the Australian Golden Faced Blue has been regarded as the best-coloured of the Budgies whose colour hovers between blue and green, a.k.a. Parblues. It is by far the best variety for Rainbow Budgerigar production because of its rich golden facial colouring plus pure blue body colour. In older Australian books, this variety is called the Yellow Faced Blue.

All young Single Factor Golden Faced Blues have blue bodies, yellow wings, and a yellow face, but turn greenish blue on the body at maturity. Young Double Factor Golden Faced Blues have blue bodies whitish wings and a very pale cream face.

Left: Single Factor Golden Faced Violet in the foreground, and Double Factor Golden Faced Violet to the rear. Note the deeper yellow colour on the face and wings of the bird in the foreground.

The Budgies that carry one Golden Faced Blue gene plus one Blue gene (i.e. Single Factor Golden Faced Blues) are a greenish colour. Those with two Golden Faced genes (i.e. Double Factor Golden Faced Blues) are the spectacular birds with a glorious golden face and a rich blue body colour.

Below: The greenish Clearwing Violet female on the left above has one Golden Faced Blue gene – i.e. she is Single Factor for Golden Faced Blue. The Opaline Violet male on the right is a Double Factor Golden Faced Normal Violet.

There is, however, a double disappointment with this variety, which is a real problem. The Single Factor Golden Faced Blues are greenish in colour, that is, not blue enough, and the Double Factor Golden Faced Blues are poor-quality exhibition birds with smaller heads and short feathering all over. I first published this fact in 1963 in the journal of the Budgerigar Society of New South Wales. In all the years since, I have never seen a Double Factor Golden Faced Blue that is a really good showbird.

The solution to this problem

This beautiful pair of Violet Clearwings are both HYBRIDS between a Golden Faced and a Yellow Faced Violet. That is they carry one gene for Golden Faced Blue and one gene for Yellow Faced Blue. They have lovely colour plus excellent exhibition qualities.

Make no mistake here, if you see a perfectly coloured Golden Faced with great exhibition qualities at a show, it is certain to be a hybrid. The pretty runts are the Double Factor Golden Faced Blues. Almost everyone, myself included, have a very difficult time in identifying these hybrids.

Left: This Australian Heritage Golden Faced Violet Normal is a hybrid. It is half Golden Faced Violet and half Yellow Faced. He has perfect colour and no judge could be certain that he is not a Double Factor Golden Faced Blue.

Since the two parent varieties have to be exhibited in separate classes at shows, these hybrids are technically unable to be exhibited. They are fakes. But who cares? They look lovely and should be accepted by judges as Double Factor Golden Faced Blues in my opinion.

It is worth noting that Rainbow Budgerigars are, in general, bred for colour only, so the smaller Double Factor Golden Faced Rainbows are perfectly OK.

How to breed a Golden Faced x Yellow Faced hybrid

If you cross a Single Factor Yellow Faced Blue to a Single Factor Golden Faced Blue, you get, on average:

25% Single Factor Yellow Faced Blues,

25% Single Factor Golden Faced Blues,

25% pure Blue and

25% hybrid Golden Faced x Yellow Faced Blues.

All of these young are useful for breeding.

Left: The male on the left in this photo is a Yellow Faced Violet Clearwing carrying one Blue gene. The female on the right is a Single Factor Golden Faced Violet Clearwing, so she also carries one Blue gene. This is the typical pairing that I use for the production of hybrid Yellow Faced x Golden Faced Blues.

English Yellow Faced Blues

At a Glance

Yellow Faced Blues have cream faces and greenish-blue body colour when spilt for blue, but Double Factor Yellow Faced Blues are identical to Normal Blue Budgies. These Double Factor Yellow Faced Blues will produce 100% Yellow Faced Blues when mated to a Blue Budgie, despite the fact that both parents are visually Blue Budgies. The best aspect of Yellow Faced is that they are very good show Budgies. They have lush feathering and a large head, whereas Double Factor Golden Faced Blues, which have a stunning blue body colour, tend to be smallish and have a smaller head.

Left: This is a male English Yellow Faced Blue Single Factor Violet Sky Normal Modern Showbird with a very evenly coloured Teal Blue body colour. It is an outstanding example of perfection in Yellow Faced Blue body colour, plus a perfectly clear cap.

The face colour in Yellow Faced Blues can vary from very pale cream, which is almost white, through to near golden.

A female Yellow Faced Blue Cinnamonwing Grey Australian Dominant Pied Modern Showbird.

A male Yellow Faced Normal (Violet) Grey Australian Dominant Pied Modern Showbird.

Golden Tops

This variety was found in a pet shop in Port Macquarie, New South Wales, Australia, by Lyn Spiers, who sent one to me for development about 11 years ago. It was from a line of Rainbows that carried almost every variety of Budgie known to science. It took me more than eight years to remove all of the messy bits such as Spangle, Dilute, Cinnamonwing, Mauve, etc, before I could work out what I had, but I eventually realised that I had struck gold.

At a Glance

I am certain that the brilliant Rainbow breeders worldwide are constantly finding new mutations that make their Rainbows look better and better. It seems that there might be around five different golden mutations that are amazingly bright. This is perhaps the best of them.

In essence, the Golden **Top** mutation leaves the Golden **Faced** Blue mutation for dead. Why? Because the Double Factor Golden Faced seems always to have poor size, head and feathering.

Two young Golden Tops: On the left a Double Factor Golden Top Mauve Rainbow, and on the right a Double Factor Golden Top Violet Rainbow. At this age Double Factor Golden Faceds Blues have pale cream faces which deepen to a golden shade at maturity.

Golden Tops have incredibly rich yellow faces, even when they are young (see below). Unlike Golden Faced Blues, the Double Factor form of the Golden Top mutation does not have poor feathering. Double Factor Golden Faced Blues are super-glued to poor size and feathering. All of this adds up to the Golden Top being by far the best of the Golden Faced Blue varieties.

Above are two birds of the same age. On the left, a young Double Factor Golden Faced Violet Clearwing. Note its pale face. On the right a young Double Factor Golden Top Rainbow. Note the rich golden head colour BEFORE the first moult. Golden Faced Blues have soft cream-coloured faces when young.

Two Double Factor Golden Tops showing off their spectacular golden foreheads.

The key aspect of Golden Tops is that both Double Factor and Single Factor forms of this mutation have good exhibition qualities. In particular, they are good-sized birds with big heads and long masks. These are Golden Top Heritage Budgies in development, but their modern relatives are truly lovely birds. Single Factor Golden Tops have a greenish body colour, much like Golden Faced Blues.

Left: A male Double Factor Spangle Opaline Grey Dilute Double Factor Golden Top. Notice that, for a pet-shop bird, his head and mask are OK – this shows the advantage of Golden Tops over Australian Golden Faced Blues. That is, Double Factor Golden Tops are every bit as good as showbirds as the Single Factor Golden Tops. His yellow face is far brighter and much more spectacular than this photo shows. Perhaps the camera is incapable of capturing Ultraviolet colours. Australian Golden Faced Blues have nowhere near this intensity or area of UV pigment on their faces, nor are their bodies and wings as free from yellow colour. And Double Factor Australian Golden Faced Blues are inferior showbirds as well.

Above: A pair of Golden Top Violet Mauve Heritage Rainbows. This is 100% real colour.

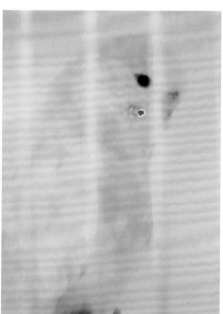

Left: A young male Single Factor Golden Top Cinnamon Clearwing Spangle Violet Sky during its first moult. I have never seen budgies go through such a spectacular colour change as these Golden Tops do. This is due, in part, to the appearance of UV pigment during the first moult. Nestlings lack the UV pigment.

Comparing Australian Golden Faces and Golden Tops

At a Glance

DOUBLE FACTOR AUSTRALIAN GOLDEN FACE	DOUBLE FACTOR GOLDEN TOP
Has a light yellow cap like a green.	Has a deeper yellow, luminous cap.
Has a strong yellow face colour.	Has a stronger, luminous yellow face colour.
Has some yellow body colour suffusion.	Has virtually no yellow body colour suffusion.
Has creamy-yellow wing colour.	Has creamy *white* wing colour.
Has UV pigment on cap and near cheek patches.	Has widespread UV pigment on its face and body.
Has poor feathering on the head and mask.	Has excellent head and mask feathering.

Superficially, the Single Factor Golden Faces and Golden Tops look pretty much alike – they differ mostly in UV pigment.

SINGLE FACTOR AUSTRALIAN GOLDEN FACE	SINGLE FACTOR GOLDEN TOP
Has a greenish blue body colour with no UV pigment on the body and wings.	Has a greenish blue body colour with UV pigment on the body and wings.

Believe it or not!

In case you might not have noticed, in sunlight, all green series budgies and yellow and golden faces have a light silvery-yellow cap, and a similarly-coloured stripe next to each cheek patch. The forehead is therefore much lighter yellow than the mask... but it glows with a pale UV colour. Below is a photo of a Lutino Budgie under strong sunlight – see the silvery-white forehead. This is not a doctored photo – it is just what your mind has never noticed!

Unlike this Lutino, (right) all

Golden Tops have a stunning rich, luminous, deep golden forehead and mask. To see one in sunlight is an unforgettable and moving experience.

All of this brings up the sad situation that, at nearly all Budgie shows, the lighting is abysmal. Thirty-year-old fluorescent tubes, that never were a balanced white light to begin with, hang about eight metres above the birds. Judges and exhibitors have no way of assessing the vibrant colours of our birds; and prospective new club members leave the hall unimpressed with our drab budgies. We need to do better.

White Caps

The White Cap is destined to become one of the top five Budgie varieties in the world. It is so incredibly beautiful and so easy to breed.

White Caps can be bred in most varieties as well; White Cap Rainbows and Clearwings in particular are heart-stopping. The Opaline in the Rainbow mix softens

and puts a uniform iridescent glow/sheen to the colour all over. Opaline and White Cap are at their best when they work together.

Left: This is a White Cap Seafoam Rainbow. This bird is an Australian Heritage Exhibition Budgerigar, and it has a very stylish head and body. In some Rainbows the colour of the wing markings is a bronze colour, which is permissible under the Australian Heritage Budgerigar Association's Rainbow Standard. The extra area of the greenish-blue on the wings is preferred.

Plain grey wing markings are penalised, except if they complement the bird's colour: e.g. a grey body colour. Here judges are permitted to show artistic judgement.

At a Glance

A White Cap Seafoam mated to a Sky Blue produces: 50/50 of Sky Blues and Seafoam White Caps, i.e. the same as the parents.

White Cap Seafoam mated to White Cap Seafoam produces:

25% Double Factor White Cap Green

50% Single Factor White Cap Seafoams, and

25% Double Factor Normal Sky.

Left, above and below: These are two young Teal White Cap Rainbows. The top one is a Teal Blue and the bottom one is a Teal Green.

The Teal Blue is a Double Factor Violet Sky White Cap Rainbow.

The Teal Green is a Single Factor Violet Sky White Cap Rainbow.

The bronze-coloured wing markings, as well as no markings at all, are considered highly attractive in the Australian Heritage Budgerigar Association's Rainbow Standard of Perfection. Judges are encouraged to use artistic licence to judge these classes.

Notice the dark cheek patches, indicating the presence of the Violet gene.

Right: Photo showing the pure white cap on a Teal Blue White Cap Rainbow.

94

Left: A Single Factor White Cap Double Factor Spangle. It is a beautiful mix of yellow, cream and white.

Below: A group of Seafoam Single Factor White Cap Clearwings: they have a white cap and wings, plus a yellow mask and an iridescent Seafoam body colour.

Note the male in the middle has a more greenish body colour, which is the case with all Green and Parblue Budgies.

Below: Two Normal White Cap Budgies.

Left is a Single Factor Seafoam (i.e. Sky Blue) White Cap. He carries one gene for White Cap and one for Blue.

Right is a Double Factor 'Light Green' White Cap. However he is not a true Green. He carries no Green genes at all. Nor does he carry any Blue genes. He is a Double Factor White Cap. Notice the patches of white on the mask near the cheek patches. This makes it very likely that breeders will create white-faced Greens from birds like the lower Budgie soon.

Left: Seafoam White Cap Rainbow. Notice the shimmering opalescence. The mixture of Opaline, White Cap, Cinnamonwing and Clearwing is a superb piece of orchestration. This is one case where the (sometimes annoying) gene-linkage between Cinnamonwing and Opaline is a blessing.

Right above: This is a Seafoam White Cap Normal Modern Exhibition male. A completely clear cap like this one is essential in all White Caps. The large round spots on his mask are excellent as well.

On the right is a Mauve White Cap Heritage Exhibition Rainbow male.

Above: We are still learning about White Caps.

Both of these Violet White Cap females have very blue body colour. Usually, it is a greenish-blue colour.

The Normal (left) has a very blue body colour and a type 1 wing pattern.

Violet is well known for reducing the yellow suffusion on the bodies of Golden Faced Blues, Yellow Faced Blues and White Caps.

For the record, the left bird is a Modern Showbird and the Rainbow (right) is a Heritage Showbird. The Rainbow also has the type 1 wing pattern, i.e. an even grey cast over the wing feathers.

Left: White Cap Seafoam Heritage Exhibition Clearwing.

A Double Factor White Cap 'Green' Rainbow. For the record, this female has no Green genes at all in her, so she is not genetically a Green. Double Factor 'Green' White Caps can never also carry the Green or the Blue gene, they are just pure White Caps.

What an amazing bird this male is! It is a hybrid between a White Cap Seafoam and a Golden Faced Sky. He is a Modern Showbird with type 1 wing pattern and truly amazing almost-orange head colour.

Other varieties

Albinos and Lutinos

Albinos and Lutinos are beautiful birds. The 'Ino' gene turns Blue Budgies into red-eyed White Budgies, and Green birds into red-eyed Yellow Budgies.

Left: This bird is a Lutino – note his red eyes.

The 'Ino' gene hides all colours except white or yellow. All other colours are still there, hidden in the genes, but they are chemically stopped from being seen. So, hidden in an Albino can be Cinnamonwing, Pied, Dilute, Opaline, Greywing, and so on.

If the yellow pigment is removed from a Lutino, you get an Albino.

To make matters even more complex, the 'Ino' gene is usually sex-linked, but very rarely, a Recessive Albino or Lutino turns up. The sex-linked hereditary mechanism is very confusing and it is made even more difficult by the fact that birds' sex chromosomes work the opposite way to human sex chromosomes.

So the best solution is to use lists of breeding results: see below.

Right: A very rare photo of a Recessive Albino male. This variety is visually identical to the sex-linked version of Albino. It has perfect camouflage in a show cage with a white interior!

Sex-linked 'Ino' matings

Albino male mated to a non-Albino female produces non-Albino males split for Albino and visual Albino females.

Albino female mated to a non-Albino male produces males split for Albino and pure non-Albino females.

Albino to Albino produces 100% Albino young.

For Lutinos, just substitute Lutino for Albino in the list above.

Right: Albino and Lutino siblings, showing the partial absence of down feathers and their red eyes.

Black Budgerigars

Black Faced Budgies originated in the Netherlands and the unrelated Black Winged mutation turned up in Venezuela. While both varieties nearly became extinct, finally they were bred into good numbers by very skilled people. The two were first combined by Roger van Delft and his partner Benjamin Seyed to create the world's first nearly black Budgie. They are also being crossed with Anthracite Budgies to create an even blacker bird.

At a Glance

Not long ago, Black Budgies were a pipe dream. But now, predominantly Black Striped Budgies are well established. What are they, how were they developed AND how can you breed them?

When you add Black Faced and Black Winged genes to Anthracite body colour, you really do create an amazing bird. The door is open to many superb new colours and patterns – imagine a Black Faced Black Winged Anthracite Banded Pied.

Anthracite Clearwings would be unforgettable too – imagine them with uber-white wings.

This is a line-up of many Black Faced and Anthracite types. From left to right:

Black Faced Single Factor Anthracite

Black Faced Violet Sky

Black Faced Double Factor Anthracite

Black Faced Green

Double Factor Anthracite

Double Factor Black Faced Grey Violet

Single Factor Anthracite Greygreen

Photo: Johan Kortenray.

Above left: Black Faced Double Factor Anthracite pair.

Above right: Black Faced Black Winged Grey. Roger van Delft and Benjamin Seyed are now pioneering the mixing of Black Faced and Black Winged Budgerigars with many other colours and varieties. Photo: Roger van Delft and Benjamin Seyed.

Yellow Faced Blackwing Cobalt Budgerigar. It will take some time for Budgie breeders to get used to these totally different Budgies. Photo: Johan Kortenray.

Cobalt Violet Black Faced Black Winged Budgerigar. The snake-like pattern on its front is amazing. Photo: Johan Kortenray.

Black Faced Cobalt Violet. Photo: Johan Kortenray.

Double Factor Anthracite Black Faced. Photo: Johan Kortenray.

Both Black Winged and Black Faced are recessive mutations, so in the first generation of an outcross to non-black Budgies, neither mutation produces any of their characteristic black colouring.

Both mutations act independently of each other, so juggling the two mutations in Double Factor form in one bird is a challenge.

Anthracite is semi dominant: in the Single Factor form it creates a darker blue or green, and in the Double Factor form you get the very dark grey.

Black Budgies are a combination of the Black Faced and Black Winged genes, plus the Anthracite mutation.

Black Faced Green Hagoromo.

The Black Faced Hagoromo and the Black Faced Black Winged Hagoromo are among the most challenging Budgie combinations to breed. The breeder is to be congratulated for this amazing degree of difficulty in production. Above is a Black Faced Green Hagoromo.

Hagoromos are the Japanese Helicopter Budgies with twin feathered helicopter rotors on their shoulders. Their heredity is complex as it does not rely entirely on conventional genes. This complex Black Faced Hagoromo variety ranks as one of the four great Budgerigar breeding triumphs alongside the Clearwing developed by Harold Peir, the Rainbow developed in Sydney, Australia, by persons unknown and the endangered Banded Australian Dominant Pied.

Interestingly, all four are largely based on modifiers that are in the DNA, but which are not genes, and also by the electrome, which is the electrical control of development of animals and plants.

It is so exciting to see the breeding of spectacularly coloured varieties of Budgies again. For far too long, colour has been neglected.

Black Faced Black Winged Anthracite.

Yellow Faced Black Winged Grey. Photo: Rashid Maruf.

Black Faced Black Winged Dun Fallow.

Black Faced Black Winged Dun Fallow Green – the green and black frontal striping is superb. Photo: Tariq Wasim.

Black Winged Grey.

Black Faced Black Winged Greywing.

Black Faced Black Winged Dun Fallow.

Photos: Louis van Zuijlen, Roger van Delft and Benjamin Seyed.

These two beautiful silvery Budgies are outstanding – a Black Winged Grey (left) and a Black Faced Black Winged Greywing (centre). In the future there will be many more artistic creations like these.

Right: Black Faced Green. Photo: Yutthana Imanothai.

Chimeras: two Budgies in one body

Right: There have been many arguments about what causes these strange birds. A recent Chimera produced by Brett Martin has settled the argument once and for all. It has bits of a Greygreen Cinnamonwing on one side and Sky Normal elsewhere. Cinnamonwing is on the Z sex chromosome and Grey and Green are not. In fact, the Grey mutation and the Green mutation could also be on different chromosomes from each other. Photo: Brett Martin

In any case, by the old theory (see below), at least two and possibly three chromosomes would need to independently malfunction or to get damaged to form this bird with three changes between sides:

1. Grey to non-Grey
2. Green to Blue
3. Cinnamonwing to Normal

Under the old theory this is simply way too unlikely ever to happen: billions to one against!

Conventional thought was that a chromosome failed to separate or to function properly in these Budgies when each one was an embryo, leading to bizarre colours appearing. That is, a DNA malfunction.

At a Glance

The weirdest Budgies in the world are odd coloured birds like the one above. They are Chimera Budgies (also known as 'mosaics' or 'half siders' to some people). Curiously, they never produce young that look like themselves.

The odds against a DNA malfunction like this happening are hundreds of thousands to one. The problem with this theory is that it fails to explain how multiple differences caused by separate genes could occur in the same bird at the same time. That is, a Budgie that is part Greygreen and part Sky Blue is not possible – but these do exist (see photo on page 106). One part is Grey plus the Green gene and the other is non-Grey plus the Blue gene. These two lots of genes are malfunctions happening in one bird at the same time: the odds of billions to one! So the theory of one malfunctioning chromosome can't explain that sort of Budgie.

Left: Sometimes the Chimera is a halfsider, that is, one half of the bird is, say, Blue and the other half is Green – with the line of demarcation right down the centre of the bird. The bird on the left is exactly that – a halfsider. Others have random patches of different colours, as is the case with the bird below. Believe it or not, sometimes the bird is male on one side and female on the other! Photo: Susan Dennis.

Right: Crested Opaline Blue and Green Chimera. Photo: Kathy Manton.

I have mated two of these Chimeras together and raised 18 young: none of them were Chimeras. Each one was just an ordinary Budgie of one sex, and without any unusual features.

CURIOSITY.

The bird on the right is nearly a halfsider. He has a Spangle left wing, but his right wing has almost no pigment.

Look closely at his left wing. It has the flightless wonder virus disease. That is, many flight feathers are missing. But the other wing doesn't have it, hinting that this virus may only attack genetically prone individuals, i.e. there is a genetic component in susceptibility to this incurable disease.

New breakthroughs

New work that I have seen with horses offers a new view on these Budgie oddities. Believe it or not, they are two different Budgies joined together. They originate as a pair of non-identical twins: two eggs inside one eggshell separately fertilised by different sperm. The two resulting embryos then fuse into one body. One composite embryo made up from the cells of two non-identical twins: two Budgies in one body.

Sometimes this compound bird is Green on one side and Blue on the other. Sometimes it is a mop on one side and a non-mop on the other. Sometimes we see a mosaic of different colours like Cinnamonwing and Normal wing colour patches on one bird. All of this fits neatly with the theory of two different birds fused together as one. It is just a neater and **much closer** variant of the conjoined twin (except that in this case, they are not identical twins). All of this is controlled by the bird's electrome.

The electrome

This is the HUGE breakthrough from a project led by Michael Levin at Tufts University in Massachusetts, USA, that solves a wide range of problems that many of us have struggled with for decades. It finally explains the basic structure and nature of animal and plant development. All plants and animals are electrical beings where every cell is electrically active, acting as tiny batteries. They form part of the development of the framework of all living things, from skeletons, repairs, and organs in animals, to the framework of plants.

The electrome uses the tiniest of electrical currents, around 0–90 millivolts, to make the template of our bodies, which genes are unable to do by themselves, e.g. two eyes, one nose, plus a backbone, etc. After laying down the structural plan, the electrome dictates which bit goes where. Ninety millivolts creates skeletal muscle, seventy millivolts creates nerve cells, etc.

So how does this relate to breeding Budgies? The voltage changes form the blueprint of our bodies, organs, etc. These voltage changes do more than just form a blueprint, however: they actually instruct the genes when to go to work and what to do and where to do it.

Classic electrome effects in Budgies would be Crest and Hagoromo structures. The bilateral symmetry and placement of the whorls in Hagoromos will be controlled by the electrome. The placement and shape of the crests/whorls will be electrome controlled, which fits in very well with my Crest theory. Obviously, the electrome is the mechanism behind Chimeras (see 'You are electric' by Sally Adee, *New Scientist* magazine, 25 February 2023).

How do we know about the workings of a Chimera?

Many horses are registered as purebreds by DNA genetic marker testing. That is, hair samples are pulled out and DNA from the root of the hairs is used to verify that the foals do indeed come from the mare and stallion listed on the pedigree certificate. It all went pear-shaped when the Quarter Horse Dunbars Gold was lodged for registration. Dunbars Gold is a brindle-coloured horse – a horse striped much like brindle dogs. This is usually a non-heritable characteristic in horses. When they sent in the hair sample of Dunbars Gold, he had two different sorts of DNA types: one from his darker hairs and one from the lighter ones. That is, he is two horses in the one body. Fully integrated into one neat body, are two different horses, **one male and one female** that were more or less mixed up as if by a blender. How weird is that? However, he looks and functions like a typical male horse.

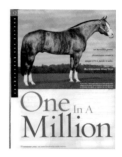

In most of the genetic literature, the geneticists called these sorts of horses, humans, Budgies, etc, Chimeras (pronounced *ky-meer-a*). The Chimera is a fictitious Greek monster with a lion's head, a goat's body and a snake's tail. It also breathed flames. The geneticists were right – that is, the Chimera horses, Budgies, etc, appear to be two different organisms joined together. This explains why they don't reproduce their strange combinations of colours. That is, they either breed as one colour, or they breed as the other. Photo: *The American Quarter Horse Journal.*

Presumably, most Chimeras are normal looking. If a horse is made up of two horses of the same colour or of two identical twins, then it would look quite normal. Even a DNA test would not reveal two identical twins in one body because identical twins have identical DNA types and sexes.

To make it all more confusing, they now have hereditary brindle-coloured horses that do pass the colour on to their foals. That is, there is now also a horse mutation for brindle, as there is in dogs. Very confusing.

On the right is a very subtle Chimera. Note the patch of violet body colour on his chest near his lower foot. BUT the vent area has violet suffusion, which is common in Violet varieties: this is a

Red Violet Olive Green Clearwing. Suffusion is blurry, but Chimera colours are very clear.

All great breeders notice the tiniest of differences. This is what makes them great. This bird's Chimera area amounts to about six feathers!

Left: A very similar Chimera in a Normal Greygreen.

Cinnamonwings

Cinnamonwings are beautiful Budgies with brown wings. They are usually just called Cinnamons. This mutation turns all melanin pigment from black to brown, which turns all body colour a lighter colour as well.

Left: This is a Cinnamonwing Violet Sky Yellow Faced/White Cap hybrid. That face colour is real, not enhanced. The White Cap gene creates these miracles.

Cinnamonwing and Opaline are both sex-linked mutations and they tend to link together, much as Cinnamonwing and Lutino tend to link together to form Lacewings. Linkage means that two genes stick together and are passed on to future generations as one single variety.

Below left: This is a White Cap Opaline Cinnamonwing Grey. The Grey gene darkens the Cinnamon wing markings considerably.

Below right: This is a White Cap/Golden Faced hybrid Sky Blue Cinnamonwing.

Most Cinnamons bred are females because of the sex linkage. Many Normal-looking males are split for Cinnamon, which means that when mated to a Normal female half of the daughters will be visible Cinnamons and half of the sons will be split for Cinnamonwing like dad. No female can be a visual Normal which is split for Cinnamon. Cinnamons tend to have pinkish feet, but these ones have a grey-pink feet.

Cinnamonwing matings go this way:

Cinnamon male mated to Cinnamon female produces 100% Cinnamons.

Cinnamon male mated to Normal female produces equal numbers of Normal males split for Cinnamon and Cinnamon females.

Normal male split for Cinnamon mated to Cinnamon female produces 25% Cinnamon males, 25% Cinnamon males split for Cinnamon, 25% Cinnamon females and 25% Normal females.

Normal male split for Cinnamon mated to Normal female produces 25% Normal males split for Cinnamon, 25% Normal males, 25% Cinnamon females and 25% Normal females.

A Normal male mated to a Cinnamon female produces 50% Normal males split for Cinnamon and 50% Normal females.

To find out more go to the sex linkage chapter on page 185.

Lacewings

Lacewings are one of the very strangest varieties in Budgies.

They are a combination of Cinnamonwing and Lutino or Albino. The 'Ino' gene and the Cinnamonwing gene both reside on the Z sex chromosome, and when both occur on one Z chromosome, they tend to link together and interact. That is, 'Ino' and Cinnamonwing are both visible in one

At a Glance

Lacewings are Albinos or Lutinos with red eyes, and white or yellow feathers plus Cinnamonwing wing colour. The wing colour is always a soft brown, but never black.

bird at the same time (which is theoretically impossible). 'Ino' also can join up for a triple display with the sex-linked Opaline gene and the Cinnamon gene, both of which are on the Z chromosome together.

Usually Albino and Lutino remove all colour except the yellow in Lutinos. Albinism and Lutino only remove melanin pigment. But in the case of Lacewings, both Cinnamonwing and 'Ino' are visible in the same bird. You would expect that the 'Ino' gene would remove all melanin colour, but it does not remove cinnamon melanin. This weird occurrence happens because the two mutations reside on the Z sex chromosome.

Gene linkage is when two genes stick to each other: they travel together and don't want to break apart. This can be because they are just very near to each other

Left: This very Modern Budgerigar is an Opaline Cinnamonwing Lacewing – three sex-linked mutations from the Z chromosome all working together. Genetically this is a Cinnamonwing Opaline Lutino.

on one chromosome or if they touch each other when the chromosomes are folded. The way we usually see photos of chromosomes looking like two sausages tied together is a brief moment during cell division. Like this:

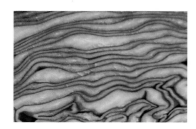

Normally chromosomes in cells are vastly long threads folded into a scribble of great complexity. Looking similar to the sliced red cabbage photo left. Sometimes, when strands of different folded chromosomes touch, they form a linkage which is re-established every time that the chromosomes fold up. They always fold the same way.

Opalines

Opalines were one of the very few Budgie mutations that occurred in the wild. Trappers sent them off with shipments of Wild Budgies to Adelaide and even to England. It is my contention that Opaline is the original colour of Wild Budgies long, long ago.

The amazing thing about Opalines is that they vary so much. Some are almost totally green or blue. This creates wonderful opportunities for creating exciting new Budgie varieties based on the Opaline.

At a Glance

Opalines are among the most beautiful Budgerigars ever developed. Their body colour rises up from their belly and breast to mix with their wing colour as well. The name Opaline reflects the opalescent nature of their mixture of green or blue with their black wing markings; reminiscent of an opal gem.

Above are examples of variability in Opaline wing patterns. The female on the left-hand side has a predominantly green wing, but the right-hand female has a predominantly black wing. Both are Opalines. The green female is very close to being an all-green bird.

By far the best creation involving the Opaline is the spectacular Rainbow variety. Rainbows have gold, cream, blue, violet and green all on the one spectacular bird. Once seen, you can never forget them. Brilliant Rainbow breeders (mostly in the Middle East, North Africa and Asia) have increased the amount of body colour on the wings, removing most of the black or grey wing markings along the way. This has created psychedelic colour effects on a living bird!

This amazing Rainbow has a huge amount of greenish-blue on its wings. It is a great tribute to its breeder. And it has a tiny crest too.

The Rainbow is a combination of the three prettiest Budgie varieties ever produced: Opaline, Yellow Faced Blue and Clearwing. This one is a brand new variety, a White Cap Bronze Seafoam Rainbow. These new varieties are being developed by the members of the Australian Heritage Budgerigar Association.

In Australia, up until about 1970, self-Blues or self-Greens were bred for showing. These were either all-Green or all-Blue Opaline Clearwings. A self-coloured object is something of one uniform colour all over. For instance, a Black Eyed White or Black Eyed Yellow is also referred to as a White Self or Yellow Self.

Right: This male bears a close resemblance to an Opaline Clearwing Green – it is almost a self-green.

Opaline is a sex-linked variety where the visibly Opaline male must carry two Opaline genes but the female only carries one. It is a recessive sex-linked variety. For details, go to 'Breeding statistics' on page 112–4.

Below left: This is little fellow is another new one – a young Double Factor White Cap Green Rainbow. His wing is almost all green. This is another example of the new Budgerigar varieties being developed by the Australian Heritage Budgerigar Association.

Below right: An Australian Golden Faced Violet Opaline with large areas of violet on his wings.

For a much more thorough look at Opalines, go to the Master Class section on Opalines on page 328.

Pastels: a new breakthrough

Around the world, Budgie breeders are beginning to take an interest in Pastels. A lot of this is due to Naomi Watts, who is the leader of our Pastel Group within the Australian Heritage Budgerigar Association.

This is Naomi Watts and some of her Pastels. Naomi can see opportunities in developing subtle Budgie colours. Men have dominated the Budgie world for way too long. As a male, I must admit that, in general, women are often far better at picking beautiful colours and beautiful colour combinations than men. It's time that more women made colour decisions and Budgie clubs will benefit enormously from this activity. Contact Naomi via the Australian Heritage Budgerigar Association's Facebook page or via @The Pastel Projects – Pastel Budgerigar Breeders United.

Right is a Bush Budgie Pastel. This amazingly beautiful Australian Golden Faced Blue Dilute turned up among my 100% pure Bush Budgies. I have been lucky enough to also breed them in Golden Faced Violet Dilute Bush Budgies as well.

What is a Pastel?

Obviously, Pastels are superbly subtly-coloured birds such as you can see in this chapter. They have long been overlooked by the Budgie fraternity. But no more! Naomi and her group, mostly women, are currently working on exactly which shades and colours will be allocated classes at exhibitions. She wants members of her group to help in deciding and naming colour effects that should be deemed classes. Anyone from anywhere in the world can join her group and take part in the decision-making. She is not interested in which mutations are involved, but rather the colour effects achieved. So, a class could be called 'Whisper Blue', 'Cream Frangipani' or just 'Seafoam'. Any bird that fits these delicious descriptions can enter the class – regardless of its genetic make-up.

In Europe, among colour Budgies, they are casually referring to these birds as Pallid. The word 'pallid' often has connotations meaning 'pale because of poor health or lacking vigour, insipid'. We chose the name Pastels because of its positivity and its use in art and fashion.

This is a complete breakaway from the usual description of Budgies by their complex genetic makeup. The 'Cream Frangipani' above is a Double Factor Spangle, Single Factor White Cap.

Naomi is thinking of having no formal judges, but rather members of the group democratically picking the prettiest bird in each class. And why not?

Below could be a 'Whisper Blue' on the left and a 'Glacier' on the right. Two different tones of blue and white. The left bird is an Opaline Cinnamon Clearwing Sky and the one on the right is an Opaline Dilute Clearwing-bred Sky.

To re-cap, none of the class or colour names mentioned here are decided upon – they are just conversation starters. None of our judging criteria are decided yet. All of the Australian Heritage Budgerigar Association's decisions are made by the members.

Pastels are not new, they have popped up individually here and there for decades... BUT no one has developed classes for them at shows. There has been no organised breeding of these beautiful Budgies. But now there is support for Pastels at last.

If you wish to breed them or even if you just want to look at the photos of these exquisite Budgies, join Naomi's Pastel Facebook page or see these birds on the Australian Heritage Budgerigar Association's Facebook page as well.

Left: Exquisite as this Dilute White Cap Sky Rainbow is, perhaps it and the Bush Budgie Pastel could be called 'Seafoam' or 'Silver Lichen'?

Left: This pinkish Budgie is a real 'rock star'. He is an Amethyst, genetically a Red Violet Fallow Clearwing. Note the pink eyes, cere and feet, and pinkish body colour.

Centre: A 'Glacier' bred by the late Hilton Smith.

Right: Another 'Seafoam' or 'Silver Lichen'? Genetically a Cinnamon White Cap Rainbow.

Saddlebacks

This is a Violet Normal Saddleback. It is a recessive mutation which appeared in Les and Barry Ryan's aviaries in Sydney in 1975. Notice the blurry greyish scapular markings, and the pale areas on the back of the head. It is easily confused with Opaline, but Saddleback never produces body colour on the wings. The main feature of Opaline is body colour on the wings. Opaline is a sex-linked variety, so it is on a totally different chromosome to the recessive Saddleback mutation, i.e. there is no relationship between the two.

Like all wing-marking pattern mutations, Saddleback is quite variable. The other wing-marking pattern mutations that vary are: Spangle, Texas Clearbody, Dutch Pied and Opaline. Saddlebacks occur in most colours and varieties.

Spangles

Spangles are typically Budgies with thin, crescent-like markings on their wings and back, plus halo-like spots on their masks when they are Single Factor for this mutation. Their body colour is slightly diluted. In the Double Factor form, the Spangles are mostly all yellow or all white, but they can have patches of body and wing colour on their body as well as the white of yellow.

Like Opaline, Spangle is very variable: it can produce bands across the belly, or wing markings very similar to Normals. Or Normal-looking birds with white or yellow tails. There is also a Clearwing-like form of Spangle.

Above left: A Teal Blue White Cap Single Factor Spangle showing the classic swank that Spangles are noted for. The Spangle is a wonderful beginners' Budgie for breeding – semi-dominant and stylish.

Above right: This is a Sky Blue Yellow Faced Teal Blue Single Factor Spangle. It is a European Exhibition Budgie with moderately extreme feathering. The markings ideally should be clearer, i.e. a thin but defined crescent at the tip of each wing feather.

Note the very long mask and neck on this Grey Spangle. Both Grey and Spangle seem to add to the feather, style and size of show Budgies. In this case the very long neck is essential to balance the newish very long mask. Long masks need long necks to complement them, otherwise they hang down over the chest. Unfortunately, most breeders fail to restore this balance, ruining the outline of the Exhibition Budgerigar.

Above left: A female Greygreen Single Factor Spangle. The body colour and wing markings are quite good. Again, note how stylish she is.

Above right: This beautiful bird is a White Cap Double Factor Spangle. Note the two or three greenish feathers on the breast.

The Spangle appears to be the opposite to the Australian and German Fallows. Whereas the Fallows appear to be linked to poor size and feathering, the Spangle appears to be linked to lush feathering and maybe to excellent posture as well. This may explain their meteoric rise in popularity as a show bird, although this linkage seems barely to have been noticed by breeders.

Right: A White (Blue) European Double Factor Spangle.

Left: A Purewing Sky Blue Spangle. It is thought to be a variant of the Double Factor Melanistic Spangle. It is similar to a Clearwing, except that its body colour is rather pale.

Right: A Banded Greygreen Spangle. The band is just above its legs. This is a hereditary feature, but it is not very easy to perfect. Much the same as the band in Banded Australian Dominant Pieds.

Left: A White Tailed Melanistic Spangle. Note the Spangle pattern on the primary flight feathers as well.

Right: Although hard to recognise as a Spangle, this is a Violet White Tailed Spangle. It is far more 'melanistic' than the Spangle variety called Melanistic. This bird even has very black flight feathers.

Strange Budgies

There are many truly strange Budgies that have appeared over the years. Perhaps the weirdest of the lot are Chimeras, a.k.a. Halfsiders or Mosaics. These are Budgies that are a crazy mix of many colours. Often they are a Blue Budgie on one side and a Green on the other. Or a male on one side and a female on the other.

These two above are true Halfsiders. Each side is totally different. Photo: Susan Dennis.

Right: This Budgie is part Green, part Blue – with a crest on top!

Above are different Chimeras with a mixture of colours. Chimeras can be very different, with bits and pieces of strange birds all over them. Photo: Susan Dennis.

Near-black Budgies

Below: Black Faced Black Winged Anthracite Budgies, which are not found in Australia at present. Photos: Roger van Delft

Chimeras

Chimeras in birds are, incredibly, TWO babies in the one egg. Sort of like much closer conjoined twins. When twins occur in an egg, there is usually not enough space for two babies, so sometimes, the two coalesce into one bird. Sometimes half-and-half configuration, sometimes not. There are genetic mechanisms that coordinate the development of all babies such that you have two legs, two arms (or wings), one head, etc. In the case of Chimeras, these mechanisms make do as best they can. These birds never breed similar birds to themselves since no ordinary genes are involved in this configuration. It is just a developmental mistake.

Below is a Chimera horse. He is Quarter Horse Dunbars Gold. It was thought that he was a brindle horse, but he is actually two horses, one male and one female joined together in differing striped areas. This was proved by DNA testing of the light and dark areas. He is, remarkably, a fully functional male horse. But he is not a brindle.

Purewing Budgies look almost exactly like a perfectly coloured Cinnamonwing Clearwing. They are not that at all. They are Double Factor Melanistic Spangles

Photo: The American Quarter Horse Journal.

(see photo right). They are just being developed in the USA. Again, they are not available in Australia, but if you breed some Melanistic Spangles together, you might produce one. Melanistic Spangles are Spangles with darker wings. Above right, is a Purewing Spangle, which is a version of a double factor Melanistic Spangle.

Near-black Budgies are an assembly of genetic black bits and pieces, none of which is available in Australia. The Black Faced mutation produces black striping on the forehead, mask and subtly on the body. When combined with the near-black Anthracite mutation, the striping is darkened considerably. Then if you add the new Black Winged mutation, you get a truly amazing feat of Budgerigar breeding. These birds are selling for vast sums of money in Asia in particular. Some people are asking if they are really Budgies? Yes they are, but they do not exist in Australia.

Budgerigar colours

Amethysts

The Amethyst Budgerigar is very new, and still quite rare. Like the beautiful Amethyst gemstone, Amethyst Budgies are a pinkish-lavender colour.

Right: This is an Amethyst Clearwing Budgerigar. The white wings set off the pink-lavender of the body colour very nicely indeed. My best Amethysts are much pinker now than when I first began. With careful selection their pinkish colour improves every generation.

Amethysts also occur in other Budgerigar varieties such as Rainbows, Fallows, Texas Clearbodies, Dilutes, Cinnamonwings, and Recessive and Dominant Pieds.

Exhibition classes for Amethysts exist within the Australian Heritage Budgerigar Association, and the singular judging criterion is that the bird that is pinkest wins.

Left: This is a piece of amethyst gemstone. Notice the amethyst crystals on the inside. Amethyst is a reddish or pinkish lavender-purple type of quartz. Comparing the amethyst gemstone with the Amethyst Budgerigar shows remarkable similarities in colour.

By far the most important thing to do in developing your own Amethyst Budgies is to find a breeder of truly rich purple-coloured Violets. It has been proven that most so-called 'Violets' lack the pinkish or reddish tinges

Right: This is my first Red Violet Clearwing Budgerigar when he was just out of the nest. He is the founding sire of all of my Red Violets via line breeding. His descendants are considerably redder now.
For the full story on Red Violets go to page 136.

that are necessary for Amethyst development. So choose your Violets carefully.

Amethyst Clearwings seem to be the best combination in this colour. The white wings and the pinkish body colour combine so well. Below are some photos of the Red Violet Clearwings from which I developed my Amethyst Clearwings.

Above are descendants of my original male Red Violet Clearwing. The female on the left is a Double Factor Red Violet Cobalt and the male is a Double Factor Red Violet Sky Blue – both are visual Violets. Mated together, they produced 100% Violet young: half were Red Violets like mum and the other half were like dad, visually Common Violets. By introducing Cinnamonwing into this line, I produced my Clearwing Amethysts.

Above left: Always a standout in a crowd, the central male is a Red Violet Clearwing. I hope that you can see the reddish tone in his body colour as against the bluer and paler colours on some of the other Violets in this shot. The female staring upwards, one perch above him to the left, is also a Red Violet; the others are Common Violets.

Above right: This is a female Opaline Clearwing Amethyst. Genetically, she is a Red Violet Cinnamonwing Opaline Clearwing.

The sex-linked Cinnamonwing gene is used to Dilute the blue component of the body colour in the Red Violet Clearwing, leaving the pinkish tones of the Amethyst. In the case of Fallow Amethysts, the Red Violet colour has again been added, but the dilution of the body colour is done by the Fallow gene itself, not by Cinnamonwing. Similarly, with the Amethyst Texas Clearbody, the Clearbody gene itself Dilutes the Red Violet to Amethyst – Cinnamonwing is not used at all.

Sadly, these same crosses produced from Modern Show Violets do not really have the pinkish tones – only the Heritage Reddish Violets from yesteryear have the reddish intensity, and when diluted, the pinkish tones. Most Modern Violets seem to be more an intense Cobalt colour than a true Reddish Violet.

In the new Australian Heritage Budgerigar Association, we have agreed (for fun) to initially judge classes of Amethysts by one single criterion only:

This is a young Amethyst Clearwing bred in December 2020. He is one of the pinkest that I have bred. Each year the young birds are getting pinker and pinker. Without doubt, gene modifiers provide the greatest opportunity to develop new and better colours and varieties in Budgerigars.

the PINKEST bird wins! So size, mask, head, posture, etc, simply don't matter at all. It will be very interesting to see how pink we get them after 10 years or so. We are selecting for the gene modifiers that change the deep blue to ever pinker shades.

There have been a few people who doubted that the pinkish Budgies called Amethysts could exist. I attach verification from leading Budgerigar expert Cyril Rogers. In 1981 in Cyril Rogers's book *The World of Budgerigars* he mentions on page 102 that in the early days of Violet breeding, circa 1953, F. Garvey's violets were: "the most brilliant and richly coloured strain of Violets in the country (UK). Garvey's were well known for their beautiful pinkish tone of Violet and no one else seemed to be able to produce this colour unless they had birds that came actually from the Garvey strain. It is now a considerable time since any bird of this particularly rosy Violet colour have been on view at the shows as the birds seen at present time are of a more bluish Violet shade."

He goes on to say: "All varieties of visual Violet birds are undoubtedly very handsome and exceedingly colourful, two of the most striking forms I have seen are the Cinnamon Violet Cobalt and the Opaline Cinnamon Violet Cobalt. In both instances, the addition of the Cinnamon character gives the birds a beautiful, soft,

This is a Dilute Amethyst, genetically a Clearwing-bred Red Violet Dilute. Clearwing-bred Dilutes are Dilutes that spontaneously appear in Clearwing breedings. Thus, this pinkish bird carries 100% of the Clearwing gene modifiers for clear wing colour, deep body colour and (Red Violet) pinkish tones.

warm, rose-tinted Violet shade."

My Amethysts are also based on my unique strain of intense Red Violet Clearwings. I hope that this helps people to understand. It is clear that the potential for Amethyst and hopefully, fully **Pink** Budgies has been noticed long ago. Violets first appeared in Europe in the 1920s, so presumably by the use of the phrase 'early exhibitors' Cyril means around the 1930s and 1940s, perhaps the 1950s at the latest.

The Amethyst has laid dormant for perhaps 60 years or so. It is long overdue to carry on the work of the early pioneers of reddish or pinkish Violets and their Cinnamon derivatives.

Rainbows also come in the Amethyst colour. They are identical to the Amethyst Clearwing, with Opaline and Australian Golden Faced Blue genes added. Dilute Amethysts are Clearwing-bred Red Violets diluted by the Dilute gene itself; no Cinnamonwing genes are involved.

This group of Rainbow Budgies features Amethyst Rainbows at the top left and also below at the lower central position. Note their light pinkish lavender colour. These are spectacularly beautiful Budgies. Photo: R. Elwell.

Where do the pinkish or reddish colours come from?

They are optical illusions. There is no red or pink pigment in the Budgerigar. But there are structural colours that are created by the scattering of light. All blue colours in Budgies are illusions created by the scattering of light. Almost all colours in hummingbirds and peafowl are also structural colours. That is, there are no red, blue, purple, gold or green pigments at all in hummingbirds or peafowl.

The blue colours in Budgies are all created by small, cloudy air bubbles inside the feather barbs. These bubbles have black-pigmented areas towards the middle of the barb. The end result is that some components of white light are scattered back out of the barb, and others are absorbed by the black inner area. The thickness of the bubbles and also of the tiny black central area determines what colours (i.e. frequencies of light) are scattered back: it could be Sky Blue, Cobalt, Mauve or Violet. With careful selection with Violets, extra reddish or pinkish colour can also be scattered back. This

Two photos of my pinkest Amethyst Australian Fallow in 2021.

is the essence of the Red Violet and also of the Amethyst. As we change the shape of the cloudy bubbles and the amount of underlying black pigment in the feather barbs, so we change the frequency of the visible light scattered back to our eyes. I have no idea how pink we can breed a Budgie, but we are making real progress.

Recently I discovered a HUGE breakthrough that explains why my red violet budgies appear deep blue/violet in photos. When I researched violet and purple with digital cameras, it turns that they can't cope with the colour red purple, they can cope with violet but not red purple or pink lavender. They can't put red and violet together as one colour when rendering photos (check this in Google).

However, you can improve the situation a bit: go to the Vivid setting on the camera, and then also slowly increase the red in the colour adjustments in iPhoto. Above are two photos of the same bird. On the left is an adjusted vivid photo of one of my red violets which matches the bird perfectly in real life. On the right is the photo as the digital camera rendered it, which is nothing like the bird's colour in real life. Note that the red adjustment shows up a bit in the background in the left picture.

So, I really do have red violet (purple) budgies, but the modern digital cameras make them look dark blue/violet. Equally the Amethyst budgies appear to be a soft blue rather than a soft pink/purple, again because the cameras can't cope.

The Red Violet budgerigar exists and in REAL LIFE it is pure magic.

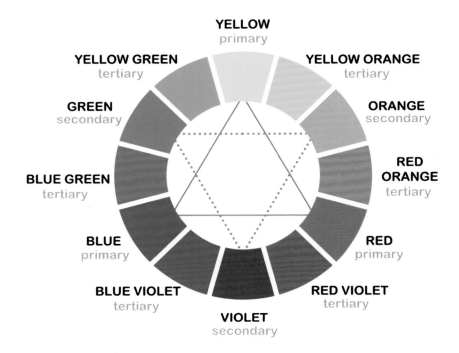

All of the photos of Red Violets and Amethysts in this book lack most of the reddish and pinkish hues that my birds carry in real life. This comparison here is the only photo that tells the real story; please go to Google to discover the pink/purple problem with iPhones etc. This is not just a budgie problem, this colour problem occurs widely in photography.

If Red Violet colour still confuses you, look above. When you add a tiny bit of red to blue, you get Violet. As you add more red, you get Red Violet. Most Violet Clearwings are Blue Violet. Red Violet Clearwings have much more red in them. If you Dilute Red Violet by using the Cinnamonwing gene, you get an Amethyst. I hope that this helps you to understand.

There are Red Violets all around the world, particularly in the magnificent Rainbows of the Arab states and in Asia. There are some truly brilliant Rainbow breeders in these areas. In Japan, Amethysts are known as Lilacs.

Anthracites

The Budgie world is zeroing in on the ALL-BLACK Budgie. With the combining of the Black Winged and the Black Faced Budgie mutations, plus the Anthracite body colour mutation, we are nearly there. Having said that, the darkest of my Violet Mauve Clearwings are as dark on the body as an Anthracite. This is the gene versus modifier game. With patience, modifiers can win out over mutations.

At a Glance

The Anthracite Budgie in its Double Factor form has the closest to black body colour yet produced. Single Factor Anthracites are just slightly darker than the bird's real body colour, so a Sky Blue turns into a Cobalt, etc.

Nonetheless, the Anthracite is a major advance in the quest to produce Black Budgies.

Double Factor Blue Anthracites.
Photo: Johan Kortenray.

Young Double Factor Blue Anthracite.
Photo: Johan Kortenray

This is a series of Black Faced Budgies. Starting from the left side, the first bird is a Single Factor Green Anthracite, the third from the left is a Double Factor Blue Series Anthracite, fifth from the left is a Double Factor Blue Series Anthracite and the seventh from the left is a Single Factor Green Series Anthracite. Photo: Roger van Delft.

Basic colour variations in Budgies

A female Light Green Clearwing, with the body colour of Wild Budgies.

A Dark Green Clearwing.

A very intensely coloured Olive Green Clearwing.

There are three variations of the basic Budgie body colour: Sky Blue, Cobalt and Mauve. All blue colours in Budgies are optical illusions caused by the scattering of light.

Right: A Sky Blue Clearwing.

Below left: A Mauve Clearwing. In Budgies, the name 'Mauve' refers to a bluish-grey colour which is rather confusing as the colour mauve is actually a pinkish purple.

Below right: A richly coloured Cobalt Opaline Clearwing showing some of the opalescence that they are famous for.

The dark, medium and light colours are caused by a simple genetic mechanism. The Light Green or Sky Blue colours are the basic colour. Then if you add one darkening gene (Single Factor) you get Cobalt, and if you add two darkening genes (Double Factor) you get Mauve or Olive.

This Amethyst Clearwing is a magnificent colour – a pinkish purple, the same as amethyst crystals. He has pinkish feet, cere, eyes and body colour because he is a Red Violet Fallow. All Fallows have pink eyes.

Still only young, this is a Red Violet Clearwing, which is an intense reddish-purple colour. If you dilute this colour using the Cinnamonwing gene, or the Australian Fallow or German Fallow genes, you will create an Amethyst as above.

When you add the yellow pigment of Green series Budgies, you turn a Grey into a Greygreen, as you can see in this Clearwing.

This is a Yellow Budgie. Yellow can be due to several different mutations – this bird is a Lutino, which shows yellow pigmentation due to xanthochromism.

The most difficult variety to produce, a Black Eyed White, which is a modified Dilute. You can also get Albinos, White Double Factor Spangles, and others.

Budgies also come in this grey colour. This female is a Greywing Grey. Note the greyish cheek patches.

The mysterious Red Violet

Over the last ten years or so, I have been breeding deep Red Violet Clearwings. They are breathtakingly beautiful, but I don't really know what modifiers create this dazzling colour.

Below is a comparison between a recent Australian National Champion Normal Violet and one of my young Red Violet Clearwings.

Clearly there is a vast difference between a Red Violet and the Common Normal Violet. The above Normal Violet is a visual Violet*, in his case I suspect that he is a Double Factor Violet Sky. That means that he has two genes for Violet and is, at base, a Sky Blue.

The Red Violet Clearwing above is a Double Factor Violet Cobalt. That means that he also carries two Violet genes, but his base colour is Cobalt. However, this does not explain why his body colour is so intense, nor where the reddish tone comes from. Obviously there is an extra colour intensifier in there which highlights the red tones.

The Reddish Violet colour is hereditary, maybe a dominant colour. It exists in some rare Heritage Normal Violets, but this is the first time that I have seen it in Clearwings. I am first of all trying to stabilise it, and also to breed up many for spreading around AHBA members. This will be an insurance policy against my losing this amazing new

---

* A 'visual Violet' is a Budgerigar that is accepted and judged as a true Violet Budgie. It can either be a Single Factor or Double Factor Violet Cobalt or a Double Factor Violet Sky.

mutation. So many new mutations or just great lines of Budgies are lost when a disaster such as a disease outbreak, a theft, or a bushfire occurs.

The Red Violet is also the base colour of Amethyst Budgerigars. As soon as I saw my first Red Violets, I thought that if I could reduce the blue from this colour, I might just get a pinkish Budgie. So I added the Cinnamonwing gene to the Red Violet Clearwings, and – bingo! – pinkish-lavender young turned up. The Cinnamonwing gene had substantially diluted the blue in the Red Violet, but had left the red colour as a superb pink.

I am still not sure if the reddish, intense colour in my Red Violet Clearwings, or the pink Amethyst colour, is due to a gene mutation or to gene modifier elements. But it is definitely hereditary. I breed 80–100 Violets each year and now about 30 of those are Red Violets.

Above is a male Amethyst Clearwing. The pinkish colour is very evident in this bird. He is technically a Red Violet Double Factor Violet Cobalt Cinnamonwing Clearwing.

Above: The females in these two photos above are visual Red Violet Clearwings. They are Double Factor Violet Cobalt Clearwings. The males are Double Factor Violet Sky Blue Clearwings. All of these birds carry the Red Violet modifier. This type of pairing will produce 100% visual Violets, half of which will be visual Red Violets.

Right: This is a visual Red Violet Clearwing, i.e. a Double Factor Violet Cobalt Clearwing with the Red Violet modifier. I haven't seen a Normal Violet with this intensity of reddish colour.

Below, we are repeating the Colour Chart so that breeders can accurately compare the colours on the wheel with actual birds nearby.

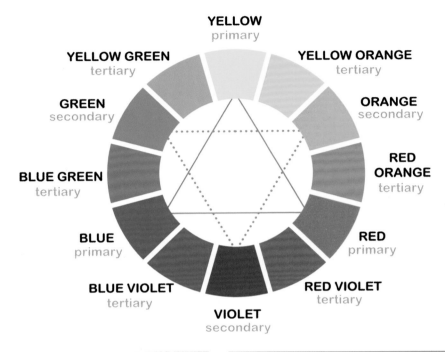

Mauve

Red Violet is a legitimate colour, but many colour-challenged Budgie breeders happily accept the Budgie on the left as a Mauve. Compare it to the real Mauve colour patch beside it.

If Red Violet colour still confuses you, look at the chart above. When you add a tiny bit of Red to Blue, you get Violet. As you add more Red, you get Red Violet. Most Violet Clearwings are Blue Violet. Red Violet Clearwings have much more Red in them. OK?

Ultraviolet colours in Budgies

Budgies possess ultraviolet pigments and can see UV colours very well. Most bird species also see UV colours but we can't. In the Budgie it has been proven that the UV pattern on the forehead and mask of adult Budgies is very attractive to the opposite sex.

Right: This is a Normal Light Green Budgie under black UV light. Note the rich yellow UV fluorescence on the forehead, and adjacent to the cheek patch. Note also that there are no other UV areas apart from the forehead and mask. This is the pattern seen on all Wild Budgies.

As any Budgie breeder knows, Budgies can't see very well in low light conditions. Visit Budgie aviaries in low light at dusk, when we can still see very well, and they will panic, flying into walls etc. So how do they find their babies to feed them in a dark nesting hollow?

Well it turns out that while Budgies have poor vision in low light in general, they do have very good vision in low ultraviolet light. All Wild Budgies have UV pigment on their cap (i.e. forehead) and UV pigment stripes on their mask parallel to and next to each cheek patch (see photo). And so do their babies in the nesting hollow or box (see photo of a baby). These UV markings act like aeroplane runway lights to facilitate feeding in low light.

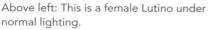

Above left: This is a female Lutino under normal lighting.

Above right: This is the same female Lutino from above, under back UV lighting showing the classic wild-type UV pattern.

Right: This is a young Budgie, still in the nest, showing the typical UV baby pattern that a parent would see in a nest.

Under black UV light, I photographed both adults and young and found that they had similar facial UV pattern, with the adults having slightly more intense UV pigmentation and the young a wider spread of UV (see photo of young bird above).

I also tested Budgies in a very poorly lit room lit only by a very weak fluorescent light, and they couldn't really see me at all. Then I turned off the weak light and turned on a fluorescent UV black light. Now I couldn't see much, but the Budgies could see my every move. So, parents presumably locate the circle and two broad areas of UV colour on each baby in the dark nesting hollow and feed it. Likewise, the babies beg the slightly more intense circle and two stripes of each parent for food.

The critical importance of UV pigment in Budgies almost certainly lies in the precise ability of adults and babies to locate each other for the regurgitation and exchange of food in dark nesting hollows. UV pigment in Budgies absorbs the UV light and emits it as visible light, adding to the overall visibility of both babies and adults.

For those wondering, UV pigment in Budgies is a sub-type of the parrot yellow pigment that Green Budgies possess*. Sadly, Blue series Budgies never produce any UV pigment at all, making them much less attractive to the opposite sex. Perhaps this is why pet shop owners so often say: "I need more Blue Budgies; I already have too many greens". Blue Budgies in a mixed colony of Budgies will not attract many mates and thus they produce less young.

A male Sky Blue Budgie.

This is the same bird under black UV light. Note that there is no UV fluorescence, except for some mucous glow above the cere.

* Australian Golden Faced Blues (both Single Factor and Double Factor) have both types of yellow pigment – parrot yellow and UV creamy yellow face markings.

This is a Double Factor Australian Golden Faced Sky Normal.

This is the same bird under black UV lighting showing the classic forehead and mask UV markings as seen in a Green bird.

English Yellow Faced Blues appear to have a pale, spread out area of UV creamy yellow pigment, and they also have the extra-intense UV on the forehead and beside the cheek-patch markings.

Above left: A female English Yellow Faced Sky Dilute in normal light.

Above right: The same female English Yellow Faced Sky Dilute as above under black UV lighting. Note the extra areas of UV yellow: full face plus wings and very little on the body. The Wild-type extra intense markings can still be seen on the forehead and near the cheek patches.

Seafoam White Caps (i.e. Single Factor White Caps) have extensive UV creamy yellow pigment all over except for the wings and the tips of the forehead feathers.

Above left: A Seafoam White Cap.

Above right: A young Seafoam Spangle. This bird is halfway through the moult and note that all new feathers are glowing creamy yellow on the head and the wings, and a greenish blue on the body. The darker purple areas are just the purple cast of the black UV light – note that the white background also appears purple.

Right: A young Seafoam White Cap Sky just out of the nest.

As a crowd attracter, what if we held UV classes at our major shows? In a blackened room out the back, with windows covered in curtains, we could have classes of glow-in-the-dark Budgies. These classes would be great for attracting people to exhibitions and even better for attracting kids to the Budgie world.

The varieties in the class could include White Caps, Yellow Faced Blues, Yellows, and so on.

White Cap Greens (i.e. Double Factor White Caps) have both parrot yellow and UV creamy yellow pigment all over except for the tips of the forehead feathers.

Right: This immature White Cap Green is just developing his white cap. White Cap Greens are born with a yellow cap which moults out to a whitish colour. At maturity White Cap Greens are indistinguishable from Normal Greens except for the white cap and a few white mask feathers near the cheek patches. Note the white feathers near the cheek patches, which suggest that a fully white face will be developed soon.

Since the intensity, spread and type of yellow pigments varies quite a bit between individual Exhibition Budgies, more research still needs to be done to confirm the precise yellow pigments and the precise yellow pigment areas in each Budgie variety. For example, some Exhibition Green or Yellow Budgies do carry excess UV creamy yellow pigment on top of their parrot yellow, presumably because breeders selected for really bright yellow or green colour in their birds. While we can't see UV pigments, we do see some fluorescence with other colours, e.g. yellow mixed with UV creamy yellow appears to our eyes to fluoresce somewhat. This phenomenon is used in dazzling yellow or orange safety vests and 'fragile' box stickers in the workplace. It is also seen in the fluorescing of white shirts and teeth under black UV light.

Left: A very clear Black Eyed Yellow from the late Peter Dodd, photographed under Black UV light, showing the spread of UV pigment over much of the bird. This creates the dazzling effect of luminous yellow. This may be the first Hi Visibility safety budgie. Well done, Peter.

143

Lastly, earlier studies made a mistake regarding parrot yellow colour. They claimed that Double Factor Green Budgies are the same colour as Greens split for Blue, when in fact the yellow is much brighter in Double Factor Green series birds (see pages 318, 319). In my Clearwings, Double Factor Greens have a much richer golden wing colour and the same applies to Black Eyed Yellows all over. This explains why in the golden era of Black Eyed Yellows, Black Eyed Whites were almost never bred. This must have happened because breeders always selected for and bred from the deepest yellow birds, which were almost always Double Factor for yellow. On investigating Peter Dodd's magnificent Black Eyed Yellows, they turned out to be both Double Factor for yellow **and** carrying UV creamy yellow all over as well. The Black Eyed Yellows of the past that were split for White were an insipid yellow colour and were culled. Black Eyed Yellow breeders take note: don't outcross to Black Eyed Whites unless your sole aim is to improve your Black Eyed Whites. Similarly, Lutino breeders should not outcross to Albinos unless your sole aim is to improve your Albinos.

The basic parrot yellow gene found in green Budgies comes in three different forms: the main parrot yellow, UV creamy yellow and the orange-red-pink series. No red, orange or pink colour can exist on a parrot unless it has the main parrot yellow gene as well (as a base). All can exist together in the one bird, but no genetically blue bird can ever have red, orange, pink or either of the yellow colours. Parblues such as Goldenfaces or Yellowfaces are not genetically blue series birds The extent of the areas of pink, orange or red on a bird carrying parrot yellow pigment (for example, on a Rainbow Lorikeet, Turquoise Parrot or Scarlet-chested Parrot) is highly variable. The amount of pink, orange and red is controlled by hereditary modifier mechanisms, making it quite easy to develop a predominantly red or pink bird (for example, a pink Bourke's Parrot), for example. Thus for showing, there are three separate groups of Budgies all of which are multiple alleles at the same gene locus: the Blue group (which includes Albinos and Whites), the Green group (which includes Yellow and Lutino), and the Yellow Faced Blue group. The Yellow Faced Blue group is not a member of the Blue group, nor is it a member of the Green group. It is a separate group by itself, often known as Parblue in other parrots. As yet we have not worked out whether the White Cap is a member of the Yellow Faced Blue group or not, nor have we worked out if it is a multiple allele at that gene locus. I have completed experiments to ascertain exactly where the White Cap belongs, and it is a multiple allele of other Yellow Faced Blues. Thus the large list of multiple alleles at this gene locus includes: Green, Blue, Australian Golden Faced Blue, English Yellow Faced Blue mutants 1 and 2, and White Cap.

Below are some photos of hybrid White Caps under normal lighting and also under black ultraviolet lighting. The brightness and increased area of UV colour clearly prove that we can breed spectacular UV Budgies in the future.

Above is a Golden Faced Blue hybridised with a White Cap. The photo on the left shows his spectacular golden face under normal light. On the right is the same bird under black UV light showing a much greater area of UV colour.

Right: Two Budgies carrying my new mutation, the Golden Top, under black UV light. Again, the UV colouring has spread considerably.

Fundamentals of genetics and breeding

Are new mutations common?

The answer is YES! Mutations are all around us, many people see them, but few people notice them. You can choose to notice them if you wish.

This mutant was photographed on 5 April 2023. There are seven young in here from one nest. The line was pure Clearwing for decades, yet a 'Normal' bird is in there among six Clearwings. This is the third round for the Golden Faced parents. So, they have been together for just on five months in one breeding cabinet. Clearwing being based on recessive genes, no Normal baby is possible. I have done no fostering nor any exchanging of eggs. Over the last 50 years, I have had three Normals appear in

pure Clearwing nests. Three mutations, or should I say three back-mutations. They have mutated back to the past. The previous two turned out to be Normals split for Clearwing.

Then there was this bird:

He looks like an Opaline. His dad was an Opaline, but his mum was a Normal. In theory you can't breed a male Opaline whose mum is a Normal. So I put his photo on Facebook as 'The rarest Budgerigar in the world', assuming that he was a mutant.

And he is. He turned out to be fertile and three generations later I am breeding what appears to be non-sex-linked Opalines, dominant ones at that too.

Below are some of his progeny, from a mating of two of his 'Opaline' young, I have bred four nests totalling 22 young – 12 Normal Violet Clearwings and 10 Opalines of both sexes in each type (more or less 50/50).

It is impossible to breed non-Opaline young from a pair of conventional Opalines. But I have a 50/50 mix of Opalines and non-Opalines in this nest, strongly indicating that this can only be a new mutation of dominant Opalines. This is a very valuable mutant for breeding better Rainbows.

When I first put the original mutant on Facebook, there were more than a few people who said that this was all nonsense. How wrong they were!

I have several mutants which are new richer Golden Faced Blues that fell out of my Rainbow breeding. Please everyone go looking for new mutations. I suspect that thousands of new Budgie mutations are hiding out around the world. Just waiting to be found. Look at my new Golden Tops below. Their colours are not artificially enhanced at all.

Above left: This is a young double factor Golden Top Violet Rainbow, not yet out of the nest. His colour is twice as good as a non-colour enhanced Golden Faced Rainbow photo. Please everyone, never colour enhance your Budgie photos.

Above right: This is a young Double Factor Spangle Double Factor Golden Top. No colour enhancement.

Breeding to the Standard

Breeding Exhibition Budgies that conform to the Standard has been one of my life's greatest joys since I was seven years old in 1954.

I adore the chest out, chin in, with a nice large head on a clean and healthy Budgerigar. I love selecting matings that stabilise the shape, colour and feathering of a beautifully balanced Exhibition Budgie.

Over many years I have had the enormous pleasure of seeing some truly amazing Budgies on the show bench. Some were mine but most weren't. I get the same pleasure from someone else's triumph as my own.

Breeding Exhibition Budgies began in earnest in the 1920s and 1930s, and today's Exhibition Budgies look nothing like the Wild Budgerigar of Australia's inland deserts. Modern Show Budgies are now enormous birds with amazing amounts of feathering when compared with the Wild Budgie.

Perhaps it is now time to review how we are going after more than 100 years of competitive breeding. Have we gone too far with the fashion-driven Exhibition Budgie. Standards of Perfection constantly move to ever-greater extremes. David Myers, one of Australia's leading bird experts, quotes his scientist father's comments on English imported Show Budgies. In 1990, he said: "They are being bred outside the limits of the species".

Which one of the two birds above would YOU choose?

This is what Budgerigar feathering SHOULD look like.

Once they were extraordinary aerial acrobats that rivalled swallows for aerial agility. Today many extreme showbirds can hardly fly at all. The relentless pursuit of ever-larger size, ever-longer feathering and ever-wider shoulders have taken a huge toll on our precious little friend.

Where do we go from here? When is enough, enough? My belief is that the Standards of Perfection are the overwhelming cause of the problems. Competition between breeders is a source of great joy for Budgerigar club members, but the welfare of the Budgerigar must be considered too. To return to the warning from David Myers, whose father, Ken Myers, Doctor of Science, Chief Research Scientist, CSIRO Division of Wildlife Research Canberra said: "They are being bred outside the limits of the species."

There is nothing wrong with breeding for larger size, larger heads, and even some directional feathering. But if we wish to breed for extremes, we simply must ensure that the poor little Budgie is able to cope as we proceed. We urgently need to work with veterinary bird experts and scientists to monitor and to remedy any problematic aspects of exhibition Budgerigar breeding. If we don't, animal welfare groups and governments will, sooner or later, take action against us, much as they did with pedigree dog groups after the showing the documentary *Pedigree Dogs Exposed* on the BBC.

The basic problem is that the changes in Standards of Perfection move invisibly without anyone being in charge of it, or even noticing the process for that matter. At every exhibition, the Standard drifts a little. Exhibitors and judges see a bird with an extra-long mask and say: "Did you see the magnificent mask on that champion Cinnamonwing!" Or: "What about the superb directional feathering on that Spangle!" This is the beginning of a more extreme Standard. It is a never-ending invisible process. Relentlessly and unnoticed, the Standard moves in new unplanned directions.

Every few years, the Standards Committees of Budgie clubs notice the unofficial changes to the look of an ideal Budgie at shows and they incorporate them into a new official pictorial Standard. Maybe even adding a bit extra to the changes to appear to be leading the march. This drift of what the 'perfect' Budgie should look like has proven to be very destructive indeed.

Modern Show Budgies often develop huge wing-feather cysts which are unknown in Heritage Budgies or Bush Budgies (see page 230). They produce feather dusters caused by selection for excess feathering (see 'Feather dusters', page 188). Many Modern Exhibition Budgies appear to avoid flying, probably because their wide shoulders cause painful arthritis. And we all are indoctrinated to say misleading words and phrases, such as 'good shoulders' instead of 'wide shoulders', or 'great directional feathers' instead of 'very long directional feathers', or 'great size' instead of 'that is a very big bird'.

These words such as 'good' and 'great', when referring to the qualities of a Showbird, make that particular feature sound totally desirable and even required by the Standard. So those nearby at the exhibition run home to breed birds like that, even if those birds have already surpassed the Standard's requirements. Rewarding birds that are bigger overall than the Standard, or those with wider directional feather than the Standard, is a dangerous and destructive practice. It is this failure to limit extremes that is doing terrible damage to Exhibition Budgies. Judges too get swept along by the show chatter, particularly if the judgement comes from a peer group leader.

Please don't think that I am against the Modern characteristics, however. What I am against is the current lack of a balanced and caring system for changes to the Standard. I am against extremes that are running wild, making a sad parody of our Budgies. So, what would I ask for?

1. All Standards committees should have veterinary advisors with the power of veto on issues such as welfare and cruelty, who will comment on the ethics of each change.
2. Research should be conducted into the downsides or side effects of all major changes to the Budgies' conformation, past and present. For example, if directional feathering extends beyond, say, 6mm on each side of the head, causing restricted vision, it needs to be classified as a fault at shows. That is, directional feathers that are too short or too long should both be penalised equally.
3. Agreement that **all** features that go beyond the ideal in the Standard must get penalised the same as if the features are below the ideal.
4. All Budgie club members should be asked to participate in all Standards issues, including proposed new colours and varieties, e.g. Pastel Budgies. All Budgie club constitutions require democratic processes, yet Standards, Varieties and Colours are controlled by committees which provide the members with very few opportunities to have their say. This really must change.

Above: These two Modern European Show Budgies have unacceptable 'directional feathering' that seriously impedes safe flying. These poor birds constantly bend their heads up and back in order to see forward.

For a more complete and rigorous look at Breeding to the Standard, go to the Master Class on 'Creating the Modern Budgerigar', on page 297.

Left: This female Modern Exhibition Budgerigar has an incredibly long mask and high 'blow' of feathering on top of her head, but she lacks the excess directional feathering in front of her eyes. Surely, this is a better head configuration. And she can see to fly.

My point is that all domestic animals should be able to have a happy and healthy life. I love bulldogs, both English and French, and I see no problem with breeding dogs with a pushed in (brachycephalic) face like much like humans have, provided that their breeding program includes working with veterinarians and scientists who can genetically reshape the breathing pipes, etc, on the inside. This can even be done quite simply by performance scores. Bulldogs can be raced over, say, 100m and their resting heart rate can be recorded before and after the run. This provides excellent information as to breathing difficulties. Then the results can be formed into a scoring system so that breeders can select which male or female they want to breed from, or which puppy they will buy.

The great thing about Exhibition Budgies is that most of the problems are on the outside of the bird and thus can easily be modified or bred out altogether.

A better vision

There is a need to begin a period of finessing our Showbirds, creating Budgies with style and balance. Tidying up the feathering and easing back a bit from extremes is essential. We need more stylish birds with smooth satin-like feathering. Better colouring and varietal characteristics are very much needed too.

There is a current (2023) movement worldwide favouring better colour and markings in Exhibition Budgies. I am so grateful for the support for my genetic discovery that Budgies have two major wing feather types – type 1 and type 2 – from key Budgie experts such as Gary Gazzard in Australia. This discovery enables elite breeders to greatly improve wing patterns in many Budgerigar varieties, from Normals to Clearwings.

I also wish to compliment the brilliant breeders who are producing truly amazingly coloured Budgies already, including breeders in North Africa and the Middle East, from Algeria to Iraq and Egypt. There are also great colour breeders in Iran, Turkey, India, Pakistan, Bangladesh, Thailand, Japan and China. The local Heritage Budgies in these areas are amazing, particularly their Rainbows, Clearwings and Hagoromos. I just hope that they never abandon these genetic masterpieces. Crossing them to Modern UK and European Exhibition birds will risk the future excellence of these superb Budgies.

The colour Budgerigars in the UK and elsewhere in Europe are new and very important. They have begun their adventure by producing outstanding, colourful, small and very healthy Budgies. I just hope that they stick to their guns in producing the future of Budgie breeding.

My point is that there is room for quite a few Budgerigar breeds, just as Canary breeders established breeds such as Norwich, Yorkshire, Gloster, Red Factor, Lizard, Frilled and many more. Each country should preserve its own Heritage varieties. Certain Budgie varieties need to be made a breed on their own, mostly because the varieties are so fragile genetically. Cresteds, Hagoromos, Rainbows and Clearwings need a separate breed ranking because crest and colour perfection are so difficult to perfect.

I breed 100% pure Bush Budgies in the original Light Green colour, plus Recessive Pieds, Violets, Mauves, Sky Blues and Dilutes. And they are SO TINY. These too need to be preserved as a domestic breed. One day, for example, we might have an online World Champion Rainbow, and I would very much look forward to seeing the best online Rainbow in the world. We need to perfect the testing for altered photos first, however. Colour alteration in particular is a real problem.

Exciting times ahead.

Left: A possible future show specimen? This male has almost no directional feather and has reduced overall feathering. Lots of pizzazz but far less extreme.

Breeding without genetics

The key is to just breed from the Budgies that you like the look of. Over the past few thousand years, breeders of dogs, goldfish, wheat and corn just bred from the individuals that they liked. They bred friendlier puppies, ever-prettier goldfish and larger seeds on wheat and corn. It really is that simple. The term 'genetics' was not even in use until the early 1920s.

At a Glance

NO GENES INVOLVED.
Have you ever wondered how long masks or large heads or coarse feathering, or even just size in budgies are inherited? All of these things are inherited, but they TEND TO BLEND! A large bird mated to a small bird produces mostly medium sized babies. Genes can't do this. These are what MODIFIERS do. Read on and you will realise that most of the hereditary aspects of the Exhibition Budgerigar are not gene-controlled at all. Modifiers which BEND THE RULES OF HEREDITY are the work horses of evolution and of domestication as well.

This Light Green Clearwing male has a nice head and posture. His length of mask is OK, and his body colour is excellent, but his wing markings are a bit too dark.

I will look for a female for him to breed with which has very clear wings and maybe a longer mask if possible. I often put it into the back of my mind and wait for the right female to appear.

Almost none of these qualities are controlled by genes except for the dominant Full Body Colour gene and the new dominant Wing Clarity gene that this male carries. He is bred from an outcross to Modern Normals, so his wing clarity is actually very good.

A Clearwing in development.

Contrary to popular opinions, breeding elite Budgies is dead easy and the science of genetics plays only a very small part in it. To cut to the chase, you don't need to use genetics at all to produce great Budgies. The vast majority of desirable hereditary qualities in Exhibition Budgies are caused by hidden armies of tiny hereditary modifiers (not genes) that create blending inheritance. So a big Budgie mated to a small one produces medium-sized young. Snout length in dogs works the same way: Long-nosed greyhound dogs mated to bulldogs produce mid-range snouts a bit like boxer dogs. The same thing happens with human skin colour.

There are thousands of modifiers in these Violet Clearwings.

So, to achieve what you want, just mate one bird to another with complementary characteristics – e.g. if your Budgie has ugly greyish wings for a Clearwing, mate it to a very clear winged bird and the young should be a much better combination of features. It is that simple.

What are these tiny modifiers? They are tiny bits of DNA that tell the genes how much or what to do. You can compare genes to factories, and modifiers to the staff and management that run the show. And there are vast numbers of these modifiers. Genes make up just over 1% of our DNA, but modifiers, etc, make up just over 78% of the DNA.

So, what bits are controlled by modifiers? The following aspects of Budgies are mostly or totally modifier-controlled: the overall size of Budgies; width of Budgies; length, width and coarseness of feathers; length of mask; size of spots; width of directional feathering; clarity of wings in Clearwings; whiteness or yellowness of Black Eyed Whites or Yellows; Pied patterns of white or yellow; intensity of Greywing wing colour; posture and frontal 'blow' of head feathers; head flecking; type of markings in Opalines, Spangles and Saddlebacks; body colour percentage on the wings of Opalines; placid personality; tendency to show off in a show cage; size and width of head; pink feet in Normals and Cinnamonwings to facilitate UV light-producing vitamin D3; and so much more …

I am a genetics nerd, but I promise to try very hard to keep this section of the book simple and to avoid technical terms whenever possible, while terms which are used are explained on the inside cover. Genetics confuses many people, so let's begin with 'like breeds like'. It is obvious that most young resemble their parents, and the sum total of all animal breeding over the millennia has been more than 99.999% based on selection for animals that look or act like mum or dad. Dog, cat, horse, cattle, and even Canaries and Budgies, have all been developed without much or even any reference to the science of genetics. For the most part, you just don't need genetics – it didn't even begin until the 1920s.

Beautiful goldfish, for example, date back over one thousand years in China. Amazingly talented Chinese goldfish breeders have created superbly coloured and shaped living works of art without the use of genetics (see page 154). Astonishingly fast thoroughbred race

Above: There are huge numbers of modifiers in this bird to eradicate the development of the yellow suffusion from his chest and stomach. He is five years old and all Golden Faced Blue get greener with age – not this bird, however.

horses are also based on simple selection and perfect records. Fast-sprinting horses produce fast-sprinting foals. Many of the leading Budgie breeders hardly use genetics at all. They don't need to.

This Normal Light Green is a Modern Showbird. None of his exhibition qualities are gene-based, they are based on bit-by-bit selection.

What will help me to breed WINNERS?

1. You can breed winners simply by studying and learning what the Standard of Perfection looks like. It is so easy today. Grab your smart phone and go to a few Budgie exhibitions. Photograph the major winners. Print them off and stick the best photos up in your aviary. Study them until you they are etched into your retinas.

2. HUMILITY is the key. Ask humble questions such as: 'What is good about this bird?', 'What do you think are this bird's best qualities?', 'What let this or that bird down?' and (here's the hard one!) 'What let my bird down?' Or, 'What do I need to improve on?'

3. Search for a mentor. Your mentor will guide you and can help you to buy some cheap birds that will breed well for you. Not all great birds cost a fortune.

4. RECORDS. Keeping useful records will help you greatly. The ultimate aim is to photograph all breeding pairs when pairing up for your records.

Below is my simple form of breeding record. It is very judgemental. This is a simple, brief record page, but it is very useful. The key bits are opinions and judgements of the parents' qualities. Forcing you to state what you are trying to achieve with each mating is essential. Maybe it will force you to get your act together. Then you must record the young at fledging and then again at maturity when you are culling. Note the abbreviations: VVV stands for 'very very very'. Words such 'fairly', 'intense' and even 'stylish' matter a lot. Include negative ones too, such as 'dirty wings' through to 'VVV dirty' for Clearwings.

This record page forces you to see how well you fared as a creative breeder and how useful each breeding bird is. The best thing is that this system creates sublime moments as you see awesome young birds emerging in your aviaries as well as the ideal future partners for them. Even ten years later this info allows you to monitor the success of all your lines of birds. Sometimes you will discover an unnoticed great male or female from long ago that turns up in the records of all really great progeny. Also, if you discover that your birds have short masks, buy at least one with a very long mask to breed into them. Constantly look out for weaknesses in your birds as well as strengths. All of this is PURE GOLD later on. I keep my records on paper sheets in folders. They withstand the dust and dirt well and they are very quick and creative to use.

Cage No: 5.	Date paired: 21/2/2022.
Male, Ring No. 574 8B4 2022 Brown.	Female, Ring No. 656 8B4 2022 Brown.
Variety: Clearwing Red Violet, split Opaline.	Variety: Red Violet Dark Green. Clearwing, split Blue.
Bred by: Me.	Bred by: Me.
Strengths: VVV clear wings, extra intense body colour, stylish, big head.	Strengths: Very large female, fairly clear wings, super body colour, great head.
Weaknesses: Needs longer mask, bigger head, and larger size.	Weaknesses: Needs more clarity on wings.
Breeding background: Bob Pitt Opaline Clearwing Violet female.	Breeding background: My breeding.
Aim of mating: To put overall size and large head into the male's line.	
Success of mating: Assessment of chicks at fledging: most young had good size and good heads. Super colour and wing clarity. Reasonably good mating.	
Assessment of chicks at maturity: Most young developed faint wing markings.	
Comments on mating: Overall, a reasonable mating, but not outstanding.	

Progeny Ring No.	Colour/variety	Quality, health, size and other comments
007	Red Violet Olive Clearwing female.	Small but well coloured VVV clear.
009	Red Violet Opaline Clearwing female.	Big bird with VVV clear wings.
014	Red Violet Clearwing male.	Super large bird, perfect colour. V Clear
018	Red Violet Olive Clearwing female.	Best bird in batch. Got the lot, VVV clear.
020	Red Violet Opaline Violet Sky Clearwing female.	Dirty grey flight feathers and light body colour.
027	Red Violet Dark Green Clearwing male.	Good size and colouring, VVV clear, head a bit small.

Posture is everything ... almost. And it is likely controlled by hundreds of modifiers. English Yellow Faced Violet Clearwing.

The ultimate of all modifier varieties, the Black Eyed White, which is a massively modified Dilute White. Not for beginners.

Forget genetics, breeding can be easy

Heredity is easy. For most aspects of Budgie breeding, all you need to do is to use common sense by compensating for the physical failings of your birds. For instance, if your birds have short masks, buy some with longer masks and breed them with your birds, or just select for longer masked Budgies among your existing birds. The young tend to average between the mask lengths of each parent. That is, no genes are involved (genes aren't into blending or averaging, they produce major, fixed effects).

At a Glance

Have you ever wondered how people over the last few thousand years were able to breed pretty and placid horses, or placid milking cattle, or friendly dogs, or larger wheat or corn grains? Or have you noticed that many of the world's most successful Budgie breeders even today don't claim to be very good at genetics?

If one bird has droopy wing carriage, mate it to one that doesn't have this problem – it is that easy. Again, no genes are involved.

159

The Yellow Faced Budgie on the left has excellent wing carriage and deportment. The Mauve on the right has droopy wings and a droopy alula, or false wing – see it pointing downwards from her wing, vertically above her right leg. This tiny 'winglet' aids stable flight. Modifiers and/or the electrome control this feathering and posture, not genes.

As outlined in the previous chapter, many qualities, from overall size to feather length to body colour, are hereditary but are not gene-based. They are controlled by modifiers.

A long mask on the male on the left and a short mask on the female on the right. All due to modifiers. That is, they are neither dominant nor recessive, they just mix together.

Right: The now banned flecking on the forehead is partially a spill-over from breeding excess spots on the mask. Careless breeding is the cause. If exhibitors at shows were not allowed to pluck excess spots from the mask (as was the case up to the 1970s), these excess spots would never have occurred. They are 100% modifier-based.

Having said that, they would make a great new variety as long as they were quarantined from other varieties.

Budgie breeding began JUST as Mendel's theories of genetics were published. Swept along by this fancy new science, Budgie breeders limited themselves to almost all Budgie colours and varieties that were gene-based. Still, over 90% of all heritable features in Budgies that breeders select for, are not gene-based. Curiously, no-one ever seems to mention this. Not even to themselves.

Here we go!

The hard work of evolution and domestication is done by teeny weeny bits of DNA called modifiers, things like tandem repeats: they modify what the genes do. Genes are like factories and modifiers are like the management and staff that runs each factory. The huge numbers of modifiers from mum and dad mix together to average out in the young. It is that easy. It is much the same as mixing black and white paint: you get grey. Evolution acts on modifiers to subtly change their effects over time.

There are a handful of modifiers that are modifier genes, i.e. genes that make small changes, but they are rare. If you need to know more, go to our 'Genetics' section in the 'Master Class' on page 346.

Genes controlling colours and varieties

Right: The 'Normal'. A Bush or Wild Budgie. Where it all began.

The Wild Budgie has a Light Green body colour plus a striped back of black, greyish-green and yellow. This is called a 'Normal', but in common usage, this name includes any Blue or Green Budgie with black-striped wings.

Dominant and recessive genes – a bit more difficult

When you mate a Fallow to a 'Normal', you usually mean a cross to any Blue or Green Budgie with black striped wings, or to any non-Fallow.

In general, however, genes are either dominant or recessive, and at any hot-spot on a chromosome, called a locus, you must have two genes present. So a pure Normal Green has two Green genes present and a pure Blue has two Blue genes present. If you mate a pure Green to a pure Blue, the young all have one gene for Blue and one for Green. These will all appear to be a green colour, but they are called Green split for Blue. That is, the Green gene dominates the Blue gene. So Green is dominant and the Blue gene is recessive (i.e. it recedes).

How it works

Pure Green crossed to pure Green will produce 100% pure Green.

Pure Green mated to Green split for Blue (split for Blue means carrying a hidden recessive gene) produces 50% pure Green and 50% Green split for Blue.

Green split for Blue mated to Green split for Blue produces 25% pure Green, 50% Green split for Blue and 25% pure Blue.

Green split for Blue mated to pure Blue produces 50% Blue and 50% Green split for Blue.

Pure Blue mated to pure Blue produces 100% pure Blue.

The above percentages will work for all dominant-recessive matings of any varieties or colours.

Some genes are only partially dominant. Spangles produce finer wing markings when they are Single Factor, and a mostly yellow or white all over when Double Factor. Other partially dominant mutations are: White Cap, Golden Faced Blue, and the dark gene. Without the dark gene, a Budgie is either Light Green or Sky Blue. With one dark gene it is Dark Green or Cobalt. With two dark genes it is a Mauve or an Olive. Violet is a darkening gene which darkens all body colours a bit when it is Single Factor and much more when it is Double Factor. Violet also adds a pinkish or reddish shade to most colours.

The specific details of the heredity of each colour or variety is included in its section or chapter. The advanced science of genetics and heredity is in the Master Class on page 318.

Most colours and varieties act independently of each other, i.e. they are all at different DNA loci. So, you can have combinations such as Violet, plus Cobalt, plus Opaline, plus Clearwing, plus Golden Faced Blue – this is called a Rainbow.

Right: A pair of Blue Bush Budgies – one gene mutation away from the Green Wild Budgie. It is now called a Normal Sky Blue. Have we lost sight of how beautiful the original Budgie is? These wild-type Blues are very beautiful. And very smart.

Sex linkage

The other main type of a gene is the sex-linked type. These genes are on the sex chromosomes; males have two Z chromosomes, i.e. ZZ. Females have one Z and one W, i.e. ZW. Sex-linked genes can only occur on the Z sex chromosomes. Almost all sex-linked genes are sex-linked recessives. The main sex-linked mutations are Albino and Lutino*, Opaline, Cinnamonwing, Lacewing and Texas Clearbody.

A male with one gene for Albino or Lutino and one for Normal looks like a Normal. If he has two Albino or Lutino genes, he is visually an Albino or Lutino. Females are different. Since sex-linked genes can only occur on the Z chromosome, she either has one Albino or Lutino gene or none at all. Albino and Lutino work the same way. One Albino gene or Lutino will make her visually an Albino or Lutino and no Albino or Lutino gene makes her look Normal.

Gene modifiers put simply

Gene mutations, for the most part, make huge, often catastrophic changes, but modifiers make minor adjustments. Both are hereditary.

We all know that genes do big things like turning a Green Budgie into a Blue one, or a Normal into a Fallow. But genes only make up around 1% of our DNA, yet 80% of our DNA is active. Clearly the remaining 79% must be the main game (See note on 'The first gene modifier insights', at the end of this section).

At a Glance

If you want to improve or perfect your Budgies, or if you want to win at shows, you must use gene modifiers. Gene modifiers, not genes, drive most of evolution and the domestication of animals, including birds. But what are they and how do they work?

The huge changes caused by genes mutating are mostly disastrous for animals in the wild. Wild Albino prey animals rarely survive. Blue or Yellow Budgies equally don't

---

* A Lutino is a yellow Albino.

usually survive long in the wild. So what do gene modifiers do? They basically tell the genes what to do. They make very subtle changes and mutate up to 100,000 times faster than genes. Thus modifiers can rapidly but subtly help wild animals to adapt to changes such as natural climate fluctuations.

In Exhibition Budgerigars, most exhibition characteristics are modifier-based. Length, width and texture of feathers are modifier-driven, as are length of mask, size of spots, directional feathering, frontal blow, posture, pizzazz, overall size, width of head, colour of feet, clarity of wings in Clearwings, colour in Black Eyed Whites and Yellows, amount of body colour on wings of Opalines, location of crests – i.e. pretty much everything to do with finessing a great showbird.

How do you use modifiers?

This is the amazing bit! You do what humble farmers have done for over 10,000 years. Select, bit by bit, for things that you need or like: bigger seeds on corn or wheat, better temperament in dogs and horses, etc. Below is an amazing silvery-white goldfish with a shortened body, double tail, long fins, a warty cap on the head, and red pigment confined to the cap, all to create the Red Cap Oranda Goldfish.

This is one of mankind's greatest breeding developments. The Red Cap Oranda goldfish. All done centuries ago without the slightest knowledge of the science of genetics.

Most domestic animals – dogs, cats, horses, cattle, pigs, chickens, sheep, guinea pigs, alpacas and goats – were developed long before Mendel discovered the science of genetics. **'Like breeds like'** and **'bit by bit'** were the methods employed. These methods involve blending inheritance.

Small to large breeds mostly medium. Black to white breeds mostly greyish.

Modifiers in the wild turned a Brown Bear slowly into a Polar Bear without a gene mutation, or rapidly modified the beaks of Darwin's finches within each El Niño cycle (three or four years). The way it works is that tiny bits of DNA that produce tiny effects can repeat themselves more and more to amplify the overall effects, thus rapidly producing massive changes.

Hereditary modifiers often live within the area where a particular gene exists. They are just short bits of DNA base pairs such as AAGT. If a gene has one bit of AAGT it might produce a little bit less colour. If it has say, three bits of this sequence, AAGTAAGTAAGT, the reduction in pigment is more extreme. An animal can have one hundred of these repeating bits of DNA, and this can create major differences.

They act as very precise and flexible volume controls on genes. Without knowing it, we use this effect to sculpt our Exhibition Budgerigars.

These bits of DNA that regulate the genes are called tandem repeats.

In case you're wondering, using genes as pretty much the sole base for varieties in Budgies over the last 90 years has significantly limited the number and beauty of Budgerigar varieties that we have produced. The Gene Theory has reduced our ability to produce living works of art. So, go ahead and bend your birds to your own will by selecting what pleases you.

Bit by bit – the first gene modifier insights

The evolution and the domestication of animals and plants is overwhelmingly due to hereditary modifier elements, not genes themselves. Only in recent years did I chance on the following brilliant discoveries.

The first person to discover gene modifiers was Nobel Prize-winning scientist Barbara McClintock who is arguably the greatest mind ever to study heredity. She is probably best known for discovering jumping genes (a.k.a. transposons). Between 1948 and 1950 she developed a theory that mobile elements regulated genes by inhibiting or modulating their actions. Her work on gene controlling elements and gene regulation was not accepted by her contemporary scientists, and from 1953 onwards she stopped publishing her research on these controllers to avoid alienation among the scientific mainstream.

To this day, her brilliant theories on gene control are not at all well understood, even by many leading geneticists. But since the publication of the ENCODE project's discovery that while genes only make up about 1% of our DNA, an amazing 80% of our DNA is active, Barbara has been totally vindicated. Barbara McClintock was right, way beyond her wildest dreams.

Genes are the factories, and modifiers are the staff and management, which run each factory. They bend genes to their will. Using a knowledge of these modifiers empowers you create tomorrow's truly great Budgerigars.

Heredity of feathers in Budgerigars

At a Glance

Most of the colours and varieties in Budgies are controlled by genetic mutations. But most of the rest, such as overall size and width of the bird, directional feathering, size of spots on the mask, length of mask, plus length, width and coarseness of feathering, are overwhelmingly controlled by lots of tiny hereditary modifiers that individually make tiny changes. With continued focussed selection, however, these tiny modifiers group together to make huge changes.

With these modifiers you get blending inheritance: for example, big mated to small produces mostly medium-sized young. Long feathers mated to short feathers produces mostly medium-length feathers. This averaging effect is the hallmark for modifier-based inheritance. Genetic mutations, on the other hand, are relatively fixed, producing major changes, and when you breed colours and varieties together, strict segregation occurs among the young produced. For example, when Green is mated to Blue, sooner or later, both parental colours reappear in the young unchanged, i.e. no blending inheritance, no averaging.

So, if you need longer masks in your birds, you simply go out and buy one or more birds with longer masks. Then cross them into your birds. If you need longer directional feathering, buy some and use them. Dead easy.

Are there any genes that control these sorts of aspects, and if so, how do they work? This is something that I have worked on since 1958, and my progress has been slow and frustrating. Since you get tiny, subtle changes with modifiers, patterns of heredity are horribly difficult to work out.

Here are some discoveries that I have made – some are reliable, others are tentative but useful:

1. "The Feather Duster or Mop gene creates long and lush feathering in the Single Factor form and a feather duster when carried in the Double Factor form. So, many breeders unknowingly select for feather duster gene because they are after 'better feathering'. Both parents who produce feather dusters are carriers of the feather duster gene and should be culled.

2. Double Factor Golden Faced Blues are almost always small birds with small heads and a short mask and short directional feathering. This is genetic linkage at its worst and it is virtually impossible to avoid. Single Factor Golden Faced Blues, however, are greenish in colour but are much better quality birds with larger heads, etc. The best solution to this problem is to cross Golden Faced Blues to Yellow Faced Blues to produce Yellow Faced x Golden Faced Blue hybrids. These look 99% the same as Double Factor Golden Faced Blues, BUT with great size, heads and feathering.

3. Some varieties have looser linkage to bad size and feathering, such as Australian (i.e. German) Fallows, Recessive Pieds and Dark Eyed Clears. With these, when you get one with good feathering, etc, either breed it to others of that mutation with good feathering or breed it to Normals to produce more valuable splits. Then take all of your inferior Fallows, Recessive Pieds, Dark Eyed Clears and your old splits to the local pet shop. Why? Because if you breed from any of your old, inferior Fallows, Recessive Pieds, Dark Eyed Clears or the old splits to improve them, you will re-establish your linkage to dreadful feathering, etc. This would be disastrous.

4. Long or messy flight and tail feathers are a terrible problem. Long feathering overall

in Budgies seems to be a semi-dominant gene or maybe modifier controlled (or worse still, both). However, these mechanisms also produce very long flight and tail feathers, i.e. they lengthen all of the feathers on the Budgerigar. Somewhere along the way, someone found a recessive gene mutation that shortens ONLY the tail and flight feathers. So you can have a Budgie with a long tail and flight feathers which is split for shorter flight and tail feathers. This leads to the problem where you cross a tiny Heritage Clearwing with lovely short tail and flight feathers to a large Modern Showbird also with short flight and tail feathers, and you produce 100% young with **long** flight and tail feathers. The good news is that all of them are split for short flight and tail feathers. So this can be fixed.

5. Directional feathering, frontal feather 'blow', dense, lush feathering, droopy alula, large round spots, long mask, wide shoulders and wide heads are all caused by modifiers, i.e. blending inheritance.

6. Crests, including Hagoromos, are very complex and will be covered elsewhere under 'Genetics'.

On the left is a lovely Budgie full of pizzazz, with almost no directional feathering, and on the right is a Budgie with enormous directional feathering. To me, the bird on the right is a mess.

On the left a long mask, on the right a short mask.

On the left, a Recessive Pied with poor head feathering. On the right, a Recessive Pied with stupendous head feathering (and little forward vision).

Improving Exhibition features in Budgies

Over the last 20 years or so, I have tried to unravel the hereditary basis of some Exhibition characteristics in Budgies. To do this, I crossed pure strains of Modern Exhibition Budgies to either pure Australian Heritage Budgies or to pure Bush Budgies. That is, I mated Budgies which were homozygous for Modern Exhibition facial and body feathering as well as modern size, to older style Budgies that were homozygous for smaller heads, short masks, no directional feathering, no frontal 'blow', short body feathering and small overall size.

Where the results indicated a strict genetic mechanism like dominance or sex linkage, I repeated the experimental matings until I had large numbers of progeny to verify my results. With these matings I produced between 50 and more than 100 offspring. This was done in part because others had put forward previous theories that my work had proven to be incorrect.

So far as I know, this is the first attempt to discover the hereditary basis of the finer Exhibition qualities in any show animal. I have had some limited success, but much more work needs to be done, if for no other reason than the fact that different hereditary mechanisms clearly create the same effects in different breeders' birds. This explains why some elite lines of Budgies don't cross well with other superficially similar lines.

For the average breeder, I recommend that you just read the blue bits below: this is all you really need to know.

Directional feathering

The bottom line: Most Modern Show Budgies carry the directional feather genes, so all Modern young also carry directional feather genes. But old-fashioned birds often lack these genes. Directional feathering appears to be a sex-linked mutation, so males with directional feathering mated to old-fashioned females with none, should produce all female young with visible directional feathering (even if it is subtle and hard to see) and male young which are split for this gene. Old-fashioned males without these genes mated to females with directional feathering should not produce any progeny with directional feathering, but male young should be split for it. **Or, put another way, males with directional feathering are far more useful and valuable than females.**

This modern characteristic leads to feathers growing out horizontally beside the cere, creating a wider-looking face and head (see photo below). My research indicates that the presence or absence of this characteristic is controlled by a sex-linked recessive gene: i.e. it works the same as Opaline or Cinnamonwing. On the other hand, the length of the directional feathering (i.e. how widely it pokes out) is controlled by modifier elements such that blending inheritance occurs (modifier elements are not genes, but they are usually in a bird's DNA and they are hereditary). Thus, a bird with very wide directional feathering mated to one with narrower directional feathering produces progeny with a mixture of lengths of directional feathering, most about half way between the parents' feathering. Lastly, my observations indicate that 'directional feathering' is a misnomer. The direction of the feather growth remains the same, it is the length of the feathering beside the cere that is altered by this gene mutation (see my separate section in this archive on 'Directional feather'). One caveat, however: there could be several directional feathering mutations but I only found one, i.e. different lines might rely on other directional feathering mutations.

This European Exhibition Budgie has extreme directional feathering which blocks its forward vision completely. This is part of its frontal 'blow' on its forehead and it surely must severely limit its ability to fly safely. Note its very long mask feathering below its beak as well. Responsible Budgerigar breeders surely must consider pulling back from such extreme exhibition breeding fashions.

The diagram above, drawn from above, shows the difference between two Budgies, one with directional feather (on the left), and one without. The right hand bird is drawn from a Bush Budgie. The other one is an older-style Budgie which has a tiny bit of directional feather.

Long mask feathering

The bottom line: This is controlled by modifier elements, so blending inheritance should occur. That is, the young birds should be mostly half way between their parents in mask length.

Frontal 'blow'

The bottom line: This is a behavioural aspect of the Budgerigar and I am confused by it. I am not sure what its hereditary base is.

'Blow' is the erection of the forehead feathers of the Budgerigar (see the Yellow Double Spangle on previous page). Male Budgies erect these feathers to show off: in general, to attract females (remember the forehead is where the sexually attractive ultraviolet pigment is concentrated). However, females erect these feathers as a sign of territorial aggression – when they raise these feathers it is usually a warning of an impending violent attack on another female or on a predator in defence of a nesting hole. Female Budgies are the more aggressive sex and they are the territorial sex; they locate and defend their territory (i.e. nesting holes in trees). Males play no part in this process – they usually only fight other males to win females, and this is usually not as murderous as female fights. It worries me that Modern Exhibition Budgerigar females with more 'blow' could be more aggressive in general and have excessive hormonal behaviour.

Long flight and tail feathers

The bottom line: these exhibition faults are controlled by a recessive mutation that shortens excessively long tail and wing feathers, leaving all other feathering long. Thus, birds of either sex with long tails and flight feathers can still be very useful for breeding if one or both of their parents had short flight and tail feathers. These long flighted and tailed birds will be split for short flights and tail.

This is a rather complex situation. In the UK in the 1940s and 1950s, it seems that Budgies occurred with longer feathers all over, maybe to protect the birds from the very cold winters (in most of Australia, winters are not that cold). The longer feathers on the body and head were considered highly attractive by exhibition breeders, but the associated long flight and tail feathers were seen as ugly. The semi-dominant gene for long, warmer feathering **lengthened all feathers,** including the flight and tail feathers. Somewhere over the following years, a second mutation popped up, which shortened **only** the flight and tail feathers without affecting the long head and body feathering. Problem solved! Well, not entirely so. All was OK until you crossed a Modern Showbird to an old-fashioned Budgerigar. To set the scene, you are crossing a Modern Showbird with long feathers all over, except for its **short flight and tail feathers,** to an old-fashioned bird with short feathers all over including **short flight and tail feathers**. This mating produces 100% birds with long feathers all over, including both **long flight and tail feathers**! The semi-dominant long feather gene has prevailed, but the recessive gene for shortened tail and flight feathers cannot (it is recessive after all). But do remember that all of these crossbred young are split for short wing and tail feathers (see Darkwing example below). It will take some years of gene juggling before this crossbred line is stabilised. Good luck! I have a chart explaining how this complex set of genes works – I can send it to anyone who is interested, but it is hard going!

This Darkwing has long, messy flight and tail feathers. However, this was an essential part of modernising this variety. He is split for short flight and tail feathers. Below is his grandson, who has better flight and tail feathering.

A big part of the challenge in modernising Exhibition Budgies lies in finessing your improvements. This bird is coming together very well indeed, particularly when measured against his grandfather. He has balanced feathering and plenty of swank.

The critical point here is to PERSIST with transitional birds like grandpa! Once you know how these genes work, you can make MUCH BETTER PROGRESS.

Darkwings are every bit as difficult to breed as Clearwings. I am so proud of this six-month-old bird!

Extra-long feathering

The bottom line: superb extra-long feathering, especially long head and mask feathering, including greater body size, occurs in Budgies carrying one semi-dominant feather duster gene (a.k.a. the mop or chrysanthemum gene). The feather duster gene in its Double Factor form causes the bird's feathers to grow continuously so that eventually it looks like the head of a mop (see photo opposite). It also causes the bird to grow to a larger body size than birds without this mutant gene. In the Single Factor form, the feather duster gene creates a superior-looking Showbird with better head and body feathering, and overall size. **These superior young usually look mediocre on leaving the nest, and don't look great until 6–12 months of age.** At some stage, maybe breeders might consider whether or not it is acceptable to breed with birds carrying this problematic mutation.

Pizzazz

The bottom line: I totally failed to understand this feature. Obviously, a healthy bird has better body posture. A well put together bird also has great posture. Excessive directional feather seems to force Budgies to pull their neck in and also to tilt their heads upward to be able to see ahead underneath the feathering in front of their eyes. This seems essential for safe flying. Rapidly growing high response animals like meat chickens, meat pigs, thoroughbred race horses, etc, often have joint and other bone problems (Developmental Orthopaedic Disease, or DOD) which can cause considerable chronic pain, resulting in poor posture. Our Modern Exhibition Budgies are rapidly growing high response birds that are much larger than their Wild Budgerigar ancestors. I am confident that large Exhibition Budgies with wide shoulders, etc, live a life of constant nagging pain due to DOD. This at least partially explains why many sit on the aviary floor for much of the time.

This is a Double Factor feather duster or mop Budgerigar.

Both of the above birds have swank: the exuberant displaying of their style and verve. They stand up straight, with their head up, chest out and chin in. They exude life and vitality! Perhaps we should not go beyond this amount of feathering, etc.

Nonetheless there are also hereditary mechanisms for the 'stand up straight, chest out, chin in' posture that seems to be a feature of all exhibition animals from horses to Budgies. So far, it has proven too difficult for me to discover a basic mechanism, but it is clear to me that birds living in pain due to DOD will hardly be able to exhibit a '*joie de vivre*'! Excess feathering, overly large size, and overly wide shoulders all militate against swank. Moderation in feathering, size and width of shoulders will produce a beautifully finessed Modern Exhibition Budgerigar with vastly better swank and pizzazz!

Both of these birds have great posture, i.e. swank.

Left is of an English Yellow Faced Violet Clearwing Australian Heritage Budgerigar.

Right is a hybrid White Cap x Australian Golden Faced Blue. He is a Modern Exhibition Budgerigar.

Inbreeding Budgies – do you dare?

We all want to breed winners, but do we dare to use inbreeding techniques? And if we do mate relatives together, how closely related can they be and what are the pitfalls and/or gains?

Recently I received from my good friend Ole Gade in Denmark, a copy of an article on inbreeding Budgerigars by Margery Kirkby-Mason and Len Dabner, published in the UK Budgerigar Club Bulletin in June 1965, and it is brilliant. Kirkby-Mason and Dabner were breeding partners in a Seaspray Budgerigar stud in Devon, England.

This 1965 article is stunning for its scientific accuracy combined with its sheer practicality. It will really help you to breed winners. It is reprinted below for your guidance in the exact form that it was published in 1965.

Human-term relationships are our guide to breeding

By Margery Kirkby-Mason and Len Dabner

It appears that the question of line-breeding cropped up in the presence of The Budgerigar Society chairman, who is known for his keenness on the subject.

So we have been asked to write a few words on line-breeding and inbreeding as our chairman has the impression that we have changed our minds on this subject and that, whereas in the past we would not entertain for one moment any idea of using related birds, but that now we did so. In fact this is not so and we are using the same method we have always used.

It is not too easy to know where to draw the line between inbreeding and line-breeding but here at Seaspray we work on the principle that if we can work out the relationship of the two birds in human terms and if it would not be allowed in humans then we do not do it with the birds either. We find that the results of using a complete outcross are almost invariably most disappointing and it is not until two or three generations later that any real improvement due to the outcrossing can be seen.

But the mating together of distantly related birds does seem to be the most successful method in the long run. We do think, however, that the mating of two closely related birds, provided they are both of high standard, does bring out that best-in-show winner sooner than the other method, but apart from the outstanding bird the rest of the stock is likely to be well below standard.

With the mating of distantly related birds there is much more even improvement over the whole stud and though it takes longer 'to get there' there comes a time when the whole stud has a strong family resemblance with many winners among them.

It is indeed true that close inbreeding doubles up on the good points but so many of us forget that it also doubles up on the bad points.

We feel so sorry when a beginner or novice tells us that he intends to mate father to daughter and so on as we feel certain he will run into trouble sooner or later – most probably sooner! There is no such thing as a perfect Budgie. There are always some faults either obvious or hidden, even in a National winner to say nothing of health faults and so after a time the beginner wonders why he has bred so many birds which are of no use to him.

Very close inbreeding might be done successfully by an extremely experienced fancier who has truly first-class stock to use and of which he has accurate knowledge for many generations both from the show points and health angle.

We always give the same advice to anyone who calls at Seaspray: "Buy the best you can afford, breed with them, keep the best (and don't let anyone wangle them out of you!), sell the rest, and buy something better". If you find a stud that you like and that you do well with then buy your stock from the same place. In this way, you will be avoiding the complete outcross and will be mating distantly related birds together which will give better results than a complete outcross would. If the breeder knows the ring numbers of the buyer's original birds he will be able to picture, within a little, what the youngsters look like and this will enable him to pick out the most suitable bird to mate with one of these youngsters so as to improve whatever point is most likely to be lacking in these birds … spots, size and so on.

Of course there comes a time when it is nearly impossible to buy the new blood which every breeder must have from time to time. We ourselves have been in that unhappy state for some years. The really outstanding bird that we should love to have is either not for sale or at so high a price that we are forced to say no. We should find it much too worrying to spend more than we could truly afford on a bird. We want to enjoy our hobby and not to have to go rushing down to the aviaries every hour or so to see if the 'wonder bird' is still alive. As every fancier knows, it is always without fail one's best bird which escapes or dies. Perhaps also our rivals feel that with nearly 65 years between us of experience of Budgie breeding we might possibly have enough knowledge to make the best use of the newcomer!

As we cannot obtain an outcross that is better than Seaspray on every point we have to buy a bird that we feel excels in some special point that we that we should like to improve in our stock. It is important here to see that the seller's stud on the whole has this improvement that we need and not in just the odd bird here and there.

It is sometimes possible to make an exchange of birds at a show, but up to now these mutual arrangements have given us no success at all in the breeding pen. However, during the last two years the owner of one of the finest studs in the country has been good enough to let us have several birds for outcrossing. We say 'been good enough' deliberately because the rivalry between her stud and Seaspray is intense, especially as we live in the same area, but always a most friendly rivalry and most enjoyable, which is as it should be. We congratulate her every time she wins best in show but she has no idea how we mutter under our breath 'Just wait until next year; we'll beat you then!'

It has been most interesting to note that 50% outcross by 50% Seaspray has not produced at all what we had hoped for. Perhaps both studs were too firmly set to blend well. But in the next generation 75% Seaspray by 25% outcross has given us much more what we are after.

However the majority of our show team is still nearly 100% K41 (Seaspray) blood but to keep up with modern trends some alteration in style has had to be made. We think we have achieved this by thinking about them differently. We find this difficult to explain but in principle it means that we have paid more attention to certain points in both birds than we had been in the habit of doing; and in turn given less attention to other points which previously we had perhaps concentrated on too much. Whether we are right or wrong, time and the show-bench alone will tell!

Well, how's that for a tour de force of inbreeding? Every single detail above is 100% in agreement with the results from my long-term genetic research into inbreeding, line- breeding and general breeding principles. It is way ahead of any attempt by any scientist or veterinarian that I have ever read, to explain the details and dynamics of inbreeding and line-breeding to exhibition breeders of any bird or animal in general.

Well done Margery and Len ... in 1965, that's more than half a century ago!

Len passed away on 6 September 1968 and Margery passed away exactly 25 years later on 6 September 1993. Both were leading judges and their Budgies were exported to many countries including the USA, Cuba, Brazil, South Africa and several European countries. Margery was a leading light on Lutino breeding in particular. Both are greatly missed. Sadly, Ole Gade has also passed away. He was one of the great budgie people that we should all listen to.

Long flight and tail feathers

For the deep genetics of this feather problem please go to 'The tale of long tail and long flight feathers' on page 306–311.

This recessive gene mutation that shortened tail and flight feathers just turned up and remains unnoticed to this day. In some ways it solved the problems … but not quite.

This totally undiscovered mutation tended to destroy most attempts to improve rare and backward colours and varieties. When a beautifully coloured small Clearwing was crossed to a Modern Showbird to improve head size and body size, long flight and tail feathers roared back to life. Both parents had short flight and tail feathers but 100% of the young had long flight and tail feathers, seeming to defy the laws of genetics.

This bird has truly horrible flight feathers.

Below: This female Clearwing has long flight feathers. She is from an outcross of a Heritage Clearwing to a Modern European Showbird. Notice that the flight feathers don't fold up neatly.

At a Glance

Long flight and tail feathers unbalance a show Budgie and look unattractive. These long feathers are a by-product of breeding long feathering on the head, mask, etc. The good news is that there is a recessive mutation which shortens only the wing and tail feathers. So, select or buy some birds that have short flight and tail feathers, but longish feathering elsewhere. Cross these to your birds with long flight and tail feathers. The first cross will likely produce 100% birds with long flight and tail feathers, but they may be split for the short flight and tail feathers recessive gene. Backcrossing among these hybrids will produce 25% with the desired feathering.

The formula for success

Be warned that if you ever backcross again to Budgies with short feathers all over, to improve colour, etc, ALL HELL WILL BREAK LOOSE AGAIN. That is, attempts to constantly outcross to improve the colour of your Clearwings (or any minor variety) or outcrosses to keep up with the ever-changing standard of perfection, will likely cause long flights and tail feathers all over again. The only way to improve and stabilise your minor varieties is to do the initial outcross to Modern Showbirds, then to constantly breed between these old-to-modern crosses. It takes longer but it will be steady progress.

And never forget that you must always select for the long and short of it: that is select for birds with long feathers overall, but with short flight and tail feathers. The birds must carry both features to be of any use.

Perfect flight and tail feathers.

Multiple alleles – a simple guide

The words 'multiple allele' strike fear into the hearts of many Budgie breeders. Gobbledygook is a fair description of these words. But is this a complex issue?

No, the basics of it are fairly straightforward.

Most mutations work alongside each other. Thus a Rainbow Budgie is an Opaline Clearwing Golden Faced Blue– all three mutations doing their own thing in one bird at one time, with maybe Violet or Hagoromo thrown in as well. Each of these mutations just gets on with its job, independently working beside other mutations.

However, this is not the case with multiple alleles: this is a **group** of mutations that push one another out of the way. They are aggressive bullies. They have strict rules that only **two** of the **group's** mutations can live together in one bird at the one time. Exactly like musical chairs with two chairs and more than two people trying to sit down.

A classic home for a **group** of multiple alleles is the one where Normal, Dilute and Greywing all fight to get in. Remember that only **two** can live there at a time. The big bully here is Normal, which is a dominant mutation which dominates both Greywing and Dilute. Greywing by itself also dominates Dilute. So you can have the following gene **pairs** in the home:

Normal and Normal, which is a visual Normal.

Normal and Greywing, which is a visual Normal.

Normal and Dilute, which is a visual Normal.

Greywing and Greywing, which is a visual Greywing.

Greywing and Dilute, which is a visual Greywing.

Dilute and Dilute, which is a visual Dilute.

But remember that the basic rule is: only two genes at a time.

And that is all there is to multiple alleles.

Pairing up

Pairing up Budgies is, for many of us, the most exciting part of each year. To assess some of your birds for colour, size, style, etc, then to select the perfect mate is a wonderfully creative adventure.

Some breeders, however, watch for natural pairs that form in the aviary – even those in love through the wire mesh to the next aviary! The loved-up pair are put together and the chemistry is wonderful to watch. And with self-chosen pairs, fertility is usually very high. Obviously, the pairs need to be compatible in all critical exhibition aspects, however.

What does that mean? Well, two enormous birds mated together will likely produce monsters and mops. Really tiny birds mated together might produce runts. Two birds with overly long flight feathers mated together could produce birds with really messy feathers, and so on.

Right: This bird has very long flight feathers. It is a very disproportioned bird and I would never breed from it. This a pity since it is also a well coloured Violet Rainbow.

So you need to train your eyes and mind to pick out really good features and really bad features in your birds. One essential method is to ask the breeder that you bought your birds from for an honest opinion on their strengths and weaknesses (ideally, you do this at the time of purchase). On each pair's breeding record page, I list all good and bad features of each bird. I then list the aim of the mating.

This aim is not necessarily to

produce a perfect bird. With Rainbows, a smart breeder would be selecting for very much clearer wings because 99% of all Rainbows worldwide have badly marked wings. That is, they have visible grey wing markings, whereas they should be just blue, and white or yellow on their wings. Getting rid of grey wing markings is a high priority because the golden face and blue body are already fairly good all over the world.

For the big European-style show Budgies, a huge blow* at the front of the head is essential. A great big golf ball above the cere ('nose') is considered perfection, and a very long mask is also essential. This is a Modern Showbird with swank or pizzazz. Note the huge golfball on his forehead and the long mask. Top breeders would like greater width of the head beside the cere, but as this impedes forward vision, I select away from it. His mask is long, but some want it to be longer than this.

A good modern head is about 30mm wide, and good mask length from the top of the cere to the bottom of the mask is 35–40mm.

Below left: This spectacular modern juvenile Clearwing has a magnificent mask, but here he is not 'blowing his head'.

Below centre: Here, the same bird is beginning to 'blow his head'. With age this will improve out of sight.

Below right: The male is a a near-perfect Exhibition Australian Heritage Clearwing Yellow Faced Violet, showing real pizzazz as it once was (circa 1962).

---

* A blow is the erection of the male forehead feathers to 'show off', usually to impress the females, although most high-quality Modern Showbirds do it, both male and female.

Selection for pizzazz is essential if you wish to win at shows. Your bird needs to stand out from the crowd. Speaking of which, do go out into your aviary and immerse yourself in Budgie gazing. Let your birds surprise you – very often a new young bird will stand out.

For instance, in the photo below, the Clearwing Opaline Cobalt, sixth from the left on the second perch from the front has the best cobalt body colour that I have ever seen. I will grab him/her to see what the breeding of this bird is, then I will try to create a line-bred group of Budgies that have that colour.

This may surprise you, but there are no true Green Budgies in this photo below. The ones that look green are Double Factor White Caps, so they have no green genes in them at all.

What about genes?

Surprisingly, genes play very little part in the heredity of exhibition characteristics. Genes play some role in colour and varieties, but not often in size, colour intensity, feather qualities, head size, spot size, pizzazz, backline, etc. If you want to win at shows, you need to pretty much ignore genes.

There are thousands of tiny hereditary modifiers that shape, colour and feather your birds. But relax, because these modifiers create blending inheritance.

So if a bird with a short mask is mated to one with a long mask, most of the young will have intermediate length masks. If a Budgie with a huge head is mated to one with a small head, the young will mostly be in-between in head size. So, when pairing up, when a bird has a fault, cross it to another bird that is strong in that area. If you constantly select for a quality that you like or need, sooner or later you will get there.

The Australian Heritage Budgerigar Association (AHBA) and our colleagues around the world are selecting for ever-pinker Cinnamon Violet Clearwings and

Fallow Violet Clearwings to create pink-lavender Budgies that we call Amethysts. And this is working very well indeed.

This is how the breeding genius Harold Peir created Clearwings back in 1930: he selected for Greywings with super-intense body colour, then selected the clearest-winged of those to become Clearwings.

You too can create Budgies of astonishing colours. The AHBA is rapidly developing many shades of Pastel Budgies – that is, beautifully pale shades of artistic colours. Below is another development, a Violet Sky White Cap Rainbow that has a magnificently nuanced Teal Blue body colour.

This is an adult White Cap Double Factor Violet Sky Rainbow. While Violet Sky White Cap Normals look a bit drab to me, White Cap Violet Sky Clearwings and Rainbows look magnificent, maybe because of the contrasting white areas.

Perhaps the great fun in breeding Budgies is creating new colours from unthought-of crosses. Who would ever have thought of a Teal Blue Budgie? See the Teal Blue colour patch below.

Teal Blue

Prepotency

You sometimes hear about a prepotent male or female. This refers to an animal that reliably passes on desirable qualities to its offspring. The great thoroughbred sire Star Kingdom passed on his ability to run fast over short distances very well: he was prepotent for sprinting ability.

On the other hand, we all have purchased wonderful birds that simply don't produce good young at all. What gives?

Well, some lines of Budgies simply don't cross well with others. Some exquisite birds never breed even one good offspring. Equally, some males or females can be homozygous for many qualities that we all want – so they breed very well. Inbreeding produces prepotent males and females … at a cost. The cost is usually health and vigour. So it pays to keep an eye out for individual birds that reliably produce great young.

We all know that a bird that produces the occasional really nice offspring is nowhere near as valuable as the one that reliably produces a strong, consistent line of good, solid young. So keeping accurate and detailed breeding records is essential. Write down opinions like 'Greatest pairing for the year' or 'Very good, even quality of the chicks'.

I am writing this because I have just recorded my best pairing ever. The female below has just produced 14 young in two nests that are all identical to herself. She is a Red Violet Dark Green Clearwing with stunning body colour and perfectly clear wings. All 14 young are identical to herself (except that a few are males!). She is a homozygous Green – she must be, because her partner is a Violet Clearwing and she has produced no Blue young.

Yet people come to me insisting that they ONLY want a Violet Clearwing. What smart breeders want is a pair that will **produce** great Violet Clearwings! Her 14 young will certainly do that!

This is the best-coloured Heritage Clearwing that I have ever bred. She is a Red Violet Dark Green and she is homozygous for Green. I never expected to produce another bird with the perfect contrast that she has. I now have 15 of them, including mum – see next page.

This is dad. He is a beautifully coloured visual Violet Heritage Clearwing. He must be a Double Factor Violet Sky, otherwise he would have produced some Violet Olive young among the 14. He worked his guts out to feed the young birds and mum, but he is not the once-in-a-lifetime bird that mum is. What a privilege to own this super female.

While this photo of the 14 young is something of a messy scrum, and it is a very poor photo, I hope that you can still see that each youngster is a carbon copy of mum. These poor young are just all terrified and confused by the glass cage front. Dad has done his job – but mum is the hero.

This stupendous female was the original mutant of the Red Violet gene. Her progeny are now spreading across Australia. After the original mating to a Violet Clearwing male, her offspring went on to produce Blue series Red Violet Clearwings. I can't begin to describe how I felt when the first Red Violet Clearwings left the nest. I was speechless. Their reddish-purple tones were truly amazing.

This may well be the first time that a photo exists of the original mutant of any Budgerigar colour or variety.

Please breeders, NEVER underestimate the ability of females to transform the quality of your Budgerigars.

Sex linkage and how it works

Birds have a topsy-turvy set of sex chromosomes. In humans, men determine the sex of the kids, but in birds it is the females who determine the sex of the chicks.

In humans, the males have XY sex chromosomes and females have XX ones. In birds the males have ZZ sex

At a Glance

Sex linkage is a messy and complex form of heredity. Here we will try to make it a little easier. The good news is that females are the great gift because they can produce non-sex linked daughters from genetically compromised lines.

chromosomes and the females have ZW. Basically, the W chromosome does nothing in relation to sex-linked genes, i.e. it is inactive.

So how do all of these letters work? To try to make things easier, we will use examples of sex-linked genes such as Cinnamon or Opaline, but you could substitute other sex linked genes such as Lacewing, Albino, Lutino, Slate or Texas Clearbody.

With sex linkage, the gene involved can only be carried on the Z chromosome. Since males have two Z chromosomes they can carry one or two sex-linked genes. Usually, if a male carries only one gene for say, Opaline, he looks Normal but he is split for Opaline. If he carries two genes for Opaline, he is a visual Opaline.

With females, it is different. She can only carry one sex-linked gene or none at all. If she carries one gene for Opaline she is a visual Opaline. If she carries none, she is obviously a non-Opaline, i.e. genetically a Normal.

Right: This is a Cinnamon Opaline Violet Clearwing. These two sex-linked varieties tend to link together and pop up in lines of Clearwings. It seems that this renders her useless for breeding because this is not a recognised variety. But this female won't ever transmit these genes to her daughters, so she has breeding value. Luckily, the Australian Heritage Budgerigar Association includes birds like this in their Pastel classes at exhibitions, so she is now desirable.

So, an Opaline male mated to a non-Opaline female produces all males that are split for Opaline and all Opaline females.

An Opaline male mated to an Opaline female produces 100% Opaline young.

A split Opaline male mated to an Opaline female produces 25% Opaline males, 25% split for Opaline males, 25% Opaline females and 25% non-Opaline females.

A split Opaline male mated to a non-Opaline female produces 25% split Opaline males, 25% non-Opaline males, 25% Opaline females and 25% non-Opaline females.

The great gift from the females

The simple bottom line is that no female, whether it is, say, a Cinnamon or not, can pass this sex-linked gene on to her daughter. Thus you can use all females to produce young females that are free of the sex-linked gene. If the male is Normal-looking, 50–100% of the female young will not be Cinnamons and they can't carry the gene either. What you see is what you get.

Often you need/want to remove the Cinnamon or Opaline gene from a line of birds. The classic need is to remove Cinnamon from your Clearwings, since Cinnamon Clearwings lack good body colour and you can't exhibit them anyway. Being sure that the Cinnamon (or any sex-linked gene) is definitely gone is the issue.

Right: This is a Normal White Cap. He is a good example of a new variety that you might wish to cross your Clearwings to.

But Modern Showbirds often carry many unpleasant hidden genetic surprises in them. Cinnamon and Opaline are two good examples of sex-linked varieties that can hide inside males. Often they also bond together in a unit. This is called gene linkage.

Often you cross a Normal male to a Clearwing female to improve head, mask and size, only to find that the male produces Cinnamon female young. You get half Cinnamon and half non-Cinnamon females, both of which are split for Clearwing. Both of these young females are useful for producing second-generation females that are free from the Cinnamon gene. In this second generation, when you mate either the young Cinnamon or non-Cinnamon to a **well-bred** Clearwing male, none of the females produced from that mating will carry the Cinnamon gene.

To repeat, all females split for Clearwing can safely be used to produce daughters that don't carry the Cinnamon gene if mated to a well-bred Clearwing male.

Having said that, if you wish to outcross your Budgies without 'contamination' from Opaline, Cinnamon or other sex-linked varieties, ALWAYS outcross to a female rather than a male. Females never have hidden sex-linked genetic secrets, so all apparently non-Opaline or non-Cinnamon females are reliably free of these genes. If you cross a **well-bred** Clearwing male to a Normal female, you should not get any Cinnamons or other sex-linked varieties (unless the Clearwing male is contaminated with Cinnamon or whatever). My Clearwings are never contaminated by Cinnamon or Opaline because I keep them apart from Rainbow or Amethyst crosses. I quarantine all elite Clearwings from all dangerous outcrosses.

The curse of mops or feather dusters

Genetic cruelty is perhaps the biggest ethical problem facing veterinary science today. Worldwide, billions of animals live short and miserable lives due to cruel breeding practices. Meat pigs (one billion at any one time) and meat chickens (20 billion per year) stand out as a sad indictment on the ruthless drive to produce ultra-rapid growth in animals. Their rapid growth produces bone and joint problems such that most are in serious pain and are crippled at very early ages.

In ornamental and pet animals, similar problems occur. Many dog breeds are seriously debilitated by extreme standards of perfection which radically change the shape or conformation of the dogs. Bulldogs are a classic example of this.

In Exhibition Budgerigars, standards requiring extreme feather bulk plus large size and wide 'shoulders' create miserable lives for the poor birds, often leading to Budgerigars that sit on the floor all day because of the difficulty and pain involved in flying.

It is not the aim of this section to oppose the production of these animals, but rather to explore better genetic practices that would still see similar 'advances', but which minimise the genetic welfare issues involved. There is no reason that bulldogs have to have breathing problems – this can be prevented by smarter breeding practices. And the bulldog can still look much the same as it does now.

This chapter is on the feather duster or mop Budgerigar. It investigates the genetic basis of the mop and how it can be avoided. It also looks at flightless and tailless wonders (circovirus) and how these can be avoided. Hopefully, we can continue to look into the issues involved in minimising genetic cruelty in other animals in future issues. We invite feedback and contributions on these issues.

I suspect that all competitive Budgie breeders produce feather dusters. One could reasonably state that the hidden recessive gene for feather dusters is present in many Modern Show Budgie aviaries.

Why? … Breeders don't want to produce feather dusters. It is embarrassing and represents a tragic loss from leading show strains. Since breeders are uncomfortable with this issue, not much solid information exists on it. There is a lot of misinformation around, so let's look at bits and pieces of information.

Feather dusters occur when a young Budgie carries two genes for the gene responsible for the appearance. That is, the feather duster gene is recessive to the gene for Normal feathering. The homozygous feather dusters produce continuously growing feathers all over, eventually creating the appearance of a head of a mop or of a feather duster. This obscures eyesight, prevents the bird from flying, mating or even from defecating properly. Equally, the bird is unable to properly, preen its feathers, or to maintain bodily cleanliness. In general these poor birds hobble around on the floor of a cage. Obviously they are unable to mate with other Budgies.

Right: This is a spectacular mop Budgie bred by Ernie Wise and Justin Fox. The bird here is very healthy and could live for six years or more with trimming, and vent and face care.

Other changes also occur. Commonly, the bird is much larger in body size and weight than its nest siblings (this mutation could be correctly be called gigantism). It can be between 50% heavier to double the weight of its siblings. It also has a deeper and different voice; Single Factor carriers of this gene often have the deeper, coarser voice too. Very rapidly after leaving the nest, feather dusters seem to adapt to a life of very little movement. They are simply unable to get around much.

In the past, it was always said that they were very short-lived: maybe no more than four to six months. With better care and feeding, however, they can commonly live to one or two years of age, a friend of mine has kept mops that lived to five or six years of age. It is thought that the huge demand that continuously growing long feathers all over causes the bird to die from exhaustion or starvation. Certainly better diet favours a longer life. Equally, human care in washing feathers and cleaning vent obstructions is very helpful. Perhaps trimming feathers that obstruct the vent, eyes or feet is a good idea.

Right: This is the same mop as previous photo. Here it is standing on a bench.

In the nest

Encountering a feather duster in the nest is a roller coaster of raw emotions. As a nest of young birds develops, one stands out as by far the best. Even before feathering properly the bird is very large with a big skull. As it feathers up, it looks better and better. The head feathering is superb and one starts to prepare one's speech to the World Budgerigar Club when accepting the trophy for 'World's Best Budgie'.

Above: From ecstasy to agony – from the big-headed bird on the left, to a corrugated mess on the right.

Then telltale lines or valleys in the head and neck feathers appear. The feathers line up in corrugations down the neck and you can see the head and neck skin through the valleys in the corrugations. Now you know that it is a feather duster. Now you know that you must hide this embarrassing failure from your mates. From ecstasy to agony in a few days… "Feather dusters? No mate, I never get them."

Why it happens

After test matings from one lovely big bird that came from a feather duster line mated to a small, runty bird (that, so far as I know, had no feather duster producing antecedents), the pattern seems fairly clear.

This first cross produced 22 young, but no feather dusters; a very fertile pairing. From the luxury of these 22 young I selected sibling pairings of large bird to large bird, large to small and small to small. When small was mated to small, 100% of the young were small and I got no feather dusters. Small mated to large birds produced 50% small, 50% large and, again, no feather dusters.

When large bird was mated to large bird, the results approximated to 50% large birds, 25% small birds and 25% feather dusters. Thus, it is fairly clear that the large birds were 'split' for the feather duster gene. When Budgies carry one gene for feather duster, they are big, bold show birds. Thus the feather duster gene is not recessive at all, but incompletely dominant like Spangle (or like the Palomino gene in horses). That is, the Single Factor form is larger overall and has more feather; it is a far better showbird. The Double Factor form is a full-blown feather duster.

As further proof of the incomplete dominance, many breeders claim that the parents of feather duster have deeper voices and a different call from Normal Budgies. That is, they have an altered voice box, much as true feather dusters do.

I repeated these matings with other Exhibition Budgies and all results were the same as above.

This superb-looking Modern Exhibition Budgie is Single Factor for the mop/feather duster mutation.

It is important to remember that this level of long and coarse feathering can be achieved by simple selection. That is, you don't need the mop gene to get this amount of feathering.

Sure, the mop gene will give coarse feathering, but this is a huge price to pay when you can achieve it in other ways.

Most breeders of Modern Exhibition Budgies have experienced the heartbreak of producing a mop Budgie. This loss from your elite lines of top showbirds is catastrophic for future breeding. One nestling appears to be the best Budgie that you have ever bred, then it turns into a mop.

If you eradicate the mop gene from your breeding lines, then all of your elite young will survive. No more avoidable losses of top-quality Budgies. No more mops to euthanase.

What should you do?

Ideally you should get rid of this gene. We don't need to spend lots of money testing for 'mop carriers' since any Budgie that produces a mop is a carrier.

In horses and cattle, dysfunctional genes like this are being tested for and eliminated these days. For example, in halter quarter horses, huge muscles are very desirable. But one gene (Hyperkalemic Periodic Paralysis – HYPP) gives you the huge muscles in the Single Factor form, but in the Double Factor form it produces a horse prone to muscle seizures and death. Now, by club law, all quarter horses in Australia must be tested and the Single Factor or Double Factor horses can't be registered or bred from.

If you decide to cull the birds, how would you decide which ones? Obviously all parents of a feather duster are 'carriers' of the gene. **Any line of Budgies where there are huge differences between the size and feather quality of the young must be suspect as feather duster producers** – particularly if the voice is deeper. Culling the various birds is then up to you.

The real cause

The real cause of feather dusters is us humans. Whenever you select for extremes in show animals, there is a big chance that you will unknowingly select for a gene that gives you your desired result, but at an awful price. For example, in miniature cattle, some are dominant dwarves. Dwarfism in cattle is semi-lethal (as it is in humans). I suggested to David Sillence, Professor of Genetic Medicine at the University of Sydney Children's Hospital, that it is the same gene as is found in humans. We funded the research through the Veterinary Science faculty and the exact same gene found in humans was found on a different chromosome in cattle. That is, one dwarf gene produces a dwarf, two dwarf genes produce a grossly distorted baby that dies at birth (in dogs like dachshunds or Jack Russells this is not the case by the way). So, carelessly selecting for VERY small cattle produces dead babies. Carelessly selecting for VERY muscled quarter horses produces disabled or dead horses.

Carelessly selecting for huge Budgies with too much feathers produces feather dusters. If the standard moved away from gross extremes in Budgies, feather dusters would almost completely disappear. Equally, fertility would dramatically improve, as would lifespan. And flightless wonders would all but disappear. Due to overall health improvements, disease would be drastically reduced and females would have dark brown ceres. Perhaps the biggest gains would be that the birds would be much easier to feed and breed, leading to beginners doing far better and staying with the clubs.

For the record, in my lines of pure Bush Budgies, and also of pure Australian Heritage Budgies, I have never had a single young feather duster. I have also never had a flightless wonder (with circovirus) or a bird with feather cysts. To test my theories, I did many (more than 100) cross-fosterings of babies, between modern overly feathered showbirds and both Bush Budgies and Heritage Budgies. No young Bush or Heritage Budgies developed into flightless wonders, nor did any get wing abscesses. My results point to the fact that all of these conditions are the result of selection for hereditary excessive feather growth. There were wing-feather cysts recorded in overly feathered Norwich Canaries back in the 1940s and 1950s, which were eradicated by breeding for less buffy, finer feathering. This is well dealt with on pages 186–187 of *Budgerigars, Canaries and Foreign Finches* by R.B. Bennett (1961).

Takeaway points

Be very suspicious of any family of Budgies where huge differences occur between the best and worst young in the one nest; particularly in relation to size and feather. That is, some are big, bold and beautiful, others are little runts. This is a fairly good indicator that at least one of the parents is carrying the feather duster gene. Another unrecorded but obvious feature in lines of Budgies which carry the mop/feather duster gene is that many young often look small and totally lacking in feather when they leave the nest, but they mature into big, beautifully-feathered adults. These birds are very likely to carry the recessive mop gene.

Be even more suspicious of animal breed clubs that breed for extreme features in their animals. Breeding for extreme brachycephalic facial features in dogs or cats, breeding for excessive feathering in birds, breeding for excessive muscling in quarter horses or excessive muscling in cattle (e.g. so-called double muscling in Belgian

Blues), all lead to the unconscious selection for nasty genes that come at a terrible price. Veterinary Science graduates have a wonderful opportunity to create awareness of these problems among exhibition animal breeders. This is a basic ethical issue for all vets.

Flightless and tailless wonders

Flightless and tailless wonders are Budgies that leave the nest fully feathered, but gradually lose mainly flight feathers and tail feathers over the first two or three years. They never recover from this progressive condition and are mostly confined to the aviary floor. Fine, grossly distorted feathers may emerge, but no unaffected ones regrow.

These three birds are all flightless and tailless wonders. They carry a virus condition that ravages overly feathered Budgies, but which has no visible effect on smaller, pure Australian Heritage Exhibition Budgies, nor on Bush Budgies. All three pictured here are modern, overly feathered 'English'-type Exhibition Budgies. None will recover from this state. None can fly. If Budgerigar breeders reduced the huge amount of feathering, this sad condition would eventually disappear forever. It would also help if all parents of feather duster young were removed from breeding lines.

The world's rarest Budgerigar

This turned out to be a new mutation: the Ocean Spray. This is the rarest Budgerigar in the world, and it is also one of the most significant Budgerigars that has been bred. A big claim, perhaps? Can I prove it? Yes I can.

It is a male White Cap Violet Rainbow, which is very, very rare indeed. But this is not the reason for my claim. This bird is a genetic freak – a Budgie that could not possibly exist. Why?

Well, he is, genetically speaking, a male White Cap Opaline Clearwing Violet. The Opaline is the key issue here. Are you aware of how Opaline works genetically? It is a sex-linked **recessive** mutation. This means that both mum and dad must carry the Opaline gene to produce a male Opaline.

Males can carry one or two genes for Opaline: if they carry one gene they look like a non-Opaline but they are split for Opaline. If they carry two genes for Opaline, they are visual Opalines. Females can only carry one gene for Opaline and if they have it, they are always visual Opalines. Since it is a recessive mutation, every male Opaline ever bred must have a visual Opaline mum. This male didn't!

His mum is a Normal White Cap, split for Clearwing, and his dad is an Opaline Blue Clearwing. To repeat, this bird can't possibly be a male. Maybe he could **look** like a male, particularly if he had an extra sex chromosome, i.e. WWZ, which is a catastrophic genetic mix-up. Birds have W and Z sex chromosomes; males are WW and females are ZW. But WWZ birds that look like males are rare as hen's teeth and infertile.

As this young miracle White Cap Rainbow was near to leaving the nest, I noted in my records that he looked like a male, but that this was not possible. He was some sort of genetic mistake, certain to be sterile.

Subsequently, his first baby hatched (left). This should be impossible. I mated him to a young female Clearwing Cobalt who laid her first two eggs on the floor. I put them in the nest box but they were infertile – see extreme left and right pinkish eggs. The other two eggs look OK. I have witnessed a miracle. If the other two eggs hatch, I should be able to learn even more about his genetic make-up.

For the record, the White Cap Rainbow miracle male came from the third round of young in one breeding season from the pair mentioned above. He was the 19th baby in one continuous set of nests. This was colossal fertility from the parents.

This miracle male does not have great size or posture, neither does he have great wing colour. He is not very clear on the wings at all, because he results from an experimental mating of small, very ordinary birds. But he is one of the most important Budgies that I have ever bred because geneticists will talk about him for a long, long time as: 'THE BIRD THAT COULDN'T POSSIBLY EXIST'.

Well, all is now clear a couple of years later. He is an Opaline lookalike! A new mutation that looks superficially like an Opaline, but which is a dominant mutation: not a sex-linked Opaline.

I paired up two of his grandchildren, both 'Opalines'* and out of 30 grandchildren (most fostered as eggs) I got 16 Opalines (nine males and seven females), plus 14 non-Opalines (eight males and six females). This is not a possible result if both of them were genuine Opalines. Doing my maths, it can only be that he is a dominant mutant that looks like an Opaline and she is likely a true Opaline. Below is a range of four of the grandchildren.

Right: A male and female 'Opaline' and a male and female non-Opaline. All are Clearwings, as were both parents. If the mother is a true Opaline and the father were not, no young would be visual Opalines. And if the father were a dominant Opaline lookalike, he would produce 50% 'Opalines' of which 50% would be male and 50% would be female. Which is what I got.

What would be genetic ratios in these young? All of the males would be split for Opaline, the two visual 'Opalines' would be Single Factor for the new mutation tentatively called the **Ocean Spray**, and the male would also be split for Opaline. The non-Opaline male would be split for true Opaline and the non-Opaline female would be split for nothing.

So, if we list the ratios of the young of the non-Opaline female (split for nothing), it goes like this:

---

* The two 'Opaline' parents are not shown here as they were on eggs.

25% Ocean Spray males split for Opaline,

25% Ocean Spray females split for nothing,

25% non-Ocean Spray males split for Opaline, and

25% non-Ocean Spray and non-Opaline females.

So, the key matings to be carried out **next** are:

1. The Ocean Spray female split for nothing mated to a Violet Clearwing male that is not split for Opaline. If the female is indeed carrying a dominant mutation for Ocean Spray, she will produce 50% Ocean Spray young of both sexes split for nothing and 50% non-Ocean Spray non-Opaline young.

2. The Ocean Spray male split for Opaline male mated to a non-Opaline female. This mating should produce:

> 1 in 8 Ocean Spray Opaline females,
>
> 1 in 8 Ocean Spray females,
>
> 1 in 8 Opaline females,
>
> 1 in 8 Normal females,
>
> 1 in 8 Ocean Spray males split for Opaline,
>
> 1 in 8 Ocean Spray males,
>
> 1 in 8 split Opaline males, and
>
> 1 in 8 Normal males.

In the first mating, if you get any 'Opaline'-looking males in the young, then the dominant Ocean Spray mutation is proven.

In the second mating, the same thing – if any 'Opaline'-looking males are produced, the dominant Ocean Spray mutation is proven.

Neither of these young males can possibly be genuine Opalines, so they must be Ocean Sprays.

What to do with a new mutation

Every so often you could well discover a totally new mutation of the Budgerigar, but what should you do with it? The following is a recipe of what to do.

1. Take at least 10–20 colour photos of the bird from all angles.

2. Prepare a new notebook to list every tiny detail of what young are bred and in what numbers, etc, etc. Record **everything.**

3. Tell no-one about this bird and do not take it to the club meeting to ask for advice YET. These actions could lead to the bird escaping or getting sick.

4. Set out to breed at least 10–20 young from the mutant. In general, crossing it to a Blue (non-Grey) Normal is best. Ideally this Normal must NOT be split for Cinnamon, Opaline or anything else. However, if it is a new colour of a Clearwing, for instance, cross it to a Blue Clearwing.

5. Next cross the young from that mating to each other or back to the parent mutant. Get heaps of young birds – 50 is not too many.

6. Record everything as the young grow up. Look at every minor detail of each young bird, write it down and take more photos. Look really hard for any similarity to the original mutant. If the mutation has produced true-to-type youngsters, press on.

7. Think of a wonderful name for your new type of Budgie. A bad name can ruin the chances of the variety taking off. Names such as 'Dusk' or 'Darkwing' can kill off a new variety right away. An exciting name like 'Clearwing' or 'White Cap' is far better.

8. NOW you are ready to show one of the young birds to your friends, maybe even take it to a club meeting. If other people like the look of it, offer some **free** to those of your trusted friends who are interested in it. Do not risk taking your original mutant anywhere. This giving away of mutant babies is THE MOST IMPORTANT STEP OF ALL. WHY? Because it is an insurance policy to protect your new discovery. A dreadful accident may kill all of this new mutation. Your aviaries may be burnt in a bush fire, or a storm may blow them down, or your birds might get a lethal disease that wipes them out, or they may get stolen, or you may get seriously ill, etc, etc. Please spread the birds around urgently. If you get greedy and think that you will make heaps of money from this new variety, the odds are that you will destroy it. Most new varieties just fade away. Be sensible and share them around for FREE.

9. It is paramount to spread some of this new variety to each state in your country to help with its eventual registration.

10. Give your results from your records to an expert in genetics to work out the pattern of heredity.

11. Ask your local club to support you in putting on a special class for your new variety at their annual show. This is a great way to assess whether people really like your new birds... or not.

12. Approach a senior Budgie person (e.g. a President or a National Judge) to support you in getting this new variety recognised (eventually) by your National Budgie Club.

13. Work with the club leaders to create a preliminary standard for this new variety. This is a critical phase. For instance, all German/Australian Fallows COULD easily have been originally called 'Red Eyed Clearbodies' and the standard would then have encouraged ever-lighter body colour and ever-darker wings.

14. Patiently wait for many gifts of stunning Budgies to flow in from those who are so grateful for your generous gift of FREE birds of this exciting new variety.

Budgerigars in India

Budgerigars in India

By Nigam Pandya

Like everywhere else in the world, Budgerigars are undoubtedly the most popular cage and aviary birds in India. In the absence of any research, it is difficult to say when exactly these pretty little parrots were first brought into the country and by whom. Not from any recorded avicultural history, but from some of the other documented records, one can say that Budgerigars had become popular cage birds by the 1950s and 1960s, and by then they were widely distributed across the country. This is evident from some of the scenes from the black-and-white era Hindi movies, where one can see Budgies not only in urban set-ups but also in rural set-ups where these birds are housed in beautifully hand-crafted bamboo cages.

I have had the good fortune to meet some of the old-time bird keepers who'd had Budgerigars in their collections since the 1950s and 1960s. A gentleman by the name of Mr Alex (I do not remember his surname) deserves a special mention here. It was in the year 1993 or 1994 that I was introduced to him by a mutual friend with an interest in birds. Mr Alex lived in a small apartment in Bandra, one of the western suburbs of Mumbai. What made me interested in visiting Mr Alex was the fact that my friend said that he had some nice Full Circular Crested Budgies. I had seen some Crested Budgies but they were either Tufted or had a crest falling down in front – never a Full Circular Crested as depicted in some of the books.

Mr Alex was more than happy to show us his birds, which were housed in the balcony of his flat. There were neat rows of box cages stacked up. Each cage had a pair of birds. On the bottom there was a longish cage with about half a dozen birds flying across – of course this was a flight cage. When I saw those Full Circular Crested birds, I was flabbergasted to say the least. Never ever, before or since, have I seen such beautiful Crested birds.

There were about eight or nine pairs of these stunning Budgies. They were all beautiful milky white with either a gorgeous shade of Cobalt, Violet or Mauve on the rump with just a few specks of dark black markings near the eyes and a fleck here and there on the wings, with a neat round circular crest on the head. Beautiful Reverse Pied Full Crested Budgerigars. It was a sight to behold. The birds were elegant, standing erect on the perch. They were longish and lean birds, like the ones depicted in some of the older books on Budgerigars.

While talking about his birds, Mr Alex mentioned that he had been maintaining his line of Budgies since the 1950s and that he was very proud of the fact that the former Maharaja of Kutch had taken some of his Crested birds to add to his collection. I asked him if he could spare some young for me. He said he could and asked me to visit after a few months. That was never to be. He passed away before I could meet him again. By the time I received the news of his passing all his birds had been disposed of as nobody in the family was interested in them.

The second set of equally stunning birds I saw was in a pet shop at a pet market in Mumbai. This was around 1996–97. There were about 18–20 birds, housed in a cage of their own, separate from other Budgerigars and birds. The birds were a stunning shade of violet that one often sees on the brinjal. A deep reddish tone of violet, the most beautiful tone of violet I have ever seen in Budgies. Much as I wanted to buy these beautiful birds, I found them to be too expensive at 1,500 rupees a pair, which was 25 times the price of normal pet-type Budgies. In hindsight it was foolish of me not to have bought them. I looked at the price and not at the value of the birds. I have become wiser now and value the bird more than the price.

From the above two examples, I am more than convinced that in a vast country like India there are thousands of knowledgeable and dedicated breeders who have been breeding and continue to breed excellent quality birds putting in decades of diligent and hard work, without being noticed by vast majority of Budgerigar keepers in the country. The need of the hour is to go out and discover these breeders and showcase their work.

The popularity of Budgerigars is at its peak and is rising day by day, thanks to social media platforms such as WhatsApp and Facebook. Today there are tens of millions in India who have Budgies as pets or as breeding birds. Barring the lull due to COVID-19 pandemic, every pet shop in India, be it big or small, in a big metropolis like Mumbai or Kolkata, or in a small non-descript mofussil hamlet, will invariably have Budgies to offer for sale. In a country where people are very price conscious, the Budgerigar is one of the most affordable pets, priced at anything between 300 and 600 rupees a pair. Apart from the affordability, people find Budgies to be easy to cater for in terms of feeding and cleaning, not to mention the small space that they require. The last criteria make these birds most attractive to city dwellers where space is always a constraint.

In spite of its huge popularity and large number of people keeping Budgerigars in India, it is unfortunate that even today the hobby is completely unorganised and without any kind of institutional support to Budgerigar keepers. In last couple of years, two or three regional societies have been formed and they remain largely regional. They cater to a small number of Budgerigar keepers, not only because of the geographical reason but largely due to the fact that most of the business of the society is conducted in the regional language and interaction between the members of the society are also in native language. This makes it very restrictive. What is needed is for such societies or clubs to conduct their business in English, which is the official language of communication at national level, or in Hindi, which is our national language. Fortunately, for starting and establishing societies or clubs, we have many models to choose from as the hobby of Budgerigar keeping has been well organised for decades in many other countries around the world, with many different kinds of societies and clubs.

Despite the lack of organisation, Indians keeping Budgies have taken to social media such as WhatsApp and Facebook exactly like a fish takes to the water. There are thousands of groups on these platforms where bird keepers regularly interact with each other and exchange ideas and their work. Hundreds of videos on Budgerigar keeping are being shared on YouTube. Many of them are in regional languages (we have 22 different languages which are officially recognised), not to mention dialects. We also have a Facebook group which has even taken the membership of WBO. Such groups have, in the last couple of years, also started organising online shows. Members of such groups post photographs of their birds on these social media platforms.

It is through such social media posts that one comes to know about the development of Budgerigars in India. There are some breeders who have managed to lay their hands on good lines of show Budgerigars from other countries. The birds from these lines can be used to develop good lines of show birds in India. A point to be made here would be that of price. The birds coming from the West are ridiculously overpriced and bought by rich and not necessarily passionate Budgie lovers. Such birds become a status symbol and rarely if at all contribute to the development of good studs in this country.

Apart from the show side of Budgies, one comes across some really exciting developments in India through social media posts. For instance, about six months ago I came across a post on a WhatsApp group which showed a photo of what looked like a White Cap Budgie. Initially I thought it to be the result of flash being used so, I asked the gentleman to send me some more photographs without the flash. To my surprise he had more than one such bird in his collection. Seeing this I talked to him on the phone and explained to him about how it could be an independent mutation of the Australian White Cap variety. I was keen to investigate and work with him if indeed it was a new or independent mutation. That still remains a dream because as soon as the gentleman learnt that it was something rare, he stopped interacting with me. He still continues to hold some of these probable White Caps in his stud.

The Hagoromo or Helicopter Budgerigar is a variety which has become very popular in India. They were brought into the country about seven or eight years ago. In all probability the strain has its roots in Egypt. As expected, the initial stock was not really very good. However, Indian breeders have really improved the Hagoromos over a period of time. Most strains established in India of these Helicopter Budgies are prolific breeders. What we need now is to improve the colours in these birds. Yet another variety which has taken the fancy of breeders is Rainbow Budgerigars. There are thousands of breeders in India breeding Rainbows. Most breeders have gone for this variety because of the exotic fancy name and also for the better price it commands because of the name. As with Hagoromos, most Rainbow strains in India could do with improvement in the vibrancy of their colours.

Apart from the varieties mentioned, there are some breeders who have been breeding good specimens of other well-known varieties, for instance German Fallows and Texas Clearbodies. In fact, I have been mentoring a person who has been breeding both German as well as English Fallows. He has been maintaining a small stud of both varieties for more than a decade now. There may be many more like him in India who are working on different varieties of Budgerigars and doing it silently without being noticed. What is needed is to discover these breeders, encourage them to showcase their work, and incentivise them to share their experience and expertise with other passionate Budgie lovers. This is possible when we have robust institutions in the form of societies and clubs supporting the work of passionate and dedicated breeders.

The future of Budgerigars in India seems to be very bright with the kind of scope we have for these wonderful little parrots. First and foremost, they are considered to be completely domesticated birds so do not come under the jurisdiction of the CITES treaty or any other Indian laws. Secondly, slowly and gradually the hobby is being organised in the form of registered societies, however small or regional they may be. Third and the most important is the potential. With a human population of 1.4 billion, more than 600,000 villages and small towns, and very large metropolises such as Mumbai, Kolkata and Delhi, each with population sizes exceeding 10 million, there is enough scope for tens of thousands of Budgerigar societies and clubs to exist and operate. There is enough scope for millions of people to join these institutions and enjoy the pure joy and happiness that keeping Budgerigars has to offer.

A Clearwing with the author.

Hagoromo Line Crested Budgerigar with very clear wings. Photo: Sandeep Vadher.

Left: Hagoromo Line Budgies. Photo: Sayandeb Bose.

Centre: A nice specimen of Texas Clearbody Hagoromo. Photo: Sandeep Vadher.

Right: Father and son Texas Clearbody. Photo: Sayandeb Bose.

English Fallows. Photo: Bakul Bhatt.

Rainbow Budgie. Photo: Sayandeb Bose.

Left: A beautiful clear-flighted show bird. Photo: Nitin Patel.

Centre: Stud of show Budgerigars. Photo: Rajdeep Rana.

Right: A nice Violet Yellow Faced Violet show male. Photo: Rajdeep Rana.

Budgerigar management

A new approach to disease control

At a Glance

Preventing disease outbreaks is essential with Budgies since they rarely recover from diseases. The two key things that are essential for Budgie health are a totally dry aviary and UVB lighting because Budgies come from the sunny deserts of central Australia. There are other issues, however, a notable one being that probiotics are useless at best and, at worst, their use after using antibiotics is bad for your birds, or for humans for that matter.

The third key thing is to find a really good specialist bird veterinarian and attach yourself to him or her. Ideally select an older vet who has had experience in the poultry industry. As a tree surgeon and arboriculturist it took more than 20 years before I was much good at my craft, and the same can be true for many vets.

Budgies are FRAGILE creatures that do not recover well from diseases. In captivity, diarrhoea often kills Budgies. Their nomadic desert lifestyle in families of about six birds the wild is excellent for avoiding contact with these sorts of diseases since most diseases need wet conditions to multiply. In captivity Budgies are surrounded by many diseases that they would not encounter in the wild. They constantly encounter poo from other Budgies which they commonly eat – thus they can hardly avoid contact with diseases any more.

1. Budgies are like American Passenger Pigeons – they breed in their millions in the wild, but they also can die in their millions when they encounter serious challenges of any sort. In extreme heat or during severe droughts, Budgies can die in their millions – they are a 'boom or bust' species.
2. In their natural environment, the individual Budgie is expendable. The evolutionary strategy of this species is to simply breed in vast numbers when times are good and thus to be able to cope with bad times even if numbers are catastrophically reduced.
3. For this reason, they also have very short lives – perhaps as little as about two or three years average in the wild. Even in captivity, most Exhibition Budgies average only about four or five years. The record longevity for a pet Budgie in a cage according to the *Guinness Book of Records* is 29 years – note that a pet cage is the PERFECT quarantine isolation unit with a perfect climate and excellent food supply.

4. Human beings, as well as many larger parrot species and cockatoos, have a very different evolutionary strategy to the Budgie. With humans, the individual DOES MATTER. It takes about 20 years to grow and educate a human, and we usually only have one baby at a time. Humans recover quite well from injuries and diseases relative to Budgies and live for a long time. (Stone Age people averaged lifespans of about 30 years, but in biblical times some individuals lived much longer, to around 60 years. Pharaoh Ramesses II lived to around 90!).

This may just mean that our approach to Budgie disease control needs to be changed. For many reasons, you could argue that we have gone down the wrong path in trying to use antibiotics to PREVENT DISEASES. Our methods of disease prevention are wide of the mark. So, let's look at some new science on everything from antibiotics to microbiomes.

Budgies absolutely adore eating oranges, which are very good for them. Oranges contribute to an acidic stomach, which discourages some diseases.

Antibiotics

Currently, many Exhibition Budgie breeders use human antibiotics purchased from a vet for Budgie disease control or prevention. Recent research on the gut microbiome in humans is showing that antibiotics do much harm as well as good. They basically upset the ecosystem inside the gut. In the guts of all animals, there is a gigantic and complex ecosystem thriving, involving billions of organisms of hundreds of thousands of species and forms of species. Each of these gut species is likely to be exclusive to that particular individual animal species. So we humans have this vastly complex soup of special organisms inside us that co-evolved with humans and can only live inside us. There are just as many cells in our gut as there are in the rest of our entire body. Thus, the human gut microbiome is by far our biggest organ.

Inside the guts of all animals are hundreds of thousands of genes belonging to the gut bacteria and other organisms that affect the development and wellbeing of the host animal. This is true for humans and Budgies alike. So, shove some antibiotics down your Budgies' throats and you may just do all sorts of damage that may indirectly over time lead to the illness or death of your birds. Using antibiotics as a preventative treatment every so often to 'clean your birds out' is a disastrously bad form of management, yet it is widely practiced by Budgie breeders.

You might be unbalancing your Budgies' gut microbiomes (a microbiome is sort of like an internal ecosystem) such that all hell breaks loose. Yes, the antibiotic may well kill the one diagnosed disease but it will almost certainly kill all sorts of other good or useful organisms as well. New research clearly indicates that it is the BALANCE of species of organisms in animals' guts that is essential for ongoing health. Even so-called 'bad' organisms are essential (in small, balanced numbers) for good health.

While the judicious use of selected antibiotics is often a life saviour for your Budgies, antibiotics kill a wide number of organisms and thus destabilise your gut. Perhaps you could compare this to spraying another ecosystem, the Serengeti National Park in Tanzania, with Roundup to control a pasture weed. Doing this would kill the native grasses as well, which would starve the wildebeest, zebras and other herbivores to death; which would then cause the lions, hyenas, leopards, vultures and many other carnivores to starve... and on it goes.

We humans are equipped to cope with this sort of gut disruption to some extent – but it is my contention that Budgies don't cope as well. This sort of disruption merely opens your poor Budgies up to more and more other problems over time. It also seriously damages the Budgies' immune systems as well, since the gut has a powerful effect on all animals' immune systems. A well-balanced gut ecosystem is essential for a healthy animal. A Budgie's own immune system and isolation for key diseases are the keys to better health, not antibiotics and similar medicines.

It is the contention here that Budgerigar health is best maintained with dry aviaries with ultraviolet lighting plus substances that promote balanced, natural gut functions. At this stage, these substances are almost exclusively natural substances such as foods and herbs.

Are probiotics any good? – an update

Probiotics have little to offer for the health of humans or birds at this stage.

Yet another scientific research project has found that the probiotics sold to the general public from pharmacies and other outlets are "mostly useless". Immunologist Eran Elinav of the Weizmann Institute of Science in Israel conducted new research looking into the gut and they found that "the concept that everyone can benefit from a universal probiotic bought from the supermarket is empirically wrong."

They also found that taking probiotics after a course of antibiotics is a very bad practice. The probiotics administered after antibiotics created a prolonged gut microbiome disturbance (up to six months), and "it's potentially harmful." Possible results from this practice are "obesity, allergies and inflammation."

The latest research absolutely nails probiotics as useless. Most scientists say that currently available probiotics are useless, but a minority have been saying that they do some good. The 'some good' statement had been the product of researching probiotics in glass containers, where they do work a little bit. BUT in human and animals' bodies, they don't work at all.

In my opinion, using current probiotics for your own health, or for your Budgies' health, is a waste of time and money. But in the future, genuinely functional probiotics will be very valuable. Maybe watch out for labels which say 'might cure something'.

This means that it is useless. Or check for the research background to all products like probiotics, particularly bird products. I have found several bird probiotics that were never scientifically tested at all.

Disease prevention

The main contenders for use in developing a stronger immune system with Budgies are the following, none of which require the involvement or approval of a vet.

- A permanently dry aviary plus vitamin D3 from exposing your Budgies to natural sunlight or UV lighting.
- Manuka honey.
- Apple cider vinegar with garlic.
- A product made from Greek oregano oil, called Orego-Stim.
- The branches of certain Australian native trees and shrubs.
- Ginger roots such as turmeric.
  Many other foods probably help too, including beetroot, amaranth and carrots.

Orego-Stim.   Liquid Gold calcium supplement.   Soluvite D vitamin D3 supplement.

Vitamin D3 is essential for a healthy immune system in Budgies and humans. Vitamin D3 acts as the hormone that drives much of the immune system. Budgies make their own vitamin D3 from exposure to direct sunlight that has **not** passed through glass, Perspex, clear fibreglass, or any other clear material. Second best is the use of Reptile One 10.0% UVB Fluorescent tube lighting – especially in birdrooms. There are also UVB LED lights that may work. I haven't tested them yet, but please remember that too much UV light can cause cancer in both humans and birds. As a back-up, use a vitamin D3 supplement such as Soluvite D Breeder from Vetafarm.

Turmeric.

Reptile One 10% UVB fluorescent light tube.

Recent research has shown that commercial vitamin D3 for humans or birds is often derived from vegetable sources. Vegetable-derived vitamin D3 is nowhere near as good as the Budgies' own vitamin D3 production or animal-produced vitamin D3. Look for the word cholecalciferol on the label – this is the best form of vitamin D. So, Reptile One lighting is by far the best source of vitamin D3.

Recently, Budgie breeder Mick Arnold sent me the following feedback on using manuka honey as I had recommended: "My first round with 10 breeding cabinets I hatched 47 chicks… I can't think of anything I have done different this year against previous years apart from the honey… These are the best results I have had in more than 20 years with Budgies."

Apple cider vinegar with added garlic has a very strong effect on my Budgies (I use Stockhealth double-strength apple cider vinegar with garlic at a rate of 2ml per litre of water – I get this product from Elenbee Bird Supplies in Australia). The day after administering it, my birds are much noisier and more active. Apple cider vinegar has been shown to improve gut health.

Manuka honey is a gentle product that you can add to the Budgies' water (blend half a teaspoon of manuka honey to 1 litre of water). It appears to nourish the gut lining, etc. My Budgies' fertility has soared since I started using it. According to current research being done with wound healing in horses by Professor Andrew Dart from the University of Sydney, manuka honey is very good, but Scottish heather honey is even better.

A new product called Orego-Stim is an emulsified oregano oil which is added to the drinking water. There is good scientific evidence that it also aids the gut health and produces healthier birds that resist diseases better. There are two different formulations of Orego-Stim: a thick milk-like white emulsion, and a much thinner diluted liquid. I use the more concentrated thick, white milk emulsion in the 1 litre bottle which is called 'Orego-Stim liquid feed additive' and I use it at the rate of 2ml of this concentrate per litre of water. There is no special rate of dilution for Budgies listed on the bottle – the dilution listed here is what I have found best from trial and error.

I guess that many other herbs, shrubs and tree parts will be of considerable help for gut health. BUT BE VERY CAREFUL – FOR INSTANCE, **CORIANDER IS POISONOUS TO BUDGIES.** The herbs that Budgies use in the wild such as Eucalyptus buds and branches plus Lemon-scented Teatree branches are likely to be very good too.

I have had a number of senior Budgie breeders look at my breeding birds too and they can bear witness to the huge numbers in each nest – for example, more than

700 young from 52 breeding cages in the first eight months of the year in 2014.

Up until recently, I rarely used antibiotics or other veterinary medicines and my birds have never been healthier. They have never had so many babies either. I have had many nests of more than eight young and some with 11 successfully raised young, which I have never even heard of before. I kept my antibiotics that I got from the vet, but I was determined not to use them unless something goes terribly wrong.

Watch out for a canker (trichomoniasis) outbreak. This is a very common problem with birds, from chickens and pigeons to parrots and finches. The cause is a tiny single-celled parasite called a protozoan. I once lost three females (canker mostly kills younger birds, and females in particular). The symptoms are green sticky droppings adhering around the vent, general listlessness, severe loss of weight and some birds dropping dead.

I used Emtryl combined with Orego-Stim for five days, after which the birds were rambunctious and very noisy again. Emtryl is known to reduce fertility for six weeks or so, thus I will need to use manuka honey and the other gut stimulators to prepare the birds for breeding.

If I get an outbreak of diarrhoea, I catch the sick birds and use a modern sulfa drug called Trimidine (available from veterinarians and made up of Sulfadimidine and Trimethoprim), which is wonderful against E. coli. But you must only use this in an emergency – it should not be used regularly for your flock treatment.

The main problem that the above system fails to beat is coccidiosis. Like canker, this is a disease caused by parasites. I use Vetafarm's Coccivet (containing Amprolium and Ethopabate) from the vet to control this disease, but only if an outbreak occurs. Baycox can also be used but it is disliked by Budgies and they refuse to drink water with Baycox in it for as long as they can. This shock to their systems leads to a moult usually within a week to 10 days (see the section 'Stuck in the moult'). New head feathers growing immediately after Baycox treatment usually develop temporary head flecking. This is an exhibition fault, but it disappears during the next moult.

Fat Budgies

I have had fat Budgies at the beginning of the breeding season every year for more than eight years. I have tried feeding different seed mixes, feeding higher protein foods, making the birds exercise more and many other tricks – all failed. It has been revealed by recent research with humans that an unbalanced gut microbiome can make people fat, so I tried the products mentioned herein – so far it seems to be working. My birds are no longer commonly obese. See article from *Scientific American*: 'How gut bacteria help make us fat and thin' by Claudia Williams.

Avian gastric yeast (megabacteria)

I had some to many birds with megabacteria (avian gastric yeast) for many years. While administering the manuka honey, apple cider vinegar, Orego-Stim and extra UVB light, no new ones have appeared over the last three years. I suspect that avian gastric yeast is a classic symptom of a compromised gut microbiome. I have tried the recommended veterinary treatments for megabacteria and I can assure you that they don't work.

Antibiotics

There is clear evidence of the decline of effectiveness of antibiotics around the world. This was always inevitable since all organisms eventually evolve to become immune to the medicines that we use to eradicate them. Perhaps it is time to try other things. See the paper by Susan Brink in *National Geographic*: 'Fatal superbugs: antibiotics losing effectiveness, W.H.O says'.

Wild parrots eating herbs

Research has shown that, in Australia, parrots eat hundreds of wild herbs, plant leaves, etc, every week in addition to the seed that they eat. Perhaps this is in part self-medication for the gut microbiome. So a wide selection of plants that are known to be safe with Budgies should be offered every week to your birds. Never use plants that are not recommended for feeding to captive Budgies.

Poo transplants

The University of Sydney is researching transferring gut organisms through faecal transplants via enemas from healthy people to other people to see what health improvements are noticed. This is a vastly superior concept to trying probiotics that contain only one or two probiotic species, as sold in shops. Maybe soon we will be able to buy special pills of safe gut organisms that survive through the stomach to release their goodies in vast numbers of different species into the gut.

Quarantine

We hear a lot about quarantine: in theory it is a good idea, but in reality it may not be so good – in the way that it is normally done. Bombarding your newly acquired Budgies with nasty antibiotics, etc, may be disastrous for the poor birds' immune systems. Certainly it has not worked well for my Budgies. What I have found useful is to create a breeding quarantine/isolation system. I put new purchases straight into a breeding cage to breed with one of my birds or with another new bird without the use of antibiotics. I find that the new birds breed really well in this isolation with my treatments of manuka honey, Orego-Stim, apple cider vinegar with garlic, and UV light supplementation (from a Reptile One 10.0% UVB tube). Along the way, they get slow contact with the diseases in my flock, which they seem to deal with really well.

New microbiome research shows that your microbiome spreads relentlessly around you all the time. So much so that it is anticipated that criminals could soon be identified by the traces of their microbiomes left at crime scenes. Your Budgies are also relentlessly spreading their gut organisms from their microbiomes such that new birds in isolated breeding cages will be inoculated sooner or later. At the end of this quarantine/isolation breeding process, I put the now healthier 'new' birds into my aviaries for the first time.

Aviaries and breeding cages

It is a good idea to build your aviaries such that you can convert them into a garden shed, or a kid's cubbyhouse, etc, should you decide to cease breeding Budgies or, perhaps, to sell your home. It is also important to talk to local Budgie breeders about what aviary/birdroom designs are best for your area. They might even help you with the building.

At a Glance

You can build your aviaries as you wish, from whatever building materials that you like, but there are certain practicalities that you need to bear in mind. In this chapter we will try to cover the essential requirements as well as the things that you need to avoid.

Garden sheds like this one can be built by a handy person or carpenter with some creativity. We built this French Provincial-style shed in three days using second-hand timber and some old hinges and it looks as though it's been there forever. Other attractive sheds are generally available in kits which any good home handy person could modify to become excellent aviaries.

Structures like these add value to any property. One of the obvious reasons for people not breeding cage birds any more is that they have a beautifully created landscaped garden and an ugly backyard aviary is just not on. Photo: Melwood Cabanas and Garden Rooms.

This is a photo from inside my birdroom. It shows an aviary with a raised gallery reaching out into the garden for light. The building is constructed from Solarspan industrial freezer material, which is made of two sheets of Colorbond steel with 50mm of polyfoam between them.

Raised galleries are very important. They allow the birds to get plenty of natural sunlight and the bird's droppings go through the wire mesh floor to the ground below. Ideally, they should have a window that can be closed when the birds need to be inside during cold weather or for noise abatement during rain.

Solarspan is sort of like giant Lego material. The sheets fit together like Lego, and they are very strong, so no frame is required. Once the concrete floor was laid, the aviary and roof took about four hours to construct. Windows are simply cut out using a reciprocating saw. Being used in industrial freezers, this material has amazing resistance to hot or cold weather. In Australia, they are now building houses out of Solarspan. This is not a paid recommendation.

Left: This is the outside of the birdroom, which is camouflaged with drab army colours in a bushland area of our garden. It is invisible from our house. This large birdroom would make a great workshop or garden shed should we ever sell.

Right: Inside the birdroom are 52 breeding cabinets and two aviaries. The cabinets are made of kitchen grade white laminated pulp board; they are more than 35 years old.

The double tube fluorescent lighting has 10% UVB lighting to facilitate good natural vitamin D3 production in the birds. The protruding nest boxes were supposed to slide inside each cage, but the builder forgot. In my opinion, nest boxes should always fit flush with the cage front to avoid knocking the nest boxes and disturbing the breeding birds.

I am opposed to using all-wire breeding cages as pulp board breeding cabinets are effectively quarantine units, which is important. Most diseases can't travel from cage to cage in pulp board cages.

Nuisance

To me Budgies produce wonderful warbling songs, but not everyone agrees. Some people hate the noise that Budgies make, and on smaller blocks of land, the neighbours can get very upset with your birdroom and birds (even though they go to horribly noisy restaurants and never complain).

Before you build your birdroom, you need to contact your local council to see what the laws on aviaries and birds are. Usually there are noise restrictions as well as restrictions about how many birds you can keep and how close to next door you can build the aviary and birdroom.

Ideally, you should build noise-reduction surfaces or designs. Tight joints and double glazing are desirable. Ceilings made from white sound-reducing tiles are good, perhaps covered with 6mm (0.25 inch) galvanised mesh. There are many noise reducing systems available.

Some Budgie breeders build the birdroom into their house next to the garage. This solves many problems.

And lastly, you should go next door to explain to your neighbours what you plan to build before building commences.

Perches are installed at a 70° angle from upright separated by 250mm.

Budgie management

Overview of contents

- Stuck in the moult
- Mobility causes morbidity
- Egg-binding
- Pink feet and vitamin D3 in Budgies
- Fostering young
- Plucking of young
- Parents attacking young that have just left the nest
- Other breeding problems
- Mites – totally misunderstood
- What harm do mites do? Plucking?
- Bird veterinarians
- Undershot beaks
- Budgie feather cysts

At a Glance

An always-dry aviary is the best way to avoid diseases.

Budgerigar management is so important. What *you* do determines everything. But there can be a tendency to blame something or someone else. When something goes wrong, always ask yourself 'What did I get wrong?' or 'What can I learn from this?' With this attitude, you can constantly solve problems and prevent them from happening again – i.e. you will grow as an expert Budgerigar keeper/breeder.

Stuck in the moult

You often hear the phrase: 'My birds are stuck in the moult.' What on Earth does this mean? It seems that the breeders are blaming the poor birds or the 'bloody weather' for the constantly moulting! The symptoms are usually bedraggled-looking birds covered in pin feathers and an aviary floor covered in feathers. And no matter what the owner seems to do, the birds keep on moulting, month after month. And if they stop moulting, a few weeks later, they start moulting all over again. They're stuck in the moult and there is nothing that you can do about it.

A carpet of feathers like this on the aviary floor might just be a sign of trouble.

What if I said that **they** are not stuck in the moult at all. What if I said that **you** were stuck in a rut, a bad habit, which was keeping them in the moult?

Think about it: being stuck in the moult is a disaster for birds, and in the wild it would probably kill them. In captivity constant moulting stunts their growth and weakens your birds, leaving them open to diseases. It is not a natural state of affairs at all – something causes it. The answer can be found in chicken farming. Often it helps to look at other bird species to get insights into caring for your Budgies. In the chicken industry, they need to control when the chickens lay eggs to even out the monthly rate of egg laying all year round. Chickens cease laying when they moult, so the chicken farmers control the moulting.

To force a moult exactly when they want it, the chickens used to be deprived of water for up to 48 hours. This cruel practice used to guarantee a moult starting within a few days. It is now banned. The shock of the lack of water forces a moult in many bird species. Can you see where I am heading? I am heading towards backing up the veterinary profession in a very big way. For a long time, vets have begged bird breeders not to use antibiotics so often. And in so many ways they were and are correct.

When you give your birds precautionary medication in their water, be it Ivermectin or antibiotics or other nasty-tasting additives, the birds simply don't drink much for several days – or however long you treat them for. This often causes a heavy moult within days, just as it does in chooks. What's worse is that as they emerge from the moult you give them another precautionary treatment against another disease outbreak, and cause yet another moult!

How do I know that this happens with Budgies? I set up experiments. About 200 birds in two aviaries were put on medication for two days and another 200 birds in two aviaries were just given plain water. The results were astonishing – all of the birds on medication went into a moult within seven days. None of the unmedicated birds moulted. I repeated this experiment twice more over two years and got the same result. I tested Ivermectin, and two antibiotics, one for each test.

Right: A young female in the moult. This is a huge drain on all Budgerigars, but particularly on Modern European Exhibition Budgies, which produce such a vast amount of feathering.

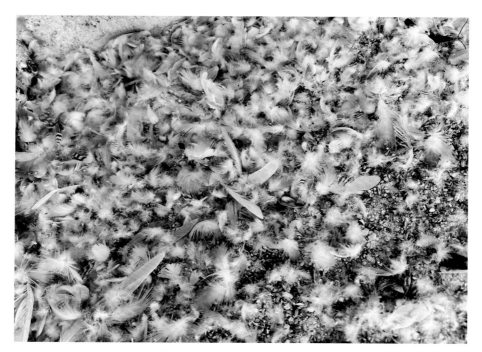

So what can you do? Well, to begin with, never again give your birds precautionary drug treatments. They do no good at all, only harm. Only treat individual birds for specific diseases if they become ill, just as the veterinarians have advised for many many years.

There are a few exceptions to this rule. Precautionary treatments for mites are essential for all Budgies except for isolated pets in small cages. Mites cause scaly face, scaly leg and feather problems, and plagues of them suck out your Budgies' blood as well. They are a massive problem in nest boxes. Regular treatment once or twice a year is essential. For treatments see 'Mites – totally misunderstood' on page 223 in this chapter.

Above and beyond everything else, a 24/7 dry aviary is the best way of preventing diseases in Budgies.

Mobility causes morbidity

Today's Exhibition Budgerigars are vastly more mobile in general than in days gone by. When I was a kid, I bought almost all of my Budgies from Greg Tunney – my mentor, 'Mr Tunney' to me – who lived nearby. Overall, most Budgie people bought only a small number of birds, all from a few local breeders.

Today, breeders buy many more birds, particularly at auctions. Often, at a single auction, one breeder might buy three or more birds all from different breeders from different cities or states. Thus sale birds travel all over the country, bringing ever more and different exotic diseases with them – which they swap with each other. Birds going to the Australian Nationals get put together in aviaries with many other birds from various breeders; again swapping diseases. Birds imported from overseas, despite quarantine, also introduce more new diseases (e.g. the flightless and tailless wonder virus). Budgie people are thus unknowingly swamping their Budgies with huge numbers of new varieties and forms of diseases, in stark contrast with times gone by. Think of COVID-19 and its effects on the human population.

Equally, modern breeding rooms are more enclosed than ever before, which creates a dangerous room that lacks natural UVB light (UVB light cannot travel through any clear material including glass, clear fibreglass, perspex, etc). This prevents the birds from producing enough vitamin D3, which is the main steroid hormone that drives the birds' natural immune systems.

Thus Modern Exhibition Budgies suffer from vastly more diseases than ever before. In response to this crisis, breeders were giving huge amounts of antibiotics and other medicines to their Budgies. As the initiator and former board member of the Australian Pesticides and Veterinary Medicines Authority (APVMA) in Canberra, I was very aware of just how bad these practices are. Overuse causes the disease organisms to develop rapid resistance to the particular drug. **Overuse of antibiotics in particular is a huge worldwide problem.**

To make matters worse, Budgies don't recover well from diseases at the best of times.

Thus I set about REDUCING the amounts of nasty chemicals that we feed to our Budgies. I researched harmless herbs and other food or water additives as well as aviary lighting that had a UVB component that helped to boost the birds' immune systems so that they didn't get sick in the first place. See the section 'Feeding Budgies' on page 231.

That beautiful pair of Budgies might just introduce new diseases. Buy some new Budgies, but not too many from different breeders.

Lastly, the proof that **mobility causes morbidity** lies with new mutations and varieties of most bird species. New colours and varieties are notorious for being sickly and weak. This is obviously the result of the rapid spreading of these highly sought-after birds from aviary to aviary at high prices (picking up more and more diseases along the way). New varieties are by far the most mobile of all birds. Hence their sickly nature. As their price drops and sales fall, the diseases largely disappear.

Egg-binding

Egg-binding should never occur if you administer a vitamin D3 liquid calcium supplement in the birds' drinking water twice a week from three weeks prior to pairing up until when you return the females to the aviary. Liquid calcium is chelated calcium, which is 100% soluble. Lime blocks and grit are largely insoluble and they mostly pass through the birds undigested. Thus liquid calcium is a way better product and it is cheaper and safer to use.

Pink feet and vitamin D3 in Budgies

Normal Budgies have blue-grey feet – or do they? Some Budgies, such as Albinos, Lutinos, Fallows, Cinnamons, Lacewings and even many Pieds, have pink feet. Does it matter?

Any judge will tell you that Normals, Clearwings, Greywings, Dilutes, Black Eyed Whites Black Eyed Yellows and Spangles – in fact any Normal-based variety – must have blue-grey feet. I believe that this is a terrible mistake.

Our 1962 Australian Heritage Budgerigar Association Perpetual National Standard does not specify foot colour at all. It is correct not to do so in my opinion.

This female Normal Australian Golden Faced Blue has pinkish feet and legs.

The point of this following section is to prove that standards requiring blue-grey feet colour need to be changed. First of all, Normal Budgies do not **all** have blue-grey feet and neither do all Budgies in the wild. It was scientifically described in 1964 by Barbara F. Brockway (*Behaviour*, Vol XXII: 3–4) that female Budgies have pink-grey feet. Males usually have darker, blue-grey feet, however.

Females have pinkish feet, presumably to produce enough vitamin D3 inside the hollow logs where they breed out of the sun, or simply to produce more vitamin D3 in the limited time that they spend outside of the nesting hollow. Low vitamin D3 = poor calcium uptake = egg-binding and death. Male Budgies do not face this challenge, hence their darker feet.

Right: Natural differences in leg and feet colours in Bush Budgies – male on the right with blue/grey feet and legs, female on the left with pink feet and legs.

As we moved our Budgies into dark birdrooms to breed and live, Cinnamons proliferated. Cinnamons got less disease problems and bred more young birds. Normals went into a sharp decline, so much so that Normals are now often quite expensive to buy. Budgies make much of their vitamin D3 on the skin of their feet, but dark feet simply don't make enough vitamin D3 in dark birdrooms, which have very little UVB light. Remember that UVB light does not travel much through glass, clear fibreglass or any clear material. But Cinnamons with pinkish feet do produce much more vitamin D3 in these dark birdrooms.

Right: This is a male Normal Yellow Faced Violet Sky. Note that his legs and feet are very pink, i.e. superbly adapted to the low lighting in birdrooms.

Light coloured skin in humans is also an adaptation to low light levels and a greater area of clothing worn in colder areas of the world such as Europe.

Pink-footed Budgies are the elite, super-adapted Modern Exhibition Budgies of the future. They survive and breed really well in dark birdrooms. Using my new systems, it is now more than ten years since I have had a single egg-bound female. Yet judges mark pink-footed Budgies down on the showbench. Why?

Vitamin D3 is made by the production of oil on the animal's skin, which the sun turns into vitamin D3. This is then re-absorbed by the skin. With birds, oil from the preen gland, just above the tail, is spread by birds during preening and is then swallowed by the birds during subsequent preening. However, much more vitamin D3 is made by the skin of the bird's feet. Per unit area of skin, feet produce 30 times more vitamin D3 than on feathered areas. Hence the evolution of pink feet under dark birdroom conditions.

If caring and advanced Budgie breeders install Reptile One 10% UVB fluorescent lights in their birdrooms, most of these problems can be avoided. These lights, which last 12 months, enable most Budgies to NATURALLY produce all the vitamin D3 that they need. This natural vitamin D3 is far better for bird's health and fertility than the vitamin D3 in dietary supplements.

Breeding problems with Budgies

Fostering young

Fostering Budgies from one nest box to another to even out numbers of young is a great idea… sometimes.

Over the years. I have done a lot of fostering of young and most of it has worked out well: a pair with 10 or 11 babies seems to cope much better when you reduce the number to seven by moving some to a pair with, say, two babies. I can't remember any pairs rejecting the babies either.

Before we look at what can go wrong with fostering, let's look at the reasons for fostering:

1. As above, to remove the strain of too many young on the parents.
2. To test whether certain birds have genetic or disease problems (e.g. wing-feather cysts, or flightless and tailless wonders). When I discovered that my Bush Budgies and my Heritage Exhibition Budgies never were troubled by wing-feather cysts, nor with the flightless and tailless wonder virus, I cross-fostered their babies to finally prove a genetic weakness in Modern Showbirds. This is very important research. Only Modern Exhibition Budgies and their hybrids get these diseases.
3. Because the female is plucking the young severely.
4. Because one parent dies.
5. Because the babies are leaving the nest way too young.

Above: Nine is too many!

219

Plucking of young

Reasons not to foster:

1. When a female plucks her young, this is often caused by tiny mites that you failed to see. At night, the mites swarm all over both female and the young, driving the female mad: hence the stress plucking. Fostering will just introduce the mites into another breeding box. So treat all cages and boxes for mites, and massage the plucked babies with Nivea hand cream which has a repulsive taste to bugies. Then return them to mum and dad's box. I suggest that you inspect the faces of mum and dad to see which one has blood on it. Then immediately remove that parent. The other parent will raise the chicks.

2. When young Budgies leave the nest way too early, it is often a sign that they are in the very early stages of French moult. Fostering them can transmit this disease from one cage to another. So, just put these early leavers back in their own nest, and maybe give them some baby Budgie formula via crop needles. Other early signs of French moult are aggressive young babies that bite and screech.

This poor young bird was severely plucked by his mum. I rubbed Nivea on him, as you can see, and he made a full recovery and is now a breeding bird in my birdroom. Nivea, Coopex and Pestene stopped the problem overnight. Budgies seem to hate the smell and taste of Nivea.

3. University research has shown that fostered baby birds don't grow quite as well. However, this is not my experience.

4. Fostering is a breach of quarantine. Breeding cages are, in effect, quarantine units. Moving other babies into a nest may introduce many diseases.

Parents attacking newly fledged young

Mature males consider young males as competition for the female and will try to chase them away. BUT, the young can't fly away since they are all in one cage. Inevitably, some males will attack their own sons. Equally females will see their own daughters as competition for their HOME – i.e. the hole in the tree, so they too will try to kill their own daughters. On the opposite page you will see just how bad this can be.

At a Glance

One of the most gut-wrenching experiences for a Budgie lover is when a parent scalps or just kills one of its own young as it leaves the nest.

But why? The Budgerigar is a nomadic species that follows the seeding grasses across the vast, hostile deserts of inland Australia. The birds only get territorial around their nesting hollow in River Red Gum trees along rivers. Here females fight to the death for a tiny hollow in a tree. They love their babies, but as with human teenagers, as they mature, the parents wish to see the back of them. As the first round of babies matures, the parents' hormones surge. They try to chase the young away to make room and food for the next brood.

Above: This young male has been savaged by his father. His eyes and eyelids are damaged, and his head is so shredded that he can't open is eyes to see. He is blind. Normally in such cases the young die from shock within 24 hours, but not so with this little hero. He found and consumed some corn, seed and water. I cleaned up his poor eyes with cotton buds and used a crop needle to inject food into his crop. If he survives, he will have a home for life with me.

Left: This is the same Budgie eating seed that he can't see.

Right: Dad sure did a lot of damage to his son. Look at the back of his neck alone. But this baby is standing on some corn, ready to eat it. He is active and getting on with survival. Fingers crossed…

Left: Eating the corn, determined to survive.

Right: This is the father. See the tell-tale blood around his face? It is vitally important to find out which parent did the damage. Getting on top of the hormonal chemistry quickly is most important for preventing further attacks.

As with all disease and injuries that happen to your birds, it is always best to regard these issues as a management issue. It is not the birds' fault, nor is it just bad luck. It is something to learn from and prevent in the future.

I regret not getting down to the birdroom by 6am that morning. I was about half an hour late. It is essential to develop a strict system of what to do every day. When you arrive at the aviary each day, immediately inspect every area to see if there are any sick, dead, or injured birds. Is there a shortage of water or seed for any birds? And so on.

In this case, removing dad is a good idea. Mum will raise the last few young on her own. Maybe feed some of the young Budgie formula with a crop needle to help mum. Any eggs can be fostered to another cage.

Lastly, this poor little bird, if he survives, will be allowed to live his life out at our aviaries no matter how deformed he looks. If we can breed from him, we will. If you don't love our little Budgie mates this much, maybe you should consider developing another hobby. These are friendly, intelligent, and beautiful little birds, and we are privileged to own them. Saving a life of one of them is a great joy and privilege as well.

Sadly, however, this bird died after fighting for two days. You can't win them all.

On the right is a crop needle: note the ball-shaped tip, and some baby bird formula.

Below right: This is a 'bomb shelter' for young Budgies to hide in on the cage floor to avoid being killed by their parents after emerging from the nest. It is constructed from a modified ice-cream container. Photo: Kathy Manton.

Other breeding problems

Right: This chick was saved because I helped it hatch. Each day, you should check your nest boxes carefully to see if there are any problems with the eggs.

In particular, you need to check all eggs to see if there are any chicks that are trapped inside their eggs. That is, if a baby is halfway out, or even if there are a few holes in the eggs, but the chick is still trapped. If the babies are dryish, halfway out and not moving much, gently drip some warm water on the bits that are stuck and use your fingernails to gently chip the egg away. Help the chick to get fully out of the egg. Try not to sever the umbilical cord. If there are only a few small holes, leave it alone and return in a few hours to see how it is going. If the holes are not bigger, or if in doubt, leave it alone until the next day.

The unhatched eggs, even if they are clear or sterile, act as hot water bottles for when mum goes out for a while, so tuck newly hatched babies over and in between two eggs. Don't throw unhatched eggs away until the hatched young are covered in down.

Right: Happy and healthy babies snuggling up to warm, unhatched eggs.

Mites – totally misunderstood

I have dealt with mites in plants and Budgies for more than 60 years, and I can assure you that they are everywhere and are impossible to eradicate. And furthermore, you have mites on yourself right now and probably don't know it.

Please just relax while I go through the mite story. Firstly, mites quickly become resistant to chemical sprays: I don't know of any other animal that develops resistance so quickly. In 1975, in sealed glasshouses, I used remote-controlled fogging sprayers (think of R2-D2 from *Star Wars*) to spread truly dreadful chemical miticides onto the plants and then left the glasshouses totally sealed for several weeks. Nothing can survive that.

Then the glasshouses were opened, aerated and watered for one week. All was perfect, problem solved… Two months later, the mites were back in all their glory without any new plants being introduced. How do you explain that? It is clear to me that mites and their eggs are brilliantly adapted to survive truly horrible conditions. Let's look at why and how. Mites are everywhere – inside the air sacs of birds (e.g. inside the bodies of Gouldian Finches), in between the veins of Budgie feathers, on areas of skin (scaly face and feet), in thousands of cracks in nest boxes, cages, aviaries, walls, ceilings, roofs, boxes, papers, and so on.

Nasty chemicals certainly kill them in large numbers, but it is clear to me that their millions of eggs secreted in cracks and hidey-holes are resistant to everything. Nothing can permeate the eggs, so the eggs wait around until the chemical killer is no longer active. Maybe

At a Glance

Mites are a total mystery for most people. More to the point, most Budgerigar breeders are in total denial about having mites at all. Like the parents of schoolchildren denying that their kids have or had head lice. I suspect that most females that abandon their eggs early or fail to incubate them have vacated their nest boxes because of mite infestation. Control is the key word. Control is not permanent. It is a temporary thing – it means bringing the mite population down to a tolerable level. If you are honest enough to admit that your birds get mites, perhaps seasonally, you will get great results in controlling them. You need to understand that you can never totally eradicate mites, but you can control them. Here is how…

it is just a set time before the baby mites hatch. Remember that pesticides and sprays usually lose their ability to kill pests in a matter of hours, particularly if exposed to sunlight.

If you sprayed for mites and your aviaries are meticulously cleaned, the mites might just wait for warm weather and all of a sudden they are back. And guess what? You are still in denial. You are a clean person and you wouldn't tolerate mites on your own body. Would you?

Well here again you would be dead wrong. Every human has eyelid (demodex) mites that live in and around their eyelash follicles. If you haven't seen **them,** SURELY you must admit that maybe, just maybe, you didn't see the mites in and around your Budgies either. At best, we only see mites during daytime when a massive plague of them occurs and they spill out into sight as tiny, pinhead-sized red dots – this colour is the blood from your Budgies seen through the mites' transparent bodies. Younger mites can't usually be seen by the naked eye.

One experienced Budgie breeder told me that they spray regularly and even under the microscope THERE WERE NO MITES in their aviaries. As if! Firstly, mites are mostly nocturnal and hide in cracks during the day. So how could you use a microscope to see into cracks? And even if you could, you would not recognise the even tinier mite eggs waiting to hatch.

What harm do mites do?

This is where the story really starts. My research has uncovered strong correlation between the presence of mites and the spread of disease, as well as behavioural problems in Budgies.

Mites are arachnids that suck blood like ticks do. Similarly to *Anopheles* mosquitos passing on malaria as they suck your blood, red mites have been found to carry poultry viruses. As yet, there has been no research done regarding disease transmission from mite to Budgies, but transmission is likely. My correlation is strong between mite seasonal activity and French moult, which is a virus known as the Polyomavirus. As the weather warms up in unheated aviaries in Australia, mites are seen and French moult begins. In colder climates, where Budgies are kept in heated birdrooms, mites would likely occur all year round. When I carry out rigid miticide spraying and medicine administration, I rarely get serious French moult outbreaks.

I have seen many Budgie breeders who have very clean nestboxes. This is an excellent idea, particularly when combined with the sprays and other products as listed below.

Above: A bird with lost flight and tail feathers due to French moult, from which he should fully recover.

Above: A severe case of French moult – this bird will almost certainly not recover.

Here is the clanger: the presence of mites also correlates with females feather-plucking their babies. This correlation is very strong between the timing of feather-plucking and mite activity. Imagine the poor female in a nest box with six young babies. Each night, thousands of mites seethe all over her, sucking her blood and creating unstoppable itching. She is driven mad!

I believe that all flying birds have what is called Obsessive Compulsive Disorder, or OCD. How could they fly if their feathers weren't perfectly cared for. So, birds constantly preen for much of the day. Can you see where this is heading? Driven mad, the females begin plucking the feathers of the young birds for relief: sort of like us biting our fingernails when we are stressed, but worse.

So, if you control mites in your cages and aviaries, I am convinced that you can dramatically reduce French moult and babies being feather-plucked. This has worked very well for me for more than 20 years. Please remember that I am constantly testing my theories, so I do still permit French moult and plucked babies occasionally during tests of new products, etc.

Plucking

One last point. Plucking has never been properly explained in my view. Some years I get heaps of plucked babies and the following year, very few, or NONE. This rules out hereditary causes because that should produce constant plucking each year. What else apart from mites could cause Budgie females, which are usually very good mums, to savagely pluck their babies? I challenge anyone to explain what else could cause erratic plucking incidents like these.

French Moult also follows the 'good year, bad year' pattern. That is, it is common to get both plucking events AND French moult occurring in the same years. This theory does not exclude the possibility that newly purchased Budgies might introduce a new super-resistant strain of mites.

How to control mites

Control is the key word. Control is not permanent. It is a temporary thing. It is not eradication. If you are honest enough to admit that, like everyone else, your birds get mites, perhaps seasonally, you will get great results. You need to understand that you can never totally eradicate mites, but you can control them. The outstanding new oral treatment for mites is Exzolt (Fluralaner). It lasts at least two weeks in chickens' bodies, but it is very expensive.

The great standby for decades has been Coopex; but why? Simple, Coopex is a formulation of Permethrin, which is one of the safest-ever fly sprays for indoor use. It is Permethrin absorbed (and maybe adsorbed – i.e. it sticks to the outside surface) into/

onto talcum powder. Thus it is a slow-release form of Permethrin. It lasts many weeks, whereas the fly spray form of Permethrin only lasts for 24–36 hours or so.

So, as the mite eggs hatch, Coopex is waiting there to kill them. Pestene Insect Powder (Rotenone plus Sulfur) is also a stable powder, and it too can control mites very well. Rotenone is a plant extract with very low toxicity to humans (but it is a fish poison). I sprinkle Pestene powder under the wooden concave floor in nest boxes, then spray Coopex in aviaries, cages and nest boxes. Using several miticides together like this is very effective since mites can't develop resistance to many chemicals at once. I also use Ivermectin at the same time. Ivermectin in Budgies' water will also kill off mites, especially scaly-face mites. But Ivermectin may cause your birds to go without water, which will initiate a sudden unseasonal moult.

Perhaps alternate Ivermectin with Exzolt. Alternating drugs also helps to prevent resistance building up.

And remember, when anything goes wrong, ALWAYS ASK YOURSELF 'WHAT DID I DO WRONG? WHAT CAN I LEARN FROM THIS?'

Importantly, a constantly dry aviary is the safest environment for Budgies. They are Australian desert nomads, thus their disease resistance is very poor.

Bird veterinarians

Bird vets are a critical part of Budgerigar management. Wild, nomadic Budgies usually live in small family groups of six to ten members in the vast Australian deserts, coming together into larger groups for breeding in River Red Gum trees along rivers. As desert nomads, they rarely come into contact with many diseases. Hence their natural disease resistance as a species is very poor. Thus, prevention is the key to disease management since Budgies just don't recover well from diseases.

Smart Budgie breeders form a close relationship with their nearest bird vet. General vets tend to avoid treating birds. Budgies are a 'live fast, die young' species, and most of us have significant numbers of them. So often individual treatment for each Budgie is financially out of the question. A flock management system is best. After one or two home visits, a good bird vet will establish a disease treatment system for you.

Usually, they will prescribe several drugs to keep on hand for treatment of specific diseases, which they will explain to you in detail. Thus you will develop a small cupboard of disease treatments ready to use in cases of emergency. You also need a hospital cage with a thermostatically controlled heating light, as Budgies are tiny and often die of the cold when sick. A quarantine cage is essential too, as somewhere to put suspicious-looking or recovering birds.

Good bird vets, particularly those older vets with experience with commercial chickens, are invaluable. But good Budgie breeders have a lot of disease-management knowledge too. The best bird vets form respectful relationships with leading Budgie breeders. Since Budgies are kept in large numbers that are subject to rapid disease breakouts, these give-and-take relationships are the only alternative to huge numbers of Budgies dying unnecessarily. Many Budgie breeders simply can't afford to visit bird vets for each and every sick Budgie, so their sick birds just die. Hence the need for vets to supply medicines to experienced Budgie breeders for emergencies.

Undershot beaks

Below is the classic parrot beak shape. The lower mandible slots neatly into a notch in the underside of the top mandible. This notch is carved into the top mandible by the action of the parrot constantly grinding the chisel tip of the lower mandible sideways into the top mandible. The notch and a shallower second notch nearby act to hold seeds and other objects in place while the Budgie husks or otherwise processes them. The grinding of the two mandibles together also creates and sharpens the needle-sharp point on the top mandible. Further sharpening occurs when the parrots chew wood and other objects: this is a self-sharpening beak.

The food that builds up under the top mandible is caused by a behavioural problem where the young Budgie fails to constantly chew its upper and lower mandibles together to shape and clean its beak while it is still in the nest box. To clean the underside of the upper mandible use a toothpick, or better still a thin metal skewer.

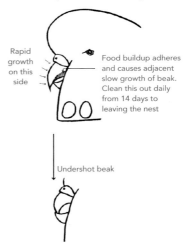

Rapid growth on this side

Food buildup adheres and causes adjacent slow growth of beak. Clean this out daily from 14 days to leaving the nest

Undershot beak

Beak chewing is also a body-language behaviour in Budgies indicating submission, and the desire to be friends. This behaviour appears to be hereditary insofar as siblings and even more distant family members seem to fail to chew and clean the upper beak.

If you failed to notice the undershot beak growing behind the upper beak, you may still be able to fix it. Firstly, clean the underside of the upper beak if necessary. I use a pair of fingernail clippers to shorten the tip of the lower beak until it is shorter than the upper beak. Try to avoid the blood veins that run inside the beak: a strong light will reveal them. Try to slope the lower beak tip shape to permit the upper beak to be in front of the lower beak when at rest.

This is a fiddly job and, as you go, you need to place the bird in a small cage a few times to relax so that you can see how much progress you have made. Maybe, the tips of both mandibles need shaping. Keeping a nail file nearby may be a good idea too.

A metal skewer – maybe blunt the tip a bit by rubbing it on a file.

This process, whether it fails or not, will not prevent the bird from feeding, but try hard not to cause any bleeding. Fresh corn on a slice of corn cob is a good food for a bird with a sore beak. Obviously I tend to get rid of lines of birds that consistently produce undershot beaks, and I never mate two undershot-beaked birds together.

Budgie feather cysts

I get very angry when I see feather cysts in my Modern Exhibition Budgies. It really upsets me when my birds are needlessly in pain. As a proud Budgie lover, I feel that we have very much done the wrong thing by our birds in creating this awful state of affairs.

Creating cysts

So what are feather cysts? These are impacted feathers that can't properly erupt from the wing or tail skin. Feathers are very complex structures that grow from a tiny genetic factory at each feather base, which uses embryonic cells called 'stem cells'.

When breeders mate Buff birds to Buff birds (i.e. coarse-feathered birds to coarse-feathered birds) and produce overly dense and long feathering, it seems that this disrupts the normal growth of healthy feathering, leading to a high risk of impacted feathers. Presumably, the factory at the feather base goes wild, over-producing stem cell variants. Hence the cheesy, swollen cysts.

More than 50 years ago it was all the rage with Norwich Canaries to breed Buff to Buff – that is, breeding overly feathered birds together. Can you guess what happened? Yep! They produced heaps of feather cysts. A huge fight ensued among breeders, with many saying that they had gone too far with buff feathering. The fight was a nasty one, but the moderate breeders won the day, changing the standard to a less heavily feathered bird. Buff to Buff matings were OUT!

Quite quickly, the cysts started to disappear and soon they were more or less totally gone. Fifty years later, we are going through the same problems with Budgies. Sadly, most bird veterinarians seem oblivious to the real cause of this problem, never advising their customers what the real problem is. For the record, I have bred about 500–700 Heritage Budgies and Bush Budgies each year for more than 20 years, NEVER to produce ONE Heritage Budgie or Bush Budgie that developed feather cysts. This is not the case with my larger Exhibition birds.

Over the last century, breeders of exhibition animals have bred for ever-greater extremes in many features:
- Pugs and bulldogs with faces pushed in so far that they can't breathe properly.
- Quarter horses with so much muscle that their legs are often deformed as they grow.
- Persian cats with pushed in faces, which also can't breathe properly.
- Dachshunds with backs so long that they have awful back problems.
- Chihuahua dogs that are so small that the females can't bear puppies safely.

We Budgie breeders have also gone to dangerous extremes. Extreme feathering is our worst problem of all in that it seriously endangers the welfare of Modern Exhibition Budgerigars.

It is obviously time for all those who care about our wonderful little birds (that rely on us for everything) to act. It is time to take a stand on reducing the massive and excessive amount of feathering that our birds are forced to live with. To bring back moderation in all things.

This issue needs to be put to Budgie club members to vote on. I am certainly very willing to put my name forward as an opponent of extreme feathering, which compromises Budgie welfare.

We need to develop a welfare code of practice for Exhibition Budgerigars, giving initial priority to the issues relating to excessive feathering and all other forms of genetic cruelty.

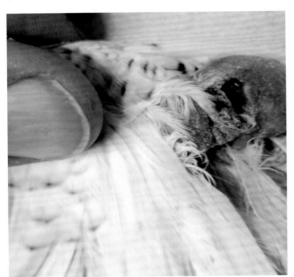 

This is a fairly typical feather cyst. Imagine the pain and misery that this poor bird goes through every day. Notice the dreadful wound where this bird has tried in vain to get rid of this painful growth.

This is the same bird. By modern exhibition standards, this is a lovely bird. By modern welfare standards, this is a sad example of cruel breeding practices.

Feeding Budgies

The basic diet

Your seed mix is very important. Clean, fresh seed from a well-run seed merchant is essential. Cheap seed containing mouse or rat urine and faeces can kill your birds in large numbers because of contamination with the bacterium *Escherichia coli*, which is commonly known as E. coli.

At a Glance

One of the fun aspects of breeding Budgies is assembling the various foods that they need. There is no right way, and your local breeders may well have the best feeding system in the world. Here are some systems offered for your consideration. Obviously, you can't just feed seed and water.

This is one of two mummified dead rats that we found in the seed mix that we used at the time. At the same time, most of our birds came down with an infection of *E. coli*. About 700 Budgies died; we shovelled them into buckets each day, crying. Laboratory tests found *E. coli* in the birds, and we found rat and mouse faeces in the seed mix as well.

Maybe the seed mix didn't cause our birds to die. The seed company told us that they did not keep seed samples from their batches of seeds. While it is possible that the *E. coli* infection came from another source, we now get our seed from another company.

Herbs and other foods

It is common to hear that some plants like kale are 'super foods' or that the Paleo diet is the way to go. This sort of nonsense comes from people with no credentials in food science or science in general. Kale, for instance, is just a variety of cabbage, as are broccoli, cauliflower, Brussels sprouts, floccoli, etc. They are all the same plant species bred in different directions.

The PERFECT Budgie seed mix

Budgies waste a huge amount of seed from seed mixes; they just seem to refuse to eat certain types of seed. The end result is that large amounts of seed are thrown out with the husks each year. Seed is expensive and this waste must be minimised, but how? The first thing to do is to give them only enough seed, and only top it up when they have eaten most of it. Otherwise, Budgies are prone to picking out their favourite 'lolly' seeds. Some breeders use a seed winnower to get rid of the husks. They then put the salvaged seed back into their aviaries.

If the Budgies are refusing to eat very much of certain seed types, then perhaps this is because that is the correct balanced food mixture for them. Perhaps Budgies know best what is the perfect ratio of seed varieties for good health. So how do we find out what is the best seed mix for Budgies?

Aviary seed mix

To find out, I set up a two-month experiment with 450 aviary Budgies in seven different aviaries. I gave them five different seed types, each in separate dishes: that is five dishes per aviary. The seed types were:

French white millet (*Panicum miliaceum*)
Panicum or common millet (*Setaria italica*)
Plain canary seed (*Phalaris canariensis*)
Red millet (*Echinochloa utilis*)
Japanese brown millet (*Echinochloa esculenta*)

I purchased bulk bags of each seed type and weighed each one. Each day, each individual seed dish was blown/winnowed to remove the previous day's seed husks and re-filled with the particular seed type. The accumulated seed dust was removed weekly. At the end of two months, the seed used was calculated by subtracting the weight of the leftover seed in both the bulk bags and in the aviary seed dishes, from the weight of the seed originally purchased. The weights of each seed type eaten over the two months was then made into a ratio for mixing seed in future. So, according to my Budgies, this is the perfect, no waste Budgie aviary seed mix.

I have expressed the ratio in kilograms (rather than a mathematical ratio) for ease of understanding:

French white millet	7kg
Panicum or common millet	10kg
Plain canary seed	23kg
Red millet	5kg
Japanese brown millet	5kg
Total	**50kg**

To double-check the results, I grew the husk and seed mix remains (i.e. the leftovers) from a general Budgie seed mix after feeding it to the same Budgies later on, and the ratios of germinated plants was remarkably consistent with the above expectations. That is, red and brown millets were the most common leftover seeds to germinate followed by French white millet. Overall, the germination results prove that most Budgie mixes are full of seed that Budgies just refuse to eat. The above ratios, in my aviaries, are the most economical to use.

It is worth noting that Budgies love hulled oats and they were initially included in these tests, but they added significantly to obesity, so the hulled oats were removed from the tests and the tests began again. During the period of these tests, no additional food supplements were given to the birds at all.

This experiment only looks at seed for aviary Budgies. We all know that breeding

Budgies need a much more varied diet, including many additional items of soft food such as vegetables, egg, protein supplements, etc. Terry Tuxford says that more canary seed is eaten when females are sitting on eggs and more panicum when they are feeding young. He also noted that his birds change seed preferences when they are moulting. I use my own aviary mix for all aviary birds but I change the amount of plain canary seed from 23kg to 30kg for breeding. There is good evidence that a period of lean quality food during the months prior to breeding increases fitness to breed provided that there is a rising plane of nutrition in the month before pairing up (i.e. higher protein, maybe soft foods with corn, oats, etc). This lean period followed by much better food mimics the natural rhythm of the seasons and removes internal fat build-up around the reproductive organs which commonly causes infertility. The rising plane of nutrition is widely used with poultry, cattle, horses, etc, to stimulate fertility. I used it to get fertile eggs from my previously infertile, rare pure Green Peafowl (*Pavo muticus*), and it worked spectacularly.

Young birds are much more prepared to eat new foods, but, as they go beyond six months of age, they become more reluctant to try new foods, including seed types. Thus, different breeders may find that their birds have different seed preferences. Equally, seed quality and freshness will affect your Budgies' choices of seeds. In this test, only top-quality fresh seed was used.

I would be very grateful for any feedback from other breeders on these issues.

Cabbage and kale, etc, are good foods when fed in moderation to Budgies, but they are not 'super foods'. There are better and worse foods in terms of health and the prevention of diseases. Garlic is one special food; recent scientific research has revealed that it has around 3,000 natural chemical compounds in it and about 574 compounds 'with potential health effects.' Garlic has been shown to contain a compound that may protect against heart attacks and another which protects against cancer. There was a wonderful article on garlic by Graham Lawton in *New Scientist* magazine on 25 July 2020, entitled 'The dark matter in your diet'.

The herb oregano has been trialled extensively by scientists involved in poultry research. There are around 55 billion chickens in the worldwide poultry industry and Orego-Stim, an oregano oil emulsion, has been shown to improve the health

of chickens by protecting the gut microbiome. It has helped my Budgies enormously. Oregano is a hardy groundcover herb which is used in pizzas and roast dinners. It is a staple part of the world's healthiest diet: the Mediterranean diet. Good for Budgies and humans!

Acidic foods help bird health by lowering the pH in the digestive system

The great 'sleeper' plant here is the humble Australian saltbush shrub. Small birds such as finches and wrens are forever eating the saltbush leaves in my garden. I planted advanced saltbush shrubs in my finch aviaries and the finches ate them to ground level until the plants died. I now grow all of my saltbushes in the garden and feed cut-off leafy branches to my Budgies and finches. I grow the creeping saltbush, which is a low-growing form of the species called *Rhagodia spinescens* (pictured left). This is a very attractive garden plant with silver foliage which grows less than one metre high – but you must ask for the low-growing form of this species.

and the gut. Oranges and apple cider vinegar are great acidifiers, as is citric acid, which is available cheaply from supermarkets. I prefer the natural products like oranges and vinegar; the best vinegar product for Budgies is apple cider vinegar with garlic (and again, part of the Mediterranean diet).

Stems and shoots of eucalypts, Lemon-scented Teatree (*Leptospermum petersonii*) and bottlebrushes are eaten by Budgies and appear to assist in good health as well.

Manuka honey has been shown in scientific research to help the immune systems of animals by assisting the function of the gut microbiome. I add it to my Budgies' drinking water (half a teaspoon per litre of water), often with Orego-Stim, about two or three days a week.

The bottom line

The key herbs, plants and natural products to feed to your Budgies are: Orego-Stim, manuka honey, apple cider vinegar with garlic, plus the usual corn, silverbeet, carrot, beetroot, oranges, capsicum (or chillies*), endive (a.k.a. chicory), leafy branches from eucalypts, bottlebrushes, Lemon-scented Teatree and rosemary, plus chickweed, winter grass, summer grass, panic veldt grass (*Ehrharta erecta*), guinea grass and amaranth.

Right is Gary Gazzard's supplementary or soft-food mix details which he has been kind enough to share with his fellow AHBA members. This is a truly outstanding mix of proven soft foods and some seeds. Gary is one of Australia's leading Modern Exhibition Budgie breeders and he is a national judge as well. Gary's care and feeding of his birds are Australia's best in my opinion.

This is what Gary Gazzard's mix looks like. Gary insists on mixing his soft food fresh each day.

---

* Birds love to eat chillies and are unaffected by even the hottest varieties. Capsicums are just chillies which lack the hot gene.

Gary Gazzard's supplementary feed or soft food

Silverbeet (ruby chard)	diced	Carrot	grated
Saltbush leaves	blender	Corn	as is
Rosemary	blender	Beetroot	grated
Broccoli	blender	Red capsicum	diced
Bay leaves	blender		(including
Mint	blender		seeds)
Chickweed	diced	Mung beans	as is

Ingredient quantities will be determined by the number of pairs of Budgies you need to feed. When you have completed preparing ingredients, add them to the mung beans and mix well. Then add seed. **Seed mix to be prepared at least 24 hours before use.**

The seed mix consists of:
    50% Peach face mix
    40% Hulled oats
    10% Saia oats

Mix seed well then add cod liver oil/wheat germ oil (normally sold combined) and also I add good oil – 50% each of recommended amount. Mix well and then let it sit for 24 hours before use.

Serving size approximately two soup spoons per dish.

Do you add probiotics?

No, you do not! Up until recently most scientists said that while in theory probiotics should work, in practice they don't as yet. A small group of scientists still claimed that they DO work, however. But recent research has proven that current (2023) probiotics do work in laboratory glass containers, but they do not work in animals' bodies. And if used after the use of antibiotics, probiotics actually do further damage in putting the gut microbiomes out of balance. So it is best to avoid them for now. Future probiotics hopefully will be very important, but not yet.

The University of Sydney is working on transferring faecal material from very healthy people to less healthy people, with very good results. We are still a long way from having commercial products available however. Again, this is something that could be an option for animals including Budgies at some point in the future.

Budgies and water

It has been claimed that Budgies in the wild can go for three weeks without water. This is obviously nonsense, but what is the truth?

I have been carefully studying my Exhibition and Bush Budgies for some years now to try to find out just how long they can survive without water. The answer is not long at all – maybe two days. After two days without water, my captive Wild Budgies are clearly in deep trouble. Mind you, common sense will tell you that flying birds can't carry stored water since it is too heavy. Flying birds have features such as mostly hollow bones and lightweight air sacs to fill up internal spaces – all to save weight.

How did a researcher get it all so wrong? Well, Budgies are very well adapted for survival in the desert. They suck up morning dew from plant leaves even in the desert. That is water. They eat green grass seeds which are quite moist too – that is, the seeds contain water. I have observed this in flocks in the wild.

Perhaps the biggest source of unnoticed water for my Budgies is from plant sap. Feed your Budgies green grass seed heads and watch closely. They chew up the stems and leaves to squeeze out and drink the sap. They do the same with silverbeet stems too. They expertly squeeze/chew out all the sap from the white stems.

Budgies also eat many bits of plant leaves, stems and buds. It is obvious that they get some excellent nutrients from plant sap; both from xylem and phloem tissues. Xylem sap contains precious micronutrients* that Budgies need, such as calcium and phosphorus from the roots, and phloem contains the products of photosynthesis from the leaves, such as carbohydrates like sugar. It is likely that scientists will one day discover that Budgies can handle phloem sap better than most animals can.

I hope that by now you have got my point: that drinking water from pools or springs is only **one** way of getting water, **especially in the desert**. Budgies do get plenty of water every day, even during droughts – just not from pools. This perhaps explains why the researcher who looked into how long Budgies could go without water got it so very wrong. He or she was just a poor observer.

This is not to say that Budgies are not geniuses at finding springs or pools of water in deserts. They are, and they may travel huge distances to find water. All of this adds up to plenty of water every day for Wild Budgies.

In captivity we feed Budgies **DRY** seed instead of the moist semi-ripe seeds that they often eat in the wild. The forbs (small herbs excluding grasses, etc) that Budgies eat in the wild are not even recorded, let alone fed to our Budgies. But other parrots eat hundreds of different plant leaves, etc, every week. Our Budgies in captivity usually have a rather moisture-deprived diet.

Clean, fresh water is essential every day for captive Budgies. But so too are stems of grasses, semi-ripe grass seeds, bits of gum tree branches with leaves still on, Lemon-

---

* Micronutrients is the new name for trace elements.

scented Teatree, silverbeet, oranges, corn on the cob, and so on. The water in all of these is very beneficial for your Budgies.

Another myth

While we are exploding myths such as three weeks without water, here is another… It is commonly reported that Budgies are in danger of dying if you even slightly overdose them with vitamin D3. I have never found this to be the case (and yes, I have carefully tried over-dosing them). Equally, I cannot find any research that verifies the poisoning of Budgies from feeding too much vitamin D3. This is a myth and stories of dead birds caused by overdose of vitamin D3 appear to be without foundation; they are an over-reaction to a slight risk.

As an aside, vitamin D3 is not a vitamin anyway! Vitamins are compounds that we need for health, but can't make ourselves. We do make our own vitamin D3 ourselves: so it is best referred to as a steroid hormone. Again, new research has shown that the vitamin D3 that we take in liquid or capsule form is often not very good. It is vegetable-based vitamin D3 which is not as useful as animal-produced vitamin D3. Look for the word 'cholecalciferol' on the bottle as this is the best form of vitamin D3. It is often far better to make your own vitamin D3 from exposing your skin or your Budgies feet to a safe level of sunlight.

Removing Budgerigar rings

Sometimes Budgies get swollen legs due to a problem with their club ring. This is a serious problem that can lead to the bird losing its leg or even dying. There are cutters that you can buy from bird sales days or from bird clubs to remove the ring. These clippers fit onto the ring and then you snip the ring off.

But some rings are made of a very hard aluminium alloy that simply can't be snipped off. There are ring cutters that are used to remove rings from human fingers, but they are too big to insert under the tiny Budgie ring. However, you can file the foot of the ring cutter down since it is usually made of soft brass.

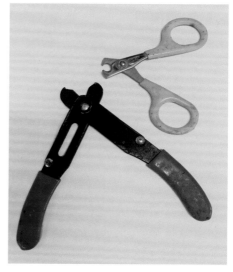

Two different types of ring snippers.

This is the human ring remover. The pointed arm on the upper right hand side in this photo is the foot that goes under the ring. I filed it down until it was thin enough to fit between the Budgie ring and the bird's foot.

This is the filed-down ring remover the right side up and ready to cut. The wheel is the cutter and there is a winder behind it out of sight. That pointed bit goes under the ring to hold the ring and it also protects the foot from the cutting disc above.

In this photo, the top disc is the winder joined to the cutting disc. My fingers are holding the lever that moves the pointed foot up towards the cutting disc. The foot has a groove along its top side that the cutting disc slots into as it cuts through the ring. This is a fiddly two-person job. I practiced on a spare ring which was not on a bird until I worked it all out. It works!

This shot shows how you could use a rubber band to keep a gentle pressure on the cutting disc. The two small fragments to the left are the two halves of a cut ring.

Types of Budgerigars

Bush Budgies

When their aviary in my backyard was severely damaged by a falling gum tree, most of the Bush Budgies remained in the open aviary and the rest returned the next day – they love their home!

But after more than 30 years of breeding them, they are not just green any more. Evolution arms all species (including us) with lots of genetic alternatives that pop up from time to time. So, over the 30 years, quite a few new colours have turned up. I have selected these colours to breed from.

There is almost no end to the number

At a Glance

Bush Budgies are so much fun to be around. They are athletic, intelligent and fly like swallows. These are rescued Wild Budgies and they are always Light Green... or are they? Mine were babies rescued from a fallen tree in the wild after a bush fire 30 years ago. They are the happiest aviary birds that I have ever seen. We should set up a club to exhibit them in all the new colours that have occurred in captivity.

Some of my Green Bush Budgies.

of mutations that can occur. And you can swap colours with other Bush Budgie breeders. Bush Budgies are becoming very popular recently because of their cheery personalities and great colours.

This is a Dilute Blue Bush Budgie. Such a pretty colour. All of these colours lie hidden under the Wild Budgie's green colouring. Remove the yellow and blue appears. Remove most of the blue and a soft whitish sky blue remains. Remove most of the black from the wing markings and a silvery grey remains.

Two young. The one on the left is a Violet Double Factor Australian Golden Faced Dilute carrying the Full Body Colour modifier. Behind is a Violet Normal Double Factor Australian Golden Faced Bush Budgie.

On a cold winter's morning – 17 Blue Bush Budgies.

This is a pair of Recessive Pieds, Blue on the left and Green on the right. Who would have thought that a flamboyant Pied mutation lurked inside my plain Green Bush Budgies.

A curious Golden Faced Dilute Blue Bush budgie.

This baby Bush budgie is a double factor Golden Faced Violet-Mauve.

Below: An adult Single Factor Australian Golden Faced Dilute Sky Blue, a.k.a. Apple Green.

Every bird in this section is a 100% pure Bush Budgie. If you want a beautiful garden aviary full of colourful healthy birds, these are the ones to get. But you may need to hunt around on social media to find them as the new colours in Bush Budgies are quite rare.

After selecting for hidden recessive colours in my original Green Budgies, every nest box now is a lucky dip; as Forrest Gump said: "Life is like a box of chocolates – you never know what you're gonna get."

Imagine an attractive aviary in your backyard full of always-happy Bush Budgies. In almost every colour.

The basics

To colony-breed Bush Budgies, you need an aviary about 2m x 2m. I suggest a roof over the entire structure plus three sides covered in, with only one side open. Put in three or four pairs and about six to eight nest boxes. Make sure that you get the more expensive nest boxes with a concave cut into the floor. Never buy a nest box with a smooth, shiny floor as this leads to splayed legs in the young. Do not buy pulp-board nest boxes as females will chew them to bits. Almost 100% of shop-bought nest boxes are utter rubbish.

NEVER FORGET THAT ALL BUDGIE FEMALES WILL DESTROY ANY WOODEN OBJECTS IN THEIR AVIARY.

Maybe get some marine ply from a hardware shop (e.g. Bunnings) and make your own nest boxes. Three ply for the sides and top, plus five ply for ends and base. The tops should be hinged. Cover the floor in sawdust or wood shavings. Make it 25cm long by 20cm wide and high. The hole in the front should be 35mm in diameter.

Maybe install a 2m-long shelf for the nest boxes. Face the nest boxes in opposite directions alternately to avoid fighting between the females.

This is what female Bush Budgies do to thin nest boxes bought from pet shops.

Three sturdy nest boxes. The outer two are made of marine ply and the middle one is a hollow branch glued onto a nest box. All are supported from the roof by U-shaped weldmesh.

Right: A hollow log from a fallen tree in a cleared area, which has been cut to size with a chainsaw. The log on each end was used as a stencil to mark out the shape on marine ply, then the shape was cut out with a jig saw. The plywood ends were attached with furniture screws which are a screw on one end and a bolt on the other. Wing nuts were then used for securing the plywood. Do not take hollow logs from bushland areas as animals use them.

Left: This is another variant of a hollow log. In this case, the nesting hole was drilled with a hole saw on an electric drill. A smaller hole was used for the perch. Note the wingnuts on top.

Below: This is a furniture screw with a wingnut attached. The screw part is screwed into the wood with a threaded cap which has a hexagonal top. Then the cap is removed and the wingnut goes on.

Right: This is the First Australian Standard of Perfection for Budgerigars in 1936, painted by noted artist Neville Cayley, Chairman of the Budgerigar club of the Royal Zoological Society of New South Wales. It is a fitting Standard of Perfection for today's Bush Budgies.

STANDARD TYPE OF MALE BUDGERIGAR
(Copyright)
ADOPTED BY THE AUSTRALASIAN BUDGERIGAR COUNCIL, 1935

Pet Budgies

At a Glance

Pet Budgies can be your best friend, but not all Budgies make perfect pets. And not all training systems work either. So in this chapter we will look at how to select a really good young Budgie and make it your best friend.

Selecting your new young Budgie

This is the most important bit. Some Budgies are naturally friendly and outgoing, but others are not. Just like people. Females are lovely, but males are mostly more outgoing and they tend to talk much better than females. Firstly, even if a hand-raised young Budgie costs $100 more, it is vastly better than one that was not hand raised, because almost 100% of hand-raised Budgies imprint on humans. Imprinting is where, up to a certain age, babies learn to accept whoever they commonly see is a family member. Just check that it was raised from no more than two weeks of age. Some people just hand feed the young birds much later – from about four or five weeks of age – and these birds are often a bit wild and hard to train.

Right: Interact with the bird that you are thinking of buying to see if it is loving and playful. Don't select the prettiest one, select the sweetest one instead. Remember that you buy the beauty but live with its personality.

Having said that males tend to make the best pets, my best pet Budgie friend (right) was a female who picked me out for HER friend in the aviary when she was nine months old. She always came to me and travelled all around my aviaries on my shoulders. Her choice.

If you can only buy a young Budgie that was not hand fed and raised, you need to take your time. Wait and watch the birds to see if there is one that comes to you: buy this one. Or put your hand in the cage of Budgies and wait for the one that is interested in your hand. If the bird is scared, get the pet shop person to put it into your cage after purchase (then the bird will only be traumatised by the pet shop person, not you). If the pet shop will not let you do these things, go elsewhere. To repeat, males are generally best as pets, and the bird should only have a half-grown tail, about 4–6cm long. Budgies with longer tails than this might be too old to train.

Training

Poor training can ruin a good bird. So be gentle and patient. Never force yourself on your bird. ALWAYS let the Budgie come to you. Then and only then will it become your friend. Budgies never forgive or forget rough handling or bullying. I oppose the 'step up' system where you push your index finger on the bird's tummy, thus forcing the bird to hop onto the finger. Birds hate being forced to do things. Offering your finger while showing the bird a treat is much better.

One simple technique is to put your caged Budgie on a table in front of you in your TV room and open the cage door. Gently place your hand in a comfortable position on the cage floor and wait. Maybe hold a treat of some fresh corn or some winter grass seed heads or endive. Watch the TV and wait for curiosity to take over. Maybe on night one, there will be no progress, but sooner or later the bird will realise that you are a friend. Let the Budgie set the pace. If the bird is very wild, turn the room light down low and place your hand in the cage and wait. This period of non-threatening behaviour on your part is a life-long investment with this Budgie.

A couple more tips. After you tame your baby budgie, its cage should be home base only. That is, the bird is out of its cage most for most of the day. Select a cage that has a huge door opening for the bird to come and go as it pleases. Do not buy two birds as they will become friends and ignore you. The ideal pet Budgie regards you as its mate for life. And talks much better.

Do not under any circumstances feed your Budgie what social media people recommend. Stick to foods as recommended in this book. They are tried and proven winners. See chapter Feeding Budgerigars, page 231. There are so many foods around that are poisonous to Budgies.

Few animals make great companions like Budgies. This one was smarter than most dogs and every bit as friendly. No wonder that the Budgerigar is the world's most popular pet bird.

This is a good cage design for a pet Budgie showing the large, hinged door. The 30cm x 30cm door allows an easy route in and out for the Budgie, with a smaller door inside the larger door. Note the smaller guillotine door open at the lower front. If you leave the large door open during the day, the Budgie will go in and out as it pleases. Allowing your Budgie freedom of movement will add to its happiness.

This gives a better view of the open large door with the open smaller guillotine door at the bottom.

Obviously, you need a strict protocol for when the Budgie is out of its cage. A lot of Budgies escape, with disastrous consequences. Simple things like automatic closing flywire doors on your house, work very well. A simple flywire spring door and flywire on your windows is all that you need to keep your Budgie safe inside your home.

Heritage Budgerigars

(a.k.a. Colour Budgerigars) – why preserving them is both necessary and urgent in all countries

Quote from Neville Cayley, from the introduction to his 1933 book *Budgerigars in Bush and Aviary*:

"One of the chief charms of the Budgerigar is its small size. This places it in a class apart from other parrots. And being an Australian species it is the duty of Australians to combat and condemn any attempt that may be made to alter its size and so spoil one of the world's most beautiful parrots."

It should be obvious from this photo that almost no-one listened to Neville.

At a Glance

This section looks into the problems with crossing brilliantly coloured Heritage Budgies from all countries to Modern UK and European Showbirds, including Clearwings, Rainbows, Hagoromos and Black Budgies. The research is based on crossing pure Australian Heritage Exhibition Budgerigars to Modern Exhibition Budgerigars. Australian Heritage Exhibition Budgerigars are bred to the very moderate Australian National Standard of 1962.

If breeders cross Australian Heritage Exhibition Budgies to Modern Showbirds to get 'better feathering', they will possibly be introducing the gene for mop (a.k.a feather duster) Budgerigars, plus the genes that facilitate the flightless and tailless wonder virus, and others that create difficulty and pain in flying and a susceptibility to wing-feather cysts.

Breeding for larger size in Budgies turns them into 'high response' breeds like meat chickens, meat pigs and thoroughbred racehorses. Put simply, high response breeds grow very large very quickly. But they must be fed a 100% perfect diet, otherwise things go wrong developmentally. But even if they are perfectly fed, problems with arthritis issues, distorted limbs, and generally short lives, are common.

It is the thesis here that in general, it is prudent not to change the basic developmental geometry and fundamental growth rates too much from the wild type of any animal. Particularly in birds. If fundamental changes are to be attempted, ongoing expert veterinary advice and assessments should be sought from specialists nominated by the appropriate universities.

To do other than this is to become involved in genetic cruelty, which will inevitably lead to government action sooner or later. It is put forward here that genetic cruelty is perhaps the world's biggest animal cruelty issue, yet it remains largely overlooked. There are currently about 34 billion poultry in the production industry worldwide. Meat pigs, meat chickens and thoroughbred race horses in particular are bred to have very fast growth rates, which often condemns them to lives of pain and misery, particularly with chronic joint problems. Modern Exhibition Budgies are just one problem species to look at.

Australian Heritage Fallow Clearwing Amethyst. A tiny bird with great charm.

Australian Heritage Clearwing Violets.

Australian Heritage Clearwing Violet Dark Greens.

Above are Australian Heritage Exhibition Clearwing Budgerigars – preserved genetically from 1962. With beautiful colours and a body not too far changed from their wild ancestors, they are healthy, functional Budgies.

There has been a recent tendency to outcross Australian Heritage Exhibition Budgies to Modern Showbirds to 'improve' them, so I thought that it would be a good idea to look at this in detail.

Firstly, are Modern Showbirds better than 1962 Heritage Exhibition Budgies? No, they are not. These are just two different arbitrary standards that two independent groups breed to. Are large, modern heads, long masks, wide shoulders, etc, better than the smaller overall size, smaller heads, narrower shoulders, shorter masks, etc, of

Australian Heritage Showbirds? No, they are not. They are just 'breed standards' like the different standards for Poodle and German Shepherd dogs: both breeds are dogs, but they are bred to different standards.

If you cross your Heritage Exhibition Clearwings to Modern Showbirds, it is the Australian Heritage Budgerigar Association's contention you will do great damage to the Heritage Clearwing breed. It has taken dedicated breeders more than 90 years to get them just right. Just like crossing a Poodle to a German Shepherd. Imagine trying to re-create a Poodle by breeding from that hybrid puppy.

Australian Heritage Exhibition Budgerigars are much closer to the shape and size of a Wild Budgie. Does this matter? Yes, it does. If you change the size, shape or feathering of any bird, you can do enormous damage to its ability to fly or to its basic health and wellbeing.

For these reasons, it is essential to monitor the basic functionality of any birds that are bred to conform to artificial man-made standards (apart from colour). The greater the change in shape, size, etc, from the wild type, the greater the need to check out the welfare of the bird. In an ideal bird society, there would be a scientific advisor to whom new changes could be referred, for assessment of the welfare impact of the proposed or ongoing change. This has never occurred, to my knowledge.

This is a UK Modern Exhibition Budgerigar. It is very far removed from the wild type of the Budgerigar. It has almost no forward vision and would fly with great difficulty.

Feathers

Changing the density, length and breadth of Budgies' feathers may well be the greatest welfare problem that Budgies have ever faced. Extremes in any physical aspect tend to cause breeders to grab onto nasty and cruel mutations that ruin animals' lives. Sadly, these breeders are often totally unaware of the hereditary cruelty that they have created. Take mop or feather duster Budgies – these are caused by an obsessive compulsion to breed ever longer and lusher feathering in Budgies. Single Factor mops have 'superbly' long and lush feathering. Double Factor mops are as described: a mop – they are dysfunctional and are usually live for only a year or two. But you can breed super long and lush feathering without using the mop gene. If all Budgie breeders culled all mop producers, soon we would have Budgies with the required feathering without carrying the mop gene. Everyone wins!

This, believe it or not, is a live Budgerigar. It is a feather duster or mop. It is the result of extreme breeding for ever-greater amount of feathering. To repeat, the feather duster gene produces long, coarse feathering in the Single Factor form. In the Double Factor form it creates this sad monstrosity. Caring breeders might note that you can breed long, coarse feathering without the feather duster gene.

Severe feather cysts on a Budgerigar's wing. This is caused by overly dense feathering. That is, it is highly heritable.

Both photos above depict Budgies with long flight feathers. They are the result of outcrossing Australian Heritage Exhibition Clearwings (one a Rainbow Clearwing) to Modern Exhibition Budgies. The recessive flight and tail feather modifier gene from the Modern bird produces this surprise when you mate Heritage to Modern Budgies.

Very long primary flight feathers: the tail feathers would also be very long. Commonly, breeders frame out the excessively long tails (as has happened here) to avoid embarrassment.

This Modern European showbird has short flight feathers, but long feathers everywhere else – particularly on its over-sized head.

If you cross the Modern European grey show bird above with short flight feathers, to a heritage budgie also with short flight feathers ALL of the babies will have LONG flight feathers.

But there are still problems with long feathering that is not based on the mop gene. In general it is based on semi-dominant modifiers. These modifiers lengthen ALL feathers on the Budgie. Long head, mask, and body feathers appeal to most breeders, however, the associated long flight and tail feathers are quite ugly to most people (see photos on page 178). They also hinder flying ability. Unknowingly, European breeders incorporated a recessive gene that left most feathers long and lush, but shortened the flight and tail feathers, which fixed the problem. But it came at a price. From my research, this gene appears to weaken the growth of the flight and tail feathers, leading to flightless and tailless wonders and also, perhaps, to wing-feather cysts. (See photos on page 230.)

I have never had wing-feather cysts on any **Pure** Australian Heritage Budgerigar or on a **Pure** Bush Budgie. The wing-feather cysts may also relate to overly Buff (i.e. luxurious and dense) feathering. This overly Buff development in Norwich Canaries caused wing-feather

This pair of Heritage Violet Clearwings has been caught mid-action in rapid, blurry-faced courtship. The female (on the left) has perfectly-conformed wings. That is, they correspond precisely with the shape and proportions of the wings of Wild Budgerigars. Note the sleek satin-like feathering all over, even though they are in a heavy moult. These Heritage Budgies are every bit as athletic and healthy as Wild Budgies are.

cysts from 1925 to 1935. It was eradicated by selecting for finer-feathered Norwich Canaries in the 1950s. This involved a 'heated controversy' within the Norwich Canary Club (see *Budgerigars, Canaries and Foreign Finches* by R.B. Bennett (1961), pages 186–187). This canary problem precisely forecasts the current problems of excessive feather and body size in Modern Exhibition Budgies.

Flightless and tailless wonders. They never recover from this condition.

My suspicion with flightless and tailless wonders is that the heavy feather production also leads to a weakening of feather growth, which facilitates the development of the virus disease symptoms such as permanent feather loss. I have never had a single flightless and tailless wonder among my Bush Budgies, nor with my 100% Pure Australian Heritage Clearwings, despite my cross-fostering and experimental mixing of flightless and tailless wonder birds among the Bush and Heritage birds in aviaries. Here I am talking about 4,000 Bush and Heritage birds over 30 years. I suspect that many Budgies of all types may well contract the flightless and tailless wonder virus, but that the Bush and Heritage types deal with it very well, with no feather loss nor any other worrying symptoms. But whatever is discovered in the years to come, it is quite definite that the flightless and tailless wonder virus only causes feather loss in the lines of Modern Showbirds imported from the UK and elsewhere in Europe.

In many Modern Show Budgies the alula (false wing) hangs down, making flight inefficient. The alula works very similarly to the bent-up wing tips on modern aeroplanes. It minimises turbulence in flight. (See the false wings on the yellow budgie on the opposite page.)

Other problems with flight

The 'desirable' wide shoulders demanded in the current Standards of 'Perfection' almost certainly stretch out and/or distort the bones supporting the wings (such as the coracoid and scapula). The greatest likelihood here is arthritic problems due to stress from overly long or poorly conformed supporting bones. From as early as three months of age, many Modern Showbirds increasingly remain on the aviary floor all day, presumably due to the pain involved in flight. X-rays might confirm this, one way or the other.

Directional feather

Directional feather is the name for elongated feathers beside the cere (nasal area) in Budgies. This elongation of previously short feathers in front of the eyes seriously impedes forward vision. This sort of thing may be semi-OK in Old English Sheepdogs, because they can walk slowly and thus avoid walking into objects. But if birds fly slowly they stall in flight, crashing into the ground.

For those who breed larger, Modern Showbirds, please note that most of these problems can be eradicated fairly easily. The big one is to cull all birds that produce feather dusters, as these parents are carriers of this effectively recessive condition. You can easily breed coarse-feathered birds without using the feather duster gene, indeed many Modern Showbirds already have coarse feathering without the feather duster gene. Buying from the ethical breeders of these types of birds (i.e. breeders who assure purchasers that they never produce any feather dusters) is advisable.

This bird has directional feathering which impedes forward vision. You can't even see its eyes. Note the yellow dagger-shaped feathers on either side of the breast – these are distorted alula (false wings) that can no longer aid in stable, efficient flight.

Extremes in all things are genetically dangerous. A nicely finessed showbird with good wing carriage, deportment, colour and markings, combined with not too much feathering is a superb sight. Extremes are just a mess, and an unhealthy mess at that.

This is one of John Hawke's beautiful Red Violet Australian Exhibition Heritage Clearwings. This bird has the outline, flight feathers, overall fine feathering, mask and head as per the AHBA Standard of perfection (see below). His crouching stance is due to the fear that all Heritage Budgies feel in glass-fronted photo cages. Better to photograph through the wires of a show cage (see photographing Budgerigars page 270 for details). Budgies rarely cope well with glass-fronted cages.

Right: The AHBA's Perpetual National Standard of Perfection. Points are lost if a bird has a greater or lesser length than 8.5 inches (216 mm).

Note that the flight feathers must be just a bit shorter than the rump body feathering. Any features that are in excess of the Standard will be penalised equally to features that are less than the Standard. Extremes of feathering and size are to be avoided. The 1962 Australian National Budgerigar Standard of Perfection was adopted by the Australian Heritage Budgerigar Association to protect and preserve Heritage Budgies.

Working with veterinary experts

It is long overdue for breed clubs to work with appropriate veterinary experts in the various disciplines so that birds and other animals can 'have the look' or 'produce the goods' without having to live a life of discomfort and misery. Without any significant physical changes to look or performance, animals can be produced that are truly amazing, when leading breeders collaborate with veterinary scientists. This sort of thing happened informally in the past with brilliant vets like Dr Len Pockley (cattle), Dr Derek Major (Horses), Dr Harry Spira (dogs) and more recently, with Richard Malik DVSc (cats). But they all did it as good citizens off their own bats. We need a system that ensures that this sort of monitoring and cruelty minimisation is the norm. We need formal arrangements to ensure an ongoing improvement of balanced and functional excellence in all aspects of animal breeding.

Budgerigar behaviour

How bright are Budgies?

I guess that most of us tend to treat our Budgies as 'things' rather than thinking, feeling, living creatures. Surely a brain the size of a pea can't be very smart?

But, Budgies manage to imitate what we say, play quite advanced games (we filmed one who played a fair game of soccer), make friends with people, escape from cages by opening doors, and they seem to show both caring and empathy for their mates.

> **At a Glance**
>
> Budgies incessantly communicate with us and with each other. Here we will try to understand what they are saying. Understanding what they are saying opens up a new world of joy with your birds.

Have I gone too far? EMPATHY? Well, new research by Andrew Gallup of The State University of New York has found evidence that suggests genuine empathy in Budgies. Budgies in adjacent cages were three times more likely to yawn within five minutes of a yawn from the bird in an adjacent cage. Even watching videos of Budgies yawning elicits yawning in Budgies.

Only chimpanzees, humans, dogs and one species of rodent have previously been shown to find yawning contagious. The opinion of animal behaviour experts is that contagious yawning is a social behaviour that shows synchronisation with, and mimicking of, others. This is the beginning of empathy. Andrew Gallup says: "Social non-mammals may have basic forms of empathy." How's that!

Obsessive compulsive birds

It is my contention here that all birds have what scientists call 'Obsessive Compulsive Disorder', or OCD. OCD is defined as having (among other things): "Persistent impulses that are intrusive; performing repetitive and ritualistic actions that are excessive and time-consuming."

Coming from a family littered with such people (including myself) it is fair for me to claim that I understand this hereditary condition intimately. Perhaps I was a bird in another life!

But why do I claim that ALL BIRDS have OCD? Think about it… All birds sit there preening for much of the day. EVERY DAY. They obsessively clean, primp and Velcro up their feathers again and again and again. Each feather has microscopic hooks and barbs which join the filaments together just like Velcro. This forms the basis of the sleek body surface and also creates the sail-like structures – i.e. flight feathers – which together make up the wings needed for flight. Birds constantly zip up their feathers. So, no OCD = no flight.

If a bird did not constantly maintain PERFECT feathers, it simply couldn't fly. Hence the fact that all flying birds have OCD.

One by-product of birds having OCD is that in captivity, where their food is pre-hulled fast food, bored birds can rapidly turn to self mutilation. They desperately need some enjoyable, repetitive thing to do! This parallels fingernail biting in humans. In parrots in particular this is a problem. Parrots constantly chew their beaks to both shape and sharpen them. The sickle-like tip and corresponding notch inside the top mandible is created by constant chewing. Never to waste anything, nature also uses this constant beak chewing as a friendly greeting signal in some bird species (especially parrots), rather like the offered handshake in humans.

If you watch cockatoos in particular, you will see them chewing their beak as strangers, both cockatoo and human alike, approach them. Almost all humans are oblivious to this 'request for indication of friendly intentions' – hence the aggression of many birds towards humans. Any polite cockatoo, on seeing another bird beak-chewing, will beak-chew in response. The dialogue goes a bit like this: 'Can I be your friend?' and the reply comes back: 'I would love to be your friend.'

This poor baby Budgie was plucked by his mum. Removed from mum and kept in a warm birdroom, he made a full recovery.

In response to beak chewing by a cockatoo, I make a beak-chewing movement by rubbing my index finger over the tip of my thumb on one hand. Many cockatoos respond warmly to this gesture, more or less 'saying': 'What a pleasant change to meet a polite, non-threatening human!'

If your parrot or cockatoo self-mutilates, you need to give the bird some outlet for its OCD. Ideally, some chewing activity that is both intricate and hard work. I have had great success with other people's near-bald Gang-gang Cockatoos by giving them lamb-chop bones and chicken-leg bones. They will spend hours quietly eating these bones, meat, marrow and all. I also gave them gumtree branches full of unopened seed capsules, she-oak branches with unopened seed capsules, hawthorn branches with fruit on them, *Isopogon* branches with unopened seed capsules on them, bottlebrush branches with unopened seed capsules on them, plus any branches or wood that they like chewing. A messy cockatoo cage is a good one, but a clean one may be a disaster. Obviously cockatoos like apples, oranges, pears and most nuts. A similar approach works well with Budgies. Fresh gum tree, Lemon-scented Teatree and bottlebrush branches keep them occupied and happy. Giving Budgies only seed, shellgrit and water is courting disaster.

Why Budgies talk

Have you ever wondered why and how Budgies talk? Pet Budgies can become amazing talkers. I have heard some that can sing songs in tune and recite phrases or poems. One Budgie – Sam Janner of Canyonleigh in NSW – could say more than 100 phrases and lines from songs. He spoke perfectly pronounced English, and you could hear him from across the room. His owner, Bonnie Janner, who trained him to talk, also spoke beautifully.

The world's best talking Budgie, according to *Guinness World Records*, is Puck. He spoke 1,728 words, which qualified him as the world's best talking bird – that is, he spoke more words than any other bird.

"Play it again, Sam!"

Why do they do it?

According to new research, it is largely to do with courtship. 'Talking' in parrots and cockatoos is largely limited to males. When male Budgie meets a female, he listens to her unique family song. Most bird species have their own family songs just as whales have regional songs. It is likely that Budgie chicks learn the family song while they are inside the egg, as has been proven in other bird species. It is also likely that mums monitor the cheeps of their babies inside the eggs as well.

To show a courting male's commitment to a female, and to prove his undying love, he carefully learns her family's song. Then he sings it back to her. She thinks: 'He loves me! He has learnt our family song.'… And they both live happily ever after.

As anyone who has trained a Budgie to talk knows, it takes some weeks for a bird to learn to copy new sounds. So he has to be very keen on a particular female to stick around that long to learn her song.

To our ears, all Budgies sound the same, but computer sonograms of their call notes revealed that the songs are all different in many ways. Notes can be different or changed around in their order, etc. Checking computer-recorded songs revealed that courting males learn the song of their chosen female, making it their own.

Male pet Budgies regard their owner as their mate, so they copy the owner's 'song' to win them over.

A bird breeder friend of mine had an interesting experience with Budgies. He was training a Major Mitchell's Cockatoo to talk in its aviary, which was adjacent to his birdroom. Each day when he fed the cockatoo the owner would say: "Hello Cocky." To his surprise, one day he became aware of small voices saying "Hello Cocky" in the birdroom behind him. Upon turning around, he was greeted with the sight of about a dozen Budgies all perched at the front of their cabinets saying "Hello Cocky" over and over again!

"Baby it's cold outside!"

Quite likely, as the Budgies were pairing up with their respective females, they heard the words "Hello Cocky", so they memorised them. What a surprise for their owner. The Major Mitchell never did learn to talk… Beautiful as Major Mitchell's Cockatoos are, they are not great mimics.

How do birds speak so clearly?

This is where to story gets really fascinating. Have you noticed that parrots clearly pronounce all consonants. When they say "cap", both the c and the p are clearly pronounced. But they have no lips!!! Or do they? Birds have unbending beaks as well as tongues that are both unable to hold back air to create the sound of consonants such as P, B, F, M, P, V and Y.

All birds have two voice boxes. Down their windpipes, in the chest area, they have a syrinx, not a larynx like us. A syrinx is a dual set of voice boxes that each perform independently. Thus birds can sing a duet with themselves! And they do! So the sounds of B, F, M, P, V, Y and so on come from deep down in their windpipes.

"She Loves you, Yeah Yeah Yeah!"

The bottom line

It is now clear that female Budgies are attracted to males that are good mimics because this signals that they are devoted partners or that they can get more food. You can read more about this in an article entitled 'The Impersonators' in the 2 May 2015 edition of *New Scientist* magazine (issue 3,019, page 41). If you Google 'best talking Budgies' you will see and hear many amazing Budgies talking via YouTube, although none talk as clearly as Sam Janner.

Budgie mothers – the best in the world

Female Budgerigars are arguably the best mothers in the world. They perform all of their tasks on their own, without family support, and with no books or apps to follow. Are you impressed?... Not really?

This is what a female Budgerigar has to do when raising a brood:

1. Very carefully select a healthy and committed male; one who will perform courtship dances, and learn her family song and sing it back to her to underline his commitment.
2. Select a nest hollow and fight to win it and keep it from other females, as well as defend it from snakes, goannas and other predators.
3. Clean out the nest hole and re-shape it.
4. Lay each egg in a central position in the nest. It is not until now that the male starts to pull his weight by regular feeding of the female.
5. Brood the eggs for about 18 days until they hatch – but generally no longer than about 28 days, as if they have not hatched by then they are infertile.
6. Brood and feed the very young chicks with very finely chewed-up food (since Budgies do not produce crop milk). To feed the tiny ones, she will turn them on their backs to help them swallow the food. Females also fit the tiny babies in gaps between the eggs for warmth and support. The unhatched eggs act like hot water bottles – this is important for when the female flies off to get food or water, or to defecate.
7. As more chicks hatch, she must arrange them so that the older chicks don't squash the younger ones. She must also feed coarser food to the bigger chicks.
8. When the big, fat chicks are old enough, the adults will begin to cut off their food supply, starting with the oldest chick first. This forces the young to leave the nest one by one. The dramatic weight loss during this period of uncertain food supply makes the previously fat chicks light enough to fly.
9. When the chicks are fledged, the female will try to chase them away in preparation for her next brood. She doesn't want her daughters to steal her nest. This explains why show Budgies often will savage their babies: in a cage, the babies simply can't get away when chased.

VIRTUALLY ALL OF THESE PROCESSES ARE COMPLETED BY THE FEMALE ALONE WITHOUT FAMILY ASSISTANCE OR ANY PRIOR TRAINING OR EXPERIENCE.

I hope that by now you have a new and profound respect for the humble female Budgerigar.

How to communicate with birds

Some of the best moments of my life have been with birds. These enchanting creatures mesmerised me as a kid and they still do at the age of 76.

I have had moments in the wild where Flame Robins have stolen hair from my head for nesting. Moments when they help with the gardening – Eastern Yellow Robins sit within a metre of me and jump down to eat insects as I dig the soil. Moments when, in concert with many other species, they scream 'snake!' and then let me catch and relocate a Diamond Python or a Green Tree Snake as they raucously cheer me on from a safe distance. Moments also in the wild when a Sulphur-crested Cockatoo or an Australian King Parrot eats food from my hand. Moments when a Rock Warbler chats to me from my workbench in the garage and nests in our nearby roof cavity while I am constructing things late at night. And hundreds of other magical experiences.

Those were all moments in the wild. As a bird breeder, I get even closer to birds in my aviaries and cages. Most great bird breeders instinctively know how to behave around birds, and the birds respond in amazing ways. I have had the privilege of an aviary full of Budgies or Gouldian Finches landing all over me; playing with my hair and clothes, exploring my face, running up and down my arms and bouncing on top of my head.

However, occasionally I meet a bird enthusiast who does not know how to communicate with birds. This section is for this person. It is their key to finding a level of happiness that they have not yet experienced. So here we go – the art and science of communicating with birds.

Birds communicate incessantly. They communicate to each other and to us. They can't help themselves. Most people can tell when a bird is scared, courting a mate or angry. Birds do communicate with their voices – all birds have two voice boxes, not one like us, and they normally use both voice boxes together. But most of their communicating is done

Right: This is a Rock Warbler feeding babies in our garage. Note the roof rafters and the nest hanging from electrical wiring. Photo: Brent Wilson

using body language: posturing, dancing or making eye, beak or other movements. These are easy to learn as they are consistent among all members of a bird species and fairly consistent across all bird species.

Notice how relaxed the birds are around me while I take photos with my phone.

Truly calm and relaxed Budgies, despite my presence.

Left: A courting pair going about their business.

Right: A terrified Double Factor Golden Faced Mauve Bush Budgie. Note her wide eyes and the feathers pulled tight against her body.

Above: Terrified and panting.

Scared birds pull all of their feathers closer to their bodies, ready for rapid escape by flying. Angry or aggressive birds may erect a crest or erect the general head feathers, crouch low or open their beaks. During courtship birds will often fly to a perch, poke out their chest, erect themselves to their full tippy-toed height and maybe even jump up and down. Males in particular do this.

In contrast to the predictability of Budgies' communications, our behaviour will change almost daily. This is very confusing and frightening for our birds. Sometimes we amble slowly into an aviary gazing at one beautiful bird. Other times we race in with a seed bucket, staring at the seed dish since we are in a hurry. Often we spring out from behind a wall and scare them. Crazy people, these humans – their body language is all over the place.

The next thing to understand is that birds are not like dogs. Dogs are predators, thus they are mostly robust, confident and assertive: i.e. not easily scared. Prey animals such as horses and most birds are timid animals that are easily scared. They are constantly worried that a hawk, snake or other predator might attack them. When they are scared they panic and run or fly away. All good horse handlers and bird people tend to move in slow motion when approaching their animals. This has a calming effect on them. Running or rapid movements will terrify your bird or horse.

Right: A male showing off, looking excited and ready to mate. This has been selected as the exhibition posture for Budgies in most countries.

How to communicate with birds

To stop yourself by being so weird and confusing, you need to develop a daily system which the birds can understand and learn to trust.

1. When approaching the aviary, call out or whistle a specific note or two that means: 'Hi guys, can I come inside?' Everything from here on in is all about good manners. Bad manners terrify your birds and many bird breeders have awful manners.

2. Learn smooth, slowish movements. Predators rapidly strike or dive at birds, friends move smoothly and create calm and confidence. All good horse handlers do this with horses. Like birds, horses are prey animals. That is, they try to escape from predators.

Singing, relaxed and showing off.

3. Set up aviary rules. I generally avoid the back area of the aviary where the tiered perches are located. The birds know that they are safe there. If I must bob under to get to the back to clean the floor or whatever, I slowly bend down and look up at the birds. Most have learned to slowly fly to the front of the aviary to get out of my way. I have good manners and wait ten or twenty seconds until the all clear is sounded then under I go.

Showing off and concentrating!

Keeping half an eye open.

4. Snakes are one of the main predators of birds, and birds are programmed to panic at the very sight of a snake. Anything long, thin and moving is a snake – it must be! No bird is likely to hang around to decide if a long, thin moving object is actually a snake – by then, if it is a snake, the bird might be dead.

You have two snakes: one either side of your shoulders – we call them arms. If you flail your arms around or, when you are close by, point at your birds, they will become terrified. This is a sign of someone who is inconsiderate or unaware of Budgerigar behaviour. If I had a cent for every time I have seen a Budgie fancier gesticulating wildly with their arms and hands at a poor Budgie in a show cage, I would be very wealthy. How could anyone not notice the poor bird cringing, or fluttering all over the cage, or pulling its feathers close to its body in sheer terror?*

The broom that you sweep out the aviary or birdroom with is also a snake. Just watch how your birds behave. They fly around like mad, trying to escape. If you doubt the snake stuff, gently disconnect an aviary perch that the birds have perched on all of their lives. Now move it around the aviary. You will see your birds flying in utter panic. Anything long, thin and **moving** is a snake. If it is only long and thin that's OK. If it always moves, like a swing, that is OK too.

So, put your hands in your pockets when you look at birds in small cages. If you must use a judging stick to get them up on the perch, remember that the stick too is a snake. So approach the bird slowly with the stick from below the cage, yet in full view. Predators like hawks and tree snakes tend to strike from above.

Hawks are another common predator of Budgies. Flailing bits of cloth like a towel, or the act of opening an umbrella, look like a hawk to the Budgies and will have a similar effect to the presence of a 'snake'.

5. Stop being a bully. To get show birds in cages to work with you, you need to make training fun. And ask yourself what reward is there for the bird if it hops up on the perch? Many bird trainers are bullies and this yields mediocre results. Never punish a bird for not complying – they will never learn from punishment.

For example, to get a bird onto a perch, most people poke at the poor bird on the floor until they can lift or scare it up onto the perch. This scares the bird even more, so the bird is inclined to jump off the perch back onto the floor.

A better way is to use the scientifically proven 'advance and retreat' method. Apply gentle pressure with your hand or, in extreme cases, with the judging stick until the bird moves towards the perch, or even looks at it. Then instantly (i.e. within half a second) turn your back and move away, retreating several steps. Repeat this a number of times, always rapidly retreating, but expecting a little more each time until the bird realises that happiness is found only on the perch. This happiness and security is the bird's reward for getting up on the perch. Never approach the cage rapidly – always do it slowly. This method works brilliantly and

* I am aware that some placid showbirds can eventually relax after brutal training, but using a gentler method of training is always better.

Terrified Bush Budgies.

all judges should use it. Or at least, those with good manners should. Also, don't stare directly at the poor bird, at least not at first. Predators stare at you just before they kill you.

Birds and dogs and horses **live in the moment**. If you don't react within half a second, these animals will not connect what **you** did with what **they** did.

6. Catching and Netting: You should be honest about this. Don't try to trick your birds. Adopt an "I'm going to catch you" whistle note, or way of walking or even a word or phrase like "Look out" (remember that no dog or Budgie speaks English – they just learn to react to sounds or movements). Don't hide your net. Focus your eyes on the bird you wish to catch. The others will probably see this and relax a bit. They can tell which bird in the flock that the hawk is chasing. Very soon, when you are in the aviary for other reasons, your birds will trust you since they recognise your body language that says: "I'm not going to catch or eat you". Mine remain on my head and shoulders as I net other birds in the same aviary.

7. Warn your friends. By now your Budgies will be becoming your friends. So knock before you enter. Whenever you do anything like inspecting a nest box, tap three times on the box. Most birds will learn to go out of the box when you tap. This cuts down on fear.

8. Play games. Try going into your aviary (especially the young birds' aviary) with a handful of green seeding grasses or other treats. Always wait for the birds to come to you, never pursue them… just wait and wait. Hold the treats near the perch and soon one confident bird (the 'influencer') will steal some seed. Gradually withdraw the seed and wait motionless until one bird lands on your arm. Within a week or so, most of the birds will land all over you. This enables you to pick out your future champions or to assess the readiness of your flock to breed. Spend time with your birds, become a part of their scenery and part of their lives.

After you gain the confidence and friendship of your birds, you can relax these

Relaxed and sleepy.   Scared and alert.

rules **a bit**. But never forget to monitor the fear postures of your birds – watch for crouching down a bit with the feathers pulled close to their body, and perhaps a fearful, wide-eyed look. Flying away in terror is disastrous.

NEVER FORGET THAT BIRDS LEARN WHEN THEY ARE CURIOUS AND RELAXED – NEVER WHEN THEY ARE FRIGHTENED. MOVE SLOWLY. IF YOU ACT LIKE YOU HAVE TEN MINUTES, IT TAKES ALL DAY. IF YOU ACT LIKE YOU HAVE ALL DAY, IT TAKES TEN MINUTES.

This is a semi-relaxed bird, curious to see what is happening below. Its mask and feathers are moderately fluffed up, which is a sign that it is relaxed. Its eyes radiate curiosity.

Be aware though that the most important rule of parrot training – whether it's Budgies or cockatoos – is never react to a bite. Pretend that no bite hurts. All parrots love the power of dominating a subordinate. Never give them that pleasure. Never hit or attack them either: birds never forgive you if you do. Be a benign, non-threatening friend.

When holding a smaller parrot like a Budgie, I let them try to bite the tip of my fingernail from above. At the correct angle they can't secure a grip on your skin, so they tend to stop trying to bite the fingernail. Birds appear to have an innate reluctance to biting beak-like growths. Fingernails are made of exactly the same substance as beaks. But once they taste soft flesh, they can become dangerous.

Back to brooms

'What about brooms?', I hear you asking, 'you said that they were snakes.' I did. Show them the broom from outside the aviary; move it very slowly inside, keeping it beside your body. A free-swinging broom terrifies all birds. Start brooming very slowly until they realise that it isn't a snake, then gradually speed up. But never sweep rapidly with a broom – this is disastrous.

Well, that's a start. Please, if you have other techniques that you use, send them in so that other people can benefit from them. Remember, good manners are everything.

Photographing Budgerigars

Modern smartphones are the best thing that ever happened to Budgie photography. The tiny lens easily squeezes between the bars on an exhibition cage. This facilitates the production of magnificent photos, which is critically important for that one-in-a-million bird like this female.

Below are some stages of learning the use of smartphones.

These are all photos of a wonderful Black Eyed White that I was lucky enough to breed. Top left is a photo with the bars out of focus, but the bird in focus. Above is similar but is taken from further away. The image on the left is useful, but the focus on the bird is soft. This is a Modern Showbird.

This is how you use a smartphone for photographing Budgies in a show cage. First of all, inspect the camera to see where the lens is located (often top right). Hold the phone up against the wires with your left hand and use the right finger to press the button. This first photo has a wire right in the middle of the shot, which is not good.

That's better! Now, the camera's lens is precisely between two wires. Being a Modern Showbird, this White Cap relaxed very quickly. These are two real photos showing both the bird and its photo.

A shot between the wires of a wire baby cage. This is an English Yellow Faced Violet Australian Heritage Clearwing.

This is a Bronze White Cap Rainbow Australian Heritage Budgerigar in a show cage. At first he fluttered around the cage, but patience enabled me to get some photos. Often a good strategy is to just ping off several shots and check back immediately to see if any are any good.

Right: A White Cap Rainbow Australian Heritage Budgerigar, almost asleep in a show cage.

Below: These are two photos of a new Golden Head Budgie. The photo bottom right is under UVB black lighting in an otherwise pitch-dark room. All of the yellow colours in this photo are in fact, UVB pigment. The UVB light spooked him a bit, so the camera was kept at a distance.

Below left: This is the same bird in the same cage under normal light. His yellow head is in real life an unbelievably dazzling golden colour. This photo is taken between the wire bars and the very placid Modern Showbird is very relaxed.

Left: A Rumped Australian Dominant Pied, photographed through the bars of a wire cage-front. It is a Modern Showbird and is fully relaxed. Rumped Pieds are either Single Factor or Double Factor Pieds, which are Double Factor for the Banded Pied modifier.

Below: Modern Showbirds, like this Golden Faced/Yellow Faced double factor Violet Sky Modern Clearwing, are usually very placid, so photographing them at this very close quarters is a bit easier. This is a rather dirty-winged Clearwing resulting from an outcross to Normals. It is about six months old and in deep moult. But notice his relatively relaxed posture and also the relaxed, erected feathers on his head. When photographing up close through the bars of a show cage, you must remain motionless for some minutes until the bird fully relaxes. Your arms will ache, but eventually the bird will accept you and relax.

Cropping of photos is very important when you are photographing through wire bars. The photo on the right is the original, and you can see the blurry vertical bars on both sides. On the left is exactly the same photo after cropping. This is a Greygreen Clearwing Modern Showbird.

It will take you quite a while to get really good at 'between the wires' photography, but is really worth the effort in learning. Here are some tips:

1. Never move your arms quickly near a Budgie, as arms look like snakes to birds and this will terrify them. Broom handles, etc, are similarly scary.
2. Move in slow motion as you approach the cage with your camera. Don't chase the bird with the camera. Instead, position the lens between the wires in front of one perch and wait for the bird to return to the perch where the camera lens is.
3. I use an Apple iPhone 13 Pro max. This is quite simply the best camera that I have ever used. The quality of smartphone cameras seems to improve every year.

Dilutes, Clearwings and Greywings

The Origin of Clearwings

No variety or colour of Budgies has had its origin recorded as thoroughly and as accurately as the Clearwing. It was even a major section in the 'Bible of Budgie breeding': the 1935 second edition of Neville Cayley's *Budgerigars in Bush and Aviary*. This book was widely distributed in the UK and Australia.

Yet in UK, Budgie breeders ignored all of this precious information and cobbled together a ramshackle guess of pseudo-genetics which went on to become the official version of the heredity of Clearwings for more than 80 years. They stated that Clearwings are a multiple allele at the dil-locus, which includes Greywing, Dilute and Normal. This nonsense survives until today because almost no one could understand the meaning of confusing terms such as 'multiple alleles' or how to disprove the theory. Some UK Clearwing breeders claim that they are unable to breed well coloured Clearwings because their Clearwings were developed from a different Greywing-like mutation. However, the Clearwings in the UK were developed from large numbers of beautiful Clearwings exported to the UK from Australia. There are records of these Clearwings being sent to the UK. How on Earth did the UK breeders lose their way?

Recently the Egyptian Clearwing breeder Walid Ali produced Clearwings every bit as perfect in colour as the Australian Clearwings. Australia never sent Clearwings to North Africa, so the basis of Walid's birds can only be UK Clearwings that finished up in Egypt. If Walid can breed perfectly coloured Clearwings using my system, surely UK breeders can too. Congratulations to Walid. You are a truly great breeder of Budgerigars. You have done what no-one else outside of Australia could do.

Two of Walid's magnificent Clearwings. Absolutely World Class.

Having gotten that off my chest, let's consign that misleading nonsense to the rubbish bin and go back to the source of all Clearwings: his name is Harold Peir, in my opinion the greatest ever Budgie breeder. How did he create Clearwings?

Yes that's right, he created them and there is no mutation for Clearwings after all. He was breeding Greywings and found that one group had much better body colour. He thought that they would look even better if they had white wings combined with the deep blue body colour. So he just selected for ever-clearer wings, and after three to five years he had created the world's first Clearwings. Awesome breeding!

Right: This is the original painting of the first Clearwing Budgie. From left to right: Dilute Cobalt, Greywing Cobalt, Whitewing* Cobalt and Normal Cobalt.

THE CLEARWING ALREADY INCLUDED THE FULL BODY COLOUR GENE.

Peir just needed to find enough modifiers to make the wings turn **white**.

Plate V

Reading from left—COBALT WHITE, GREYWING COBALT, WHITEWING COBALT, COBALT

Harold Peir's recipe

So what all humble Clearwing breeders worldwide need to do is to follow Harold Peir's recipe, which is recorded in several books. This is the Holy Grail of Budgie breeding because it opens up how to breed everything from longer masks to perfect colour in all Budgies.

1. Get perfect body colour because this bit is controlled by one dominant gene: i.e. it is both stable and easy to manage. This gene is called the full body colour gene and Budgies with it are widely available. Buy some soon.

2. Next, begin the long task of clearing up the wings. You need to assemble hundreds of modifiers as Harold Peir did. Modifiers are not genes but they are the bosses of

---

* Whitewings and Yellowwings are now called Clearwings.

the genes. Harold got some Yellow Budgies from Japan; at the time, the Japanese breeders had the best Yellows. These are called Black Eyed Whites and Yellows in Australia and Yellows of light suffusion in the UK. He 'stole' the wing clarity from the Yellows by crossing them to his Clearwings-to-be. Since the body colour is a simple gene, any body colour damage to his Clearwings from this cross was easily fixed. Also Yellows are just modified Dilutes, so he got rid of any Dilutes produced.

3. Now the long task ahead. Modifiers are little bits of DNA that have tiny effects on animals. They rapidly mutate and one bird may have more than 100 wing colour modifiers alone. When you mate two birds together their young are roughly half way between mum and dad in looks. So if mum has very clear wings and dad has dirty wings, the babies are a mixed lot roughly half way between the two. It's a bit like mixing white paint with black paint: you get grey paint.

4. As you get more and more advanced in wing clarity, outcrossing them becomes more and more destructive. So, the only way forward is to select **within** your already crossed Clearwings. Outcrossing to birds with no clear wing modifiers yet again is a disaster.

Improving the quality of Clearwings as Modern Showbirds

Improving the quality of Clearwings to keep up with the ever-changing standards of perfection is a very problematic activity. When you cross a beautifully coloured Clearwing to a Modern Showbird you will destroy the varietal characteristics of the Clearwing. Remember that there are hundreds of modifiers needed to make up a Clearwing with beautifully clear wings and rich body colour. And modifiers do not behave like genes. They produce tiny changes. **Standards change over time forcing constant crosses of Clearwings back to Modern Showbirds, ruining the Clearwings every time.** If Clearwings were a mutation, there would be no problems like this at all.

So what to do? The necessity is to avoid these constant outcrosses. Firstly, I must say that constantly changing Standards makes no sense at all. It drives birds to extremes that are very cruel to the birds. The AHBA has created a permanent Standard that can never be changed, except for fixing mistakes or adding new colours and varieties.

The best solution to a problem like this is to establish hybrid Heritage x Modern Budgie lines, based on where the JUDGES think the Standard is going, e.g. Will masks need to be longer yet again? Do we need even higher frontal blow? etc.

Every outcross to a Modern Showbird bird must involve buying the very best Normals. This will help to minimise the number of outcrosses per decade. Lastly, Clearwing and other colour breeders must

The Holy Grail.

push hard for the judges to award fair marks for colour in showbirds. At the moment they are not doing that.

Never forget that all Clearwing breeders MUST maintain the dominant full body colour mutation in all Clearwings as it frees you up to concentrate on better wing clarity as well as body colour and overall exhibition qualities.

Clearwings – how to modernise them

All over the world, for more than 80 years, Clearwing Budgerigars have proven to be virtually impossible to modernise. Even in Australia, large Modern Clearwings rarely have wings that are clear, and often their body colour is poor as well.

So Clearwings come in two types: tiny old fashioned Exhibition Budgies with superb clarity of wings and astonishing body colour, or larger Modern Showbirds with awful body colour and disappointing grey wings. So the question arises: Can they ever be modernised and still look like 'real' Clearwings?

The answer is YES! And here follows the way forward.

This male is an outstanding type of Clearwing to cross to a Modern Showbird. He has very clear wings, a reasonably good head, great body colour and some OK feathering. If you can't get this quality, you could use Black Eyed Yellows or Whites (Whites or Yellows of light suffusion), which have really clear wings due to the same hereditary modifiers.

Firstly, you need a strategic plan. It is this: you must produce a line of Clearwings where every bird has excellent body colour so that you are then free to concentrate on perfecting the wing colour. Since full body colour in Clearwings is a dominant gene, it is reasonably easy to get a line where 100% of the Budgies have superb body colour.

So, go for it. Cross three of the best of your Clearwings that have excellent body colour to three of your best Modern Normals to develop an impressive group of Normals split for Clearwing. Then mate split Clearwing to split Clearwing to produce 25% Clearwings*. Since Normals don't usually carry the full body colour gene, you will need to hold any resulting pale body coloured young in reserve in case you need them.

---

* You can mate any Normal-looking good quality babies from these matings back to Clearwings and if they don't produce any Clearwing babies, at least you have produced some more split Clearwings to breed with.

These are two photos of the result of just such a split-to-split mating. What a great base for future breeding. This female is a White Cap Golden Faced Blue hybrid with full body colour. You might as well use this cross to introduce some new colour into your Clearwings as well if the quality is good enough. Never forget that ONE GOOD BIRD can turn a stud around.

Another Clearwing bred from a split-to-split mating after hybridising well-coloured Clearwings with Modern Showbirds.

Now the fun begins. Now that you have your base of stable, Modern Clearwings with great body colour, you are free to create the clear wing colour. Yes, create! Clearer wings are created by using hereditary modifiers that are in the bird's DNA, but which are not genes.

Using modifiers is a dual operation. In Clearwings, modifiers are numbered in their hundreds or even thousands just for wing clarity in one bird. Each modifier does a tiny bit. And there are different families of wing 'cleaners'. My research indicates that there are two basic groups for clarity; one modifier for paler markings, and the other for dazzling extreme yellow or white. Around the world, breeders have a form of dull, indistinct wing markings that can produce clear but blurry wings. But there is the extreme clear effect that is also necessary as well, so their birds' wings don't have that muddy and drab look. The drab wings plus no full body colour produces Budgies which are drab all over!

It is paramount that the full body colour was established in 100% of your Clearwings that you are now developing – it is easy to insert a dominant gene, which then leaves you free to tackle the more messy task of clearing up the wings, which are more difficult and less stable (modifiers like tandem repeats mutate about 100,000 times faster than genes).

This is a Light Green Normal split for Clearwing. He has a huge amount to offer if you are breeding Modern Clearwings.

On with the job

When Clearwings have young, the different wing colour effects of each parent average out in the offspring, i.e. if the male has dark markings and the female has fairly clear wings the young average out at not quite as clear as mum. But if you look closely, there will always be some that are a bit clearer than others. I have a very precise system of managing this. I rank all of my Clearwings on their breeding page in degrees of clarity, from VVVV dirty to clear, and on to VVVV clear at the other extremity. It takes no more than one or two seconds to put down its ranking, e.g. 'VV clear' or 'V dirty' or just 'clear'. This builds up to describe how each pairing fares, and what are the breeding strengths of most of the progeny. So a compatibility chart builds up: how to combine a balanced grouping of the necessary modifiers. Then you just select each year for ever more clear wings.

For some years I thought that there was a linkage between larger size and longer, coarser feathering to Normals. Increasingly, I am of the opinion that there is no linkage at all. That is, breeding a large, well-feathered Clearwing is easy enough.

Another magnificent Clearwing bred from a Clearwing cross to Modern Showbirds. In producing the split Clearwings, it is of the utmost importance to cover all necessary aspects of a Modern Showbird. This male has the long mask and good feathering that is required.

This bird has excellent posture as well. It is so important that you cover all bases when you are developing Modern Clearwings.

Yellows, Whites, Dilutes, Greywings and Clearwings

These days there are strong opinions about these colours. Which ones should have classes at shows? How can you tell a Clearwing from a Greywing or a Dilute from a Greywing? How do you identify a Cinnamon-Clearwing combination? What is a Clearwing-Greywing combination?

To sort it all out, perhaps it's best to go back to the beginning.

At a Glance

Dilutes and Greywings are mutations. Clearwings, Black Eyed Yellows and Black Eyed Whites are human-made varieties based on gene modifiers. Clearwings are modified Greywings, and Black Eyed Yellows and Black Eyed Whites are modified Dilutes (Darkwings are modified Black Eyed Whites or Yellows). Due to the complexity of the gene modifiers, outcrossing Clearwings or Black Eyed Yellows or Whites to any other variety does enormous damage to the colour and markings of both varieties. This process should always be left to talented, specialist breeders.

History

- The Dilute gene produces yellowish/green or whitish/blue birds with greyish wing markings. These are seen on occasion in wild flocks and some were exported to Europe in the 1800s. The yellowish birds were bred in 1872 in Belgium and the blue series Dilutes (a very light blue body colour and greyish wing markings) were bred in the UK by 1920. Claims that Yellow Dilutes were imported back to Australia in 1900 are misleading. Mr C.H.A. Lienau of Adelaide did import some Yellows circa 1900, but all died without breeding (see *Budgerigars in Bush and Aviary* by N. Cayley, page 45).

- Greywings were bred in the 1920s in Europe. By the early 1930s Greywings were established in Australia. They had greyish wing markings and about 50% colour intensity.

- Clearwings were developed from Greywings in the 1930s in Australia in the aviaries of Harold Peir in Sydney. It is generally accepted that the variety was further established in a wider range of colours by John Catt of Carlingford, New South Wales, and the variety was honed to perfection by Harley Yardley of Fivedock, New South Wales. By the time that Harley Yardley had finished with Clearwings, they had almost fully Normal body colour and pure white or yellow wings – but, at base, they were still genetically Greywings (see later on).

Interestingly, John Catt is generally referred to in Budgerigar books as J. Catts, but his name was in fact, John Catt (without the 's'). The Catt family were prominent orchardists and nursery people in the Carlingford and hills area of Sydney and they are still active nursery people to this day. From 1925, they were pioneering the growing of citrus and summer fruit plants and John was a leading breeder of Budgerigars as well. John's backyard originally featured a long birdroom with indoor flights behind the house where single pairs of Budgies also bred in cages. This was quite innovative at the time.

Harold Peir was also a market gardener in the Sydney region. His surname is often misspelt as Pier, which has hindered research into the history of Clearwings. Curiously, Peir's original family name was Saint Pierre and some members of Harold's family still adhere to this form and spelling.

Genetics

There are arguments as to whether these three varieties are separate mutations at all, but my research has revealed that there are only two basic mutations: i.e. Dilute and Greywing, plus the original Normal type with black wing markings. These are called multiple alleles and there are thus three at this locus – Normal, Dilute and Greywing.

The Greywing mutation has in fact been developed into at least three sub-types:
1. Original Greywings with 50% grey wing colour and 50% body colour.
2. Greywings with very dark grey wing colour (and maybe 100% body colour).
3. 'Clearwings' with 100% body colour and pure white or yellow wings.

These three Greywing-based varieties are all due to various genetic modifiers acting upon the basic Greywing mutation.

From left to right: 1. Similar to original full body coloured Greywing Dark Green. 2. Intense wing and full body coloured Greywing, 3. Full body coloured 'Clearwing'.

The Dilute mutation has been developed into four separate varieties also:
1. Dilutes with light (about 10%) body and wing colour.
2. Black Eyed Whites and Black Eyed Yellows.
3. Darkwings, Black Eyed Yellows or Whites with a dominant wing darkening gene.
4. Dilutes with deep body colour, but clear wings; Clearwing-bred Dilutes.

From left to right: 1. Pale Dilute Bush Budgie, 2. Black Eyed Yellow, 3. Darkwing, 4. Clearwing-bred Dilute.

All of this explains why crossing any of these varieties with another yields rather messy results. That is, the babies tend to be halfway between the two parents in appearance due to the modifiers.

There is a genetic hierarchy in the first cross:

Normal is dominant to Clearwing, Dilute and Greywing.

Clearwing is dominant to Dilute but the offspring have full body colour and greyish wing markings.

Clearwing blends with Greywing, because both are the same mutation with different modifiers which blend together.

Greywing is dominant to Dilute.

Confusion

Despite all of the above, it is very hard to distinguish one variety from another. All modifier-based varieties tend to blend when crossed together. Genes usually give you major changes that are fairly consistent in appearance and very reliable in ratios. Modifiers make subtle changes that accumulate into major changes that are rarely consistent or statistically predictable.

This much is certain:

- Primitive or badly bred Dilutes and Clearwings can have a wing colour that is indistinguishable from Greywings. Never let anyone tell you different. At a show some years back, four judges misidentified a grey Clearwing of mine: three identified it as a Dilute and one judge identified it as a Greywing. None got it right, and these were top-notch judges.
- Clearwings bred from outcrosses to Normals can have really dirty grey wings but very light body colour, making them impossible to distinguish from Greywings.
- Dilutes bred accidentally from Normals usually have very dirty grey wings and also a strong amount of body colour.
- Dilutes bred from Clearwings can have very clear wings yet quite dark body colour for a Dilute. They are often very attractive to look at.

Four Clearwings developed from crosses with 100% pure Normals. In each case, one of my very clear Clearwings was mated to a Normal, then two of the Normals split for Clearwing were mated together. Look at the range of wing colours, all originating from my Clearwings. These results totally disprove the theory that the different wing and body colours in Greywings are due to different Greywing mutations. There is only one Greywing mutation, but there are many modifiers that alter Greywings considerably. Every Budgie (Normals included) carries invisible modifiers that affect Clearwings and other varieties.

- Cinnamon-Clearwings can easily pass as straight Clearwings. At a show, I once saw a major winner in a Clearwing group that was a Cinnamonwing-Clearwing. And how do you identify a Cinnamonwing-Clearwing? They have very clear wings (sometimes with a hint of light brown wing markings in the sun). They have about 50–60% of Normal Clearwing body colour. They tend to have finer feather and therefore smaller-looking heads. They have light pink coloured feet. Test the theory by recording the plum eyes among newly hatched Clearwing chicks then comparing the colour of these chicks with their non plum-eyed siblings.

Back to history

It is a simple fact that only in Australia were the three varieties developed to accentuate and thus define the differences. This happened around the 1930s, 1940s and 1950s. During this time, Clearwings were invented. Yes, invented. It's clear to me that the basic or original Clearwing had grey wings and poor

This is a Cinnamonwing Clearwing Red Violet, a.k.a. an Amethyst Budgerigar. Note the very pale cheek patches, the very pink feet, the very clear wings and the very pale body colour for a Violet.

body colour. We see them today when we cross well coloured Clearwings to Dilutes or Normals. Our greatest ever Budgie breeder, Harold Peir, created the variety out of his own imagination. That is, he thought 'What If?'' What if I accentuated the contrast between wing and body colour? What if I bred for super-dark body colour and yet totally clear wing colour?' Harley Yardley perfected Peir's dream, but the rest of the world simply never shared the dream (or Harold's and Harley's abilities).

Strange as it may seem, new Budgie varieties were highly mobile during the late 1920s and 1930s. Clearwings, Greywings, Darkwings and Dilutes were both exchanged and exhibited between Sydney, Melbourne and Adelaide in Australia. Club records from these times clearly prove that breeders regularly travelled interstate, presumably by train, to exhibit and sell their new varieties, within a year or two of their origin. This led to a rapid explosion of numbers of all new Budgie varieties.

At the same time as Clearwings were developed, various breeders, notably Harold Peir, began the process of developing a pure yellow Dilute (Lutinos did not exist in Australia at the time). They created the concept of Black Eyed Yellow. They selected for ever clearer overall colour until they hopefully reached a pure yellow (or rarely, white) bird. The Black Eyed Yellow variety (Yellows of light suffusion) was subsequently developed to have near perfect yellow colour by about the 1950s. Harley Yardley had outstanding birds of this variety, as did breeders around Sydney, Melbourne, Adelaide and Newcastle.

To achieve this spectacular colour, they incorporated another diluting gene, the Cinnamon gene. The Black Eyed Yellow was, for the most part, a composite of two diluting genes: Dilute itself plus Cinnamonwing. Some non-Cinnamon Black Eyed Yellows also existed (you identify them by their purple/grey feet as against the pink feet of the Cinnamons). By the 1950s, when I bred Black Eyed Yellows, all of my babies were born with plum eyes. These were Yardley Yellows and they **all** carried the Cinnamonwing gene.

Greywings were refined too. They originally were stabilised at 50% wing colour and 50% body colour. Later on, Greywings with even more intense

This is one of the best Black Eyed Whites that I have bred. It is a Cinnamon Dilute. I began breeding this very difficult variety in 1956. These are called 'Whites of light suffusion' or similar names in countries other than Australia.

body colour were produced in Australia, and today the body colour is required by the standard to be "approaching full intensity". Australia also produced Greywings with super-intense dark grey wing markings – I have never seen one of these without the deep body colour as well. Alistair Home, Australia's greatest Greywing expert, has confirmed this observation.

So, three varieties that were originally confusing and barely distinguishable became totally different over time, even though only two base mutations plus the original Wild-type Black Winged ever existed: Greywing and Dilute.

My declaration

I feel that I really understand this group of three varieties. I have bred all of them and out-crossed all of them except **true** Greywings. I have relied on Alistair Home for most of my Greywing genetics and history because I did not want any Greywing genetic contamination of my Clearwings, Dilutes, etc. But I herewith declare that, to save my life, I couldn't identify some of the birds of each group.

- I have Clearwings that I have bred that I couldn't possibly pick from Greywings (except that I know the breeding).
- I have Dilutes that I couldn't possibly pick from Greywings (except that I bred them).
- I have seen birds at many shows in classes of Dilutes, Greywings and Clearwings but I have no idea of their genetic make-up.

I must go on to say that judges who wrong-class any of these confusing birds are letting us all down badly. If a specialist breeder like myself can't pick one from another, what right has a judge to disqualify a bird? Mark the birds down for poor colour by all means, but don't disqualify them because you have underestimated the overlaps between the three varieties.

How the colours work

Mendel discovered the gene, but genes by themselves don't decide all that much in the real world. Genes don't mutate all that often and are too rigid and conservative to provide the flexibility needed in evolution. Most change is created by the so-called junk DNA. Vast repeating nonsense-like strands of DNA act as volume controls for the genes. They rapidly and subtly crank down: colour intensity, the areas of pied markings, overall size, size of spots, length of feathers, directional feathers, etc, OR they crank them up.

Scientists claimed that only about 1% of the billions of base pairs on chromosomes form protein-coding genes, and that the rest was relatively inert, i.e. 'junk'. They were wrong then and many still are. The 98–99% is the main game. Abundant research has shown that these tandem repeats, switches and other bits actually do most of the work.

The ENCODE project discovered that 80% of the DNA is, in fact active. Some

From left: Cinnamon White Cap Seafoam Rainbow, Amethyst Clearwing Australian Fallow, and Teal Blue White Cap Rainbow. Using modifiers and the occasional gene mutation, there is no limit to the magnificent colour combinations we can all create.

scientists created the myth of modifier genes. Little genes that did subtle jobs. Nonsense. To clear the wings on a Clearwing, we unconsciously select for lower volumes of melanin deposition in wing feathers. This is done by modifiers, not genes. We wind down the volume of the wing colour by using the volume controls for the Clearwing gene itself. Modifier genes do exist, but they are relatively uncommon.

With Clearwings, Yardley and others used sheer brilliance to identify and amplify the controls to wind down wing colour while they ramped up body colour. Genes alone were not involved.

They wound down **all** of the colour in Black Eyed Whites and Yellows and stabilised the 50% colour in early Greywings.

The real problem

The real problem is that we classify all varieties by mutation. Why? There is no need to do this. Most pigeon, chicken, duck, dog, cat and even goldfish varieties are classified by appearance. At the end of the day, it doesn't really matter what the genetic make-up is. All that matters is how pretty the bird appears, whether its colour is hereditary, and how closely it conforms to the standard.

If we let go a bit on the genetic stuff, we could produce the following:

- Clearwing-bred Dilutes with subtle blue or green body colours yet really clear wings. These beautiful Pastel varieties already exist, but there are no classes for them at shows.
- Breathtaking Light Blue or Apple Green Dilutes with silvery wings. Currently Dilutes are more or less just suffused birds in the Budgie standard.
- Clearwings with a body colour haze on the wing. We could steal this haze from the Normals with body-colour suffused wings. Often this body colour suffusion has no

relationship to Opalines. These could well replace Opaline Clearwings since their all blue or all green wings should look much more attractive. These would be the perfect blue or green 'self-coloured Budgerigar' – i.e. blue or green all over. I have begun on this project and it is going well.

Those three above would set artists' hearts racing. They could be so much prettier than current varieties. While we investigate these new possibilities, we simply must continue to breed the Black Eyed Yellow and Black Eyed White (Yellows or Whites of light suffusion). I believe that these little Aussie wonders need to be conserved at all cost.

Summary

Clearwings and Black Eyed Yellows are overwhelmingly a creation of the human mind. They are not mutations and they rely mostly on volume controls on genes. Never pretend that you can reliably pick Clearwings, Dilutes and Greywings apart. Let's shape future perfection by rewarding good colour over bad. But let's wrong-class nothing and ban nothing. The Australian Heritage Budgerigar Association is developing classes for Pastel budgies which will help greatly. We are seeking contact with other Pastel breeders worldwide.

Creating the Modern Budgerigar

Breeding winners

Desirable features could include:
- overall larger size or wider shoulders
- a longer mask or bigger spots
- coarser feathering
- longer feathering
- wider directional feathers
- more frontal blow of feathers
- clearer wings in Clearwings
- less head flecking

At a Glance

Contrary to many beliefs, if you wish to improve the quality of your Budgies by careful selection, it is virtually certain that genes will not be significantly involved in the changes. New scientific discoveries have reduced the role of genes to bit-players in evolution, and in the domestic breeding of plants and animals.

When you select for such things as listed above, you are using **hereditary modifiers** that are not genes. In other words, it is dead easy. There is no dominance, no recessiveness, and no sex linkage involved. Nothing complex to master.

When breeding elite Exhibition Budgies, selecting for tiny changes in important aspects of perfection is what we all do. These tiny changes are caused by modifiers. They modify the genes. You might imagine genes as tiny factories and these modifiers would be the staff and management that run them. For example, the Dilute gene removes most of the colour on a Budgie, but many modifiers can remove whatever colour and markings that are left.

This makes sense. After all, gene mutations make huge hereditary changes under a rigid system that, in the wild, is usually catastrophic for the animal. A mutant white sparrow has little chance of surviving for very long in the wild. Evolution requires a gentle, gradual and flexible system for change: i.e. modifiers. This system is what all animal breeders have always used to create domesticated animals. Genes actually play a much smaller part. These modifiers are what humanity has used for thousands of years to breed domestic animals and plants. It is summarised by the saying: 'Like breeds like.'

To test if Clearwings could be large, I bred a line of them. This bird is more than 30cm long. His head is well beyond the zero mark.

What are modifiers?

There are two known types of modifiers: active assemblies of DNA modifiers, which are not genes, and the newly discovered electrome. Both of these modifier groups organise, change or instruct genes on what to do. To repeat, genes are the factories, and modifiers are the staff and management that run those factories.

Non-gene DNA modifiers

They are what was once named 'junk DNA'. Not long ago this junk was thought by geneticists to have no purpose at all. Then, the Encyclopedia of DNA Elements (ENCODE) report issued from a worldwide assembly of the leading DNA laboratories has discovered that 80% of your DNA is active, but only just over 1% is made up of genes.

This Golden Faced/Yellow Faced Violet Clearwing is full of modifiers. Modifiers for large head, long mask, clear wings, large size, wide shoulders and rich body colour.

There are short bits of DNA repeated to form strands called tandem repeats. These are made of the four bases in DNA which have the initials of G, T, A and C, lined up in a precise order. You can get a group of DNA bases such as GTAC **repeated** from two to 100 times. The more repeats of the bases GTAC, the more that the gene that they control responds. Imagine the strands of GTACGTACGTAC, etc. Just one or two GTAC tandem repeats will do very little. A hundred GTACs in a row will make a huge difference.

Tandem repeats are inherently unstable and mutate up to 100,000 times more often than genes do. As I said, they are very flexible. As an example, Clearwings are genetically Greywings with many tandem repeats bleaching out the greyish wing colour. But, surprisingly, the full body colour of all true Clearwings is an independent dominant gene mutation not a modifier. However, the bird below has extra-powerful body colour modifiers as well as the full body colour mutation to create amazing body colour.

In the early days of Exhibition Budgie development, the United Kingdom chose to base their colour and variety development almost 100% on genes. Australia, on the other hand, chose modifiers for many of their colours and varieties. Clearwings, as already mentioned, are modified Greywings. Black Eyed Whites and Black Eyed

Yellows are modified Dilutes. Darkwings are Black Eyed Whites and Black Eyed Yellows plus a gene mutation that re-darken their modified wings. Australian Banded Pieds are a Dominant Pied gene mutation plus a band-shaping gene mutation plus many many modifiers to tidy up and straighten up the band. Red Violet Clearwings are Double Factor Violet Cobalt Clearwings with modifiers that both intensify the violet colour plus shift the violet colour more into the red end of violet. Opaline has many modifiers that change the wing and back patterns considerably. Australian Golden Faced Blues are significantly improved in their golden colouration by modifiers.

The key to perfection in Clearwing colour is CONTRAST. This female has perfectly coloured wings and unbelievable body colour. All of this is due to modifiers.

How do you use modifiers to improve your birds?

This is SO SIMPLE. If the masks on your birds are too short, buy a couple of long masked birds and cross them to your lines. On average, the babies from crosses to your lines will have masks about halfway between those of their parents (this is how DNA modifiers usually work – sort of like mixing paint). After that, just keep selecting for longer masks in each generation. The same applies to all modifier-based characteristics. This is what good breeders have done since time immemorial.

The electrome

This is the HUGE breakthrough that many of us have awaited for decades. It finally explains the basic structure and nature of animal and plant development. All plants and animals are electrical beings where every cell is electrically active, acting as tiny batteries. They lay down the framework of all living things, from skeletons, repairs and organs in animals, to the framework of plants. See the article 'You are electric' by Sally Adee in *New Scientist* magazine on 25 February 2023.

The electrome uses the tiniest of electrical currents, around 0–90 millivolts, to make the template of our bodies, which genes are unable to do by themselves – e.g. two eyes, one nose, plus a backbone, etc. After laying down the structural plan, the electrome dictates which bit goes where. Ninety millivolts creates skeletal muscle, seventy millivolts creates nerve cells, etc.

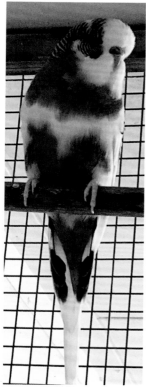

This amazing Violet Australian Dominant Pied is near perfect in terms of pied symmetry, including his chevron (v-shaped) band and his freedom from spots on his mask. Can you see the two horses' heads looking away from each other on his stomach? Now that is symmetry! All done with modifiers.

So how does this relate to breeding Budgies? The voltage changes form the blueprint of our bodies, organs, etc. These voltage changes do more than just form a blueprint, however: they actually instruct the genes when to go to work and what to do.

Classic electrome effects in Budgies would be Crested and Hagoromo structures. The bilateral symmetry and placement of the whorls in Hagoromos will be controlled by the electrome. The placement and shape of the crests/whorls will be controlled by electromes, which fits in very well with my crest theory.

Early Hagoromos often had neural dysfunctions, i.e. brain damage, probably due to a hole in their skull. They called them 'star gazers'. From the huge numbers being bred these days, the Hagoromo breeders have gotten rid of this problem. This accomplishment will have been done by electrome modifications. I suspect

A classic Hagoromo.

This photo shows the 'dot' of the centre of the facial feather whorl on all birds. Usually, it is hidden under the cere, but in the case of the Monk (Quaker) Parakeet, it is visible a few millimetres above the beak. This proves the existence of the facial whorl, which creates the aerodynamic face in birds. Photo: Christopher DeNatale

All bilateral symmetry in Budgies, for example the straight line pied band and symmetrical pied wings on Australian Dominant Pieds, will be electrome based.

Baby pinfeathers show how the feathers grow. Imagine the central dot of a whorl under this young bird's cere. This whorl forces all head feathers to aerodynamically hug the skull.

that the shape of every feather on a bird, such as curled body contour feathers, are controlled by electromes. At the base of every feather is a tiny factory producing growth and details (for further information try an online search for 'topology').

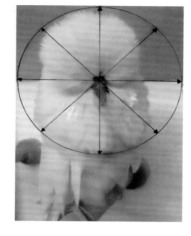

Right is the 'Modern face' on a Double Factor Spangle showbird. The arrows show how the facial feathers grow out and backwards from the central dot hidden underneath the cere. In essence this is a facial crest or whorl. Scientifically, however, this is a whorl. It is not really a crest because crests are a group of feathers that can be erected. Think of a Sulphur-crested Cockatoo or a Galah. However, the erectile head feathers (i.e. blow) that Exhibition Budgies now have ARE true crests.

You and I, plus Budgies, have whorls all over our bodies. We have a whorl at the back of our head and hairy male humans show many whorls all over their bodies. Budgies have one whorl underneath their cere that shapes all facial feathers, curving them back for streamlined flight. There are two wing whorls, one on each scapular, again for streamlined flight. The electrome also plays a huge role in disease control, possibly including cancer. It looks like the electrome can also play a role in destroying resistance of diseases to antibiotics. This is a potentially huge health breakthrough.

The electrome will also play a big part in Chimeras; i.e. in assembling two sibling bodies into one bird inside the egg.

Right: This is a half-sider Chimera. A different bird on each side – two siblings fused together. Curiously, the left side has the wingless wonder virus, but the right side doesn't. Maybe there is heritable resistance to this virus?

Above: Photo of the pinfeather whorl (a.k.a. crest) on the shoulder of the wing of a baby Budgie. This whorl shapes all shoulder feathers neatly around the shoulder joint for efficient flying. All birds have this configuration.

Going forward

I developed both Red Violet Clearwings and Amethyst Clearwings by noticing the variation in the reddish or pinkish sheen on some Violet and Cinnamonwing Violet birds. I dreamed of creating ever-better red or pink tones in these birds. So, I just retained and bred from the best of them. It took about seven generations to get there. I challenge you to dream up better colours or patterns in your own birds of any variety – it is not very hard at all. I should mention that DNA modifiers (tandem repeats) are unstable, so you will need to constantly upgrade them, otherwise they will decline.

I was lucky enough to breed a number of Black Eyed Whites with very good white body and wing colour, and I bought an Ernie Wise White Dilute with modern head and feathering. Four generations later, I had amazing Black Eyed Whites (see photos). It can be done – all with DNA modifiers; not with genes as such.

Above: An aviary full of Black Eyed Whites – a modifier-based variety.

Right: As close as I ever got to perfection in a Black Eyed White. All her colour perfection is modifier-based, and so is her feathering.

Creating the Modern UK Budgerigar

The Modern UK and European Exhibition Budgerigar is a very complex construction. Apart from most colours and varieties, its heredity is not really understood, so this is an attempt to give breeders a better insight into what is going on in the size, shape, feathering and many other aspects. Every aspect of Modern Exhibition Budgies is hereditary, but almost no genes are involved at all.

During the 1950s in the UK, breeders began selecting for Budgies with larger heads and overall greater size. Soon, lush and long feathering appeared all over these Exhibition birds. For a while, breeders selected for ever-bigger heads caused by lusher and longer feathering, until the birds became cumbersome and problematic. Long flight feathers impeded flight, and luxuriant vent feathering impeded successful mating and fertilisation. The birds had become dysfunctional.

Breeders began a long process of refining and shortening the feathers on the body, wings and tail, while retaining the amazing head and mask feathering: the modern 'Carrot Shape' (see 'Long tail and flight mechanisms' on page 178). They also developed wide directional feathering and a behavioural alteration where the birds

This is a Modern Australian Opaline Light Green Normal Budgie, featuring the carrot-like shape. Notice the long mask, the towering forehead and the large spots.

held their head feathers erect most of the time. Directional feathering is made up of longer feathers between the cere and the eyes on the sides of the forehead. This and the erect head feathering created the appearance of even bigger heads.

How did they do it?

Well, no one did any proper research into the hereditary aspects of it, they just selected for 'improvements'. This is the basic sort of selection used by humanity for thousands of years, in selecting ever better tiny changes in plants and animals: wheat with slightly larger seeds, apples with slightly larger fruit, or wolves with slightly more placid temperaments (i.e. domestic dogs).

Genes do not do this sort of tiny bit-by-bit change. They make huge differences such as producing Albinos or Dilutes or Opalines. So what hereditary mechanism is at play here? What drives tiny incremental hereditary changes that eventually add up to major changes? Here we leave the outdated world of Mendelian genetics and enter the world of modifiers.

Hereditary modifiers

This phrase is the key to understanding 95% of all heredity. It is the main game. Mendelian genetics is only a tiny part of heredity. Modern Exhibition Budgies and all other examples of plant and animal 'excellence' are in general due to hereditary modifiers such as tandem

Top-quality Australian Heritage Clearwings are 95% modifiers, made up of tandem repeats and the electrome. These controllers of genes create spectacular colours, create magical posture and pass them on to their babies.

Big head, short flight feathers and pizzazz! This male is a Seafoam White Cap Rainbow Australian Heritage Exhibition Budgerigar. You can have style and colour without huge size and too much feathering. There is room for both types of Budgies.

repeats and the newly discovered electrome. These modifiers are located in all plant and animal DNA. Mostly, each group of modifiers controls the expression of one particular gene. You could regard the genes as factories and the modifiers as the management and staff that run the factories. Each gene could have from 0 to 100 of a particular modifier that tell it what to do. One modifier might make barely noticeable change, but 20, all ganged together, will make a clearly visible change, and 100 of them can make huge changes.

It takes thousands of different modifiers to create the Modern Exhibition Budgerigar. Some create long or coarse feathering all over while others limit the coarse feathering to only certain areas: e.g. the head. And with modifiers, you get blending inheritance: that is, the young are roughly halfway between mum and dad. But this is best seen within closely related lines. That is within lines of similar exhibition birds.

As long as you breed Modern Budgie to Modern Budgie, all is fine. However, if you mate a Modern Exhibition Budgie to a 1962 Heritage-style Budgie, all hell breaks loose. There are vast numbers of modifiers that are totally different between these two groups, so the hybridising results are, in a word, catastrophic. In brief:

1. In the UK, in about 1950, Modern Showbirds were being developed with huge amounts of feathering caused by modifiers.
2. Then breeders developed another hereditary mechanism to shorten the ugly bits of feathering: long flights, long tail feathers, etc, were drastically reduced. But they retained the long feathers on the head and mask to dominate and create the 'carrot shape'.
3. In a way, the modern bird is a hand-grenade: tightly held together, but ready to explode if you pull the pin. Genetic mechanisms fighting among themselves to keep some feathers long, and others short.
4. If you cross one of these Modern Budgies to a short-feathered 1960s bird, you immediately remove the 'hold everything together' modifiers, leaving the 'long feathers all over' modifiers to explode. You have pulled the pin. The young are almost like messy feather dusters.

The electrome

The electrome is the biggest discovery in science in a long time. All bodies of animals and plants are strongly affected by an electronic system called the electrome, which lays down the blueprint for all bodies of animals and plants. Here, we are only looking at the electrome's effect in modifying genes. The electrome controls the growth of arms, wings, everything. They neatly explain how Chimeras (half-siders) successfully unite, how all crests and Hagoromos develop, and why some Hagoromos create holes in the bird's skulls causing neurological problems.

The electrome controls genes much as the bits of DNA called tandem repeats do. As I have long said: genes are just the factories and tandem repeats and the electrome includes the workers and management that control them.

How much damage have you done? Can you fix it?

This is the nub of the issue. If the pure 1960s-style Heritage Budgies that you crossed to were Clearwings, they too have vast numbers of hereditary modifiers, but in their case the modifiers are for body and wing colour. You are now juggling an impossibly great number of modifiers for just about everything. BUT since Standards of Perfection constantly drift on to ever-greater extremes, soon you will need to outcross again to catch up with yet **Another New Standard!** Put simply, Clearwings don't have a chance. And this is the reason for Clearwings doing so badly in terms of wing and body colour in the UK and Europe. UK and European breeders have not been able to breed Clearwings with good body colour and clear wings since they arrived from Australia in 1935. That is, for around 70 years. It is not that they are bad breeders, but rather that they have been fed the wrong inheritance mechanisms to achieve better colour and feathering.

Some of the older leaders in the UK and Europe are still feeding out the wrong hereditary theories, thus, in my opinion, sabotaging the Clearwing and many other modifier-based varieties. Put another way, ruining the fun that their

Whatever else, this Modern Showbird is a mess. These sorts of bloody feathers are way too common. The cause is excessive feathering that tends to rupture. There is a need to ease back a little on the excess feathering and finesse the Modern Show Budgerigar.

This is the Perpetual Standard of Perfection, chosen by the Australian Heritage Budgerigar Association. It was originally the Australian National Standard of Perfection in 1962. It can never be changed except for adding new colours and varieties or for fixing any errors. This prevents the 'show drift' which pushes Budgies to unacceptable extremes.

members could have had in breeding many beautiful Budgerigars.

If Clearwings were a simple mutation, this problem would not occur. But, we have to deal with the 'curse of the ever-changing standard'. One simple answer is to put modifier-based varieties with superb colour or wonderful crests into Heritage classes at shows, to be judged under an older Standard of Perfection which can never be altered. This is what we have done in Australia. These birds will be a very useful hereditary colour reservoir for improving the colours of Clearwings and other modifier-based varieties and colours that are exhibited in the Modern Exhibition classes.

The curse of the Standard

One area of concern is that all of us see today's Standard as a finished, stable image. It never occurs to us when we see a winning bird, that it is a snapshot in time of a conformation that is intrinsically bound to change; in fact, the Standard is changing at every show every week. It drifts unnoticed to ever-greater extremes.

At every exhibition, it changes slightly. Over a year it moves quite a lot. I call this 'show drift'.

This inevitably creates a non-level playing field. The judges who travel to show after show, either exhibiting or judging, absorb an exquisitely accurate view of the changing trends in the Standard. So, without being totally aware of it, they have a clear **vision of the future**: i.e. where the evolving standard is heading. This enables them to breed ahead of the Standard, thus virtually guaranteeing them success as an exhibitor. The ordinary exhibitor has much less of an idea of what is winning, and may even have left their best bird at home.

So, judges have a considerable advantage over the average exhibitor. It should be understood that most judges judge for free, so as hard-working club officials, they do deserve both trust and support. This is not corrupt behaviour, but it is **insider knowledge**.

Nonetheless, the bird is stylish and has pizzazz. A slightly smaller bird with less feathering and narrower shoulders would be better for the bird's welfare.

However, the wing markings are terrible. They are a mix of greyish green, yellow and black. The type 1 wing pattern with jet black and clear yellow would be much better.

It is time to re-evaluate the Standards and give the club members their say as to what is best.

There are two simple, alternative answers to this problem:

1. Create a permanent Standard that can never change – **thus ending 'show drift'.** This is the solution that 100% of the Australian Heritage Budgerigar Association's members voted for. The only exceptions are for changes such as fixing mistakes, and the addition of new colours and varieties.

   OR

2. The judges' committee sends out to all members, say, six monthly updates (with photos) on **where the Standard is heading**: i.e. what fashion trends have

The Budgerigar
Association of America
**PICTORIAL
IDEAL 2002
SIDE VIEW**

This is a case of taking the Standard of Perfection to extremes. This huge bird's forward vision is obviously impeded. This huge amount of feathering is clearly beyond the ability of this species to sustain.

arisen and/or how much more of certain features are now required. If continuously changing Standards of Perfection are to continue, it would be, in my opinion, quite improper not to keep club members constantly up to date on changes in judging priorities.

No system is perfect. Some judges can easily identify who owned or bred particular Budgies in a class at a show. Or maybe one recognisable bird to be judged has won Grand Champion at the previous show, so it is well known. This is inevitable, but judges should be trusted to do the right thing, even if the exhibitor is a friend. Overall, judges are hard-working and devoted people. It is their system that is unfair. We just need to give them a better system to work with.

It is time to consider the 'Colour and Standards Committees' that most clubs have. Democratic constitutions require the members to make all-important decisions, yet these committees largely dictate what they think is best. When you look at most modern Standards of Perfection, it is clear that they have gone way too far. The Standards cause wing-feather cysts, flightless and tailless wonders, bloodied foreheads, blocked vents, and feather dusters. Australian Heritage Budgerigars and Bush Budgies almost never get these problems.

The phrase to cover this modern breeding is 'genetic cruelty'.

Precisely the same problem occurred in Norwich Canaries between 1930 and 1940. In R.B. Bennett's 1961 book *Budgerigars, Canaries and Foreign Finches*, he states: "The craze for size appeared to take precedence over all else, with the result that a huge, ungainly bird was being produced, long-feathered and excessively browed. Unfortunately size seemed to be the most important factor, and consequently a great deal of double-buffing* was resorted to. Feather-lumps developed rapidly on scapulars and body, no doubt due to the excess feather and abnormal size, and the supremacy of the Norwich Plainhead began to wane."

Modern Exhibition Budgies are losing popularity and are encountering the same health issues. After the excesses of the 1940s, Norwich Canary breeders reduced the size and feathering of Norwich Canary and its popularity and health gradually recovered.

Are we able to learn from history?

Directional feather

To win on the show bench today, you simply must have directional feather. But how do you develop it in your birds? I have spent some years trying to sort it all out, and I am starting to make some headway. There are two issues to look at... What is directional feather, and how is it passed on from parents to chicks?

What is emerging is rather strange, so please bear with me. The way it seems to work

---

* Double-buffing is when two overly feathered birds are mated together.

is quite simple, but it may rattle your cage a bit. Please willingly suspend your disbelief until you have finished reading this attempt to sort it all out.

What is directional feather?

Try as I might I can't find any significant change in the direction of feather growth in birds with superb directional feather. It mostly seems to be longer feathers at either side of the cere, rather than a major change in the angle of growth.

As I have tried to work out Crested Budgies, it emerged that they aren't crested at all, but rather have feather whorls. Feather and hair whorls are very common in normal birds and mammals. You have one on the back of your head. Whorls act to change the direction of feather or hair growth to aid in streamlining, to avoid hair or feather snags as the animal brushes against hard objects and also to shed water efficiently.

Some wild species of parrots, e.g. Monk (Quaker) Parakeets, have a feather whorl just above the cere.

This is a young miniature Albino Budgerigar which did not develop directional feather and which was bred from birds which did not carry any directional feather genes. Note that his pin feathers are angled exactly the same as directional feathers are. Note also how all the facial pin feathers form a radial crest: they all radiate out from the same point towards the top of the cere, between the nostrils.

In this position, a few feathers overhang the cere, some go to the left and others to the right, but most go straight back over the skull. In this way the whorl is very useful. If the centre of the whorl moves a few millimetres back towards the middle of the skull, you would call this a full circular crest. But in the wild Monk Parakeets it is virtually invisible due to the central dot being right in the cleft at the middle of the cere.

I am now almost certain that all birds and definitely all parrots are crested. That is, they have a whorl on the front of their head. Please just read on …

The centre of the whorl is covered by either the cere or the beak itself. That little dot that marks the centre of the whorl on the heads of all wild birds is overgrown by the beak and cere as the embryo develops in the egg. All that remains is feathers growing back over the skull and to the left and right of the cere: that is, the whorl moulds the feathers over the head in a superbly streamlined way. The central dot disappears under the cere, etc.

Note that the widest part of the head on a Budgie with directional feather, when viewed from above and behind the bird, is either side of the cere. A bird that does not carry the directional feather gene is widest between the eyes. This right-hand bird is drawn from a wild Budgerigar. This drawing is slightly exaggerated to show the differences.

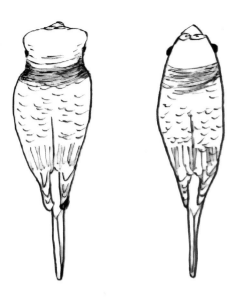

So, directional feather is the end result of a facial feather whorl which is identical to what we call a crest in Budgerigars.

So what has changed?

If my theory is correct, all that has changed is that the feathers on either side of the cere are longer than they used to be. The length of these 'directional feathers' pushes them out in front of the eyes. It is also remotely possible that something has changed the angles of the whorl as well.

How is it passed on?

Mercifully, it seems to be passed on really simply as a sex-linked recessive gene: that is, it is identical to Cinnamonwing or Opaline in its mode of transmission. So, let's do some numbers:

1. A male with superb directional feather mated to a female with none (and no history of it) will produce:
   All males with no directional feather (but split for it) and
   All females with directional feather.
   … males can be split for directional feather, but females can't.
   However:
2. A female with superb directional feather mated to a male with none (and with NO family members with directional feather) will produce:
   All males with no directional feather (but split for it)
   All females with no directional feather and **not** split for it.
   … that is, females with superb directional feather, when mated to males with no directional feather, will never produce any babies with directional feather unless the male is split for it.
3. If you mate a split male from mating #1 above, to a non-directional feathered female, you get:
   25% males split for directional feather
   25% males not split for directional feather

25% females with directional feather

25% females not carrying the directional feather at all.

… so only one female out of four babies (on average) will have directional feather.

To go beyond these matings, just look up charts for either Cinnamonwing or for Opaline and substitute the words directional feather for either Opaline or Cinnamonwing and you will get the expectations.

In my matings, it is looking like the gene for directional feather could be linked to Cinnamonwing or Opaline, but I am not convinced. What I am getting is lots of females that are Opaline Cinnamonwing birds with lovely directional feather. I suspect that other matings will see this as coincidence. Nonetheless, it proves the genetic basis of directional feather: sex-linked.

What about extra-wide directional feather?

This is emerging as a gene volume control issue: that is, blending inheritance. Long directional feather to shortish directional feather gives mostly medium-length directional feathers.

Although Mendel's work indicates that blending inheritance can't happen, in fact it does and it's very common.

So, once you have directional feather in all of your birds, as you select gradually for longer and longer buffalo horns (feathers) so your birds will get more of it.

So much of exhibition qualities are controlled by gene volume controls. These are long sections of DNA that are not genes, but they do control the extent of influence of one or more genes. So nature (or breeders) can ramp up the effect of almost any gene. Or ramp it down for that matter. You can get:

- Clearer wings on Clearwings
- Less yellow pigment on the bodies of Yellow Faced Blues
- Coarser or finer feathers
- Bigger or smaller birds
- Bigger or smaller spots
  … and so on.

Some of you must still be grumbling about the crest bit of all this. If all Budgies are crested, what on Earth are true Crested Budgies?

I suspect that what we call Crested Budgies either:

a. Have the centre of the whorl (crest) genetically moved further back on the head, or

b. Have a second whorl just behind the normal one. This is not so silly since you do get Budgies with multiple crests on their backs, wings and even chests.

By now I suppose that you all think that I am mad. Maybe you're right. Let me know your experiences and thoughts.

A story of love and hate

If there is one thing that bedevils Budgie breeders it is the dreaded issue of **long tail feathers and long flight feathers**. Particularly when you try to produce that very **loooong mask or a big head!** Long tails and flights are also a problem when you try to upgrade old-fashioned varieties such as Clearwings. My discoveries confirm that long tails, long flight feathers and curly, messy flight feathers, etc, are the same basic thing, all by-products of the one hereditary mechanism that is not a gene. It is a modifier that produces tiny changes in feather length. In this section, for simplicity, I will refer to long primary flight feathers and/or curly secondary flight feathers as long flights.

The feathers are covering its eyes.

This pair of 'clearwings' is the result of crossing Clearwings to European Exhibition Normal Budgies to 'improve them'. Note the long and messy primary flight feathers on the Blue male and the long, droopy primary flight feathers on the Green female. These birds are the result of a disastrous crossing: note the very heavily marked wing feathers and the absence of full body colour in the male. The female's body colour is OK, but her wing markings are dreadful.

Back in the 1960s when the first English Budgies arrived in Australia, the Australian judges used to often wrong-class long-flighted and long-tailed Budgies. They refused to judge them. During those early introductions of English Show Budgies into Australia, virtually 100% of the hybrid Australian/English birds had excessively long flights and tails, even though their parents all had short tails and flights.

This is a young Clearwing that is the result of outcrossing to European Exhibition Budgies. Look at how the secondary flight feathers are overgrowing the primary flight feathers. By maturity, the secondary flight feathers will be a jumbled mess. In many ways jumbled up secondary flight feathers are the worst of all long wing feathers.

It is now more than 50 years later and it has taken me this long to work it all out. And the theory is a weird one:
a. There is no gene specifically for long tails and flights.
b. But long tails and flights **are** hereditary.
c. And the problem is fairly easy to fix.

This is a 50-odd year mystery for me, so perhaps it is useful to explore the mystery as it unfolded.

More than 25 years ago I decided to try to upgrade two Australian Heritage varieties: Clearwings and Australian Clearbodies (a.k.a. Darkwings). So I crossed tiny purebred Australian Heritage Clearwings with fine feathers, to Modern Exhibition Normals with modern, coarse feathering. All of the young had enormously long tails and flights, but both parents had very short tails and flights. Every feather on the parent Heritage Clearwing was fine and very short. The Modern Exhibition Normal parent had overall coarse feather and lovely, short and tidy tail and flight feathers.

This cross between two contrasting lines, each of which was totally purebred for the characteristics under scrutiny (i.e. overall feather length and short tail and flight feathers), is precisely the method pioneered by Gregor Mendel for identifying the underlying genetic patterns. I bred around 300 babies from this type of cross over many years: Heritage Budgies with **short** tails and flights to Modern Budgies with **short** tails and flights, to produce 300 babies, all with **long** tails and flights.

It was this mating of purebred old style to purebred new style that yielded the answer. This is the classic sort of cross used in genetic research to this day, and it is the lack of this type of disciplined mating (plus a lack of meticulous record keeping) that has prevented Budgie breeders from making urgently needed breeding breakthroughs. Mating two relatively Modern Showbirds together will never allow you to discover the underlying mechanisms so that you can conquer long tails and flights. Nor will it help you understand most other hereditary exhibition qualities either.

Very long primary flight feathers: the tail feathers would also be very long. Commonly, breeders frame out the excessively long tails (as has happened here) to avoid embarrassment.

Can you guess the answer that emerged to the long flight issue?

The problem was not with the Budgies but with myself. The hybrid birds that I had produced had long feathers on the mask – great! Long feathers on the head – great! Long feathers on the body – great! And long feathers on the tail and flights – yuck! The birds all had longer feathers all over – what else would you expect the long feather hereditary mechanism to do? This is what the basic long feather mechanism does. It was only my selective viewing that screamed "the tail and flight feathers are too long". Put another way, we tend to notice the long tails and flight feathers (since we **hate** them) but not to notice that these ugly tails and flight feathers are caused by the same hereditary mechanism that causes the long mask and head feathers that we **love. They are all one and the same thing: all feathers are longer!**

This Violet Rainbow has long and messy primary flight feathers which are too big to fold up neatly. Its colour has also been artificially enhanced.

The theory

So, I thought that I should try to come up with a theory that explains what could be going on. Obviously, a mechanism that increases the length of a Budgie's feathers will lengthen ALL of the Budgie's feathers equally: including the wing and tail feathers. Thus, early large-headed birds in the UK in the 1940s and 1950s had dreadfully long tails and flight feathers. To tidy the large-headed birds up a bit, exhibition breeders must, without realising it, have found a mutation or other hereditary mechanism that shortens ONLY the wing and tail feathers leaving the long head, mask and body feathers alone. The theory goes this way:

1. The hereditary mechanisms for long feather originated in England or elsewhere in Europe and proliferated because of the cold weather and also from selection pressure from exhibition breeders for larger heads and longer masks.
2. This long feather hereditary mechanism acts a bit like a semi-dominant gene.
3. Originally **all** long-feathered birds had long tails and flight feathers, which looked messy and which infuriated judges. This is recorded in several UK Budgie books of the time, for example Cyril Rogers's 1981 book *The World of Budgerigars*.
4. Eventually a recessive mutation for disproportionately short tails and flights occurred at a different gene locus. That is, a gene that allowed the feathers on the head, mask and body to stay long but which shortened the tail and flight feathers.
5. This mutant gene for disproportionately short tail and flight feathers is recessive to the gene that normally controls the **proportionate** length of tail and flight feathers in wild Budgies.

This pair of Australian Heritage Clearwings have beautifully balanced and coloured wings. They have short flight and tail feathers, and short feathers everywhere else.

Right: This Modern European Showbird has short flight feathers, but long feathers everywhere else: particularly on its head. If you mate the Clearwings above with short flight and tail feathers, to this bird with short flight and tail feathers, but long feathers everywhere else together, you will get 100% of babies with LONG flight and tail feathers (and reasonably long feathers everywhere else).

Pure Australian Heritage Clearwings are homozygous for the old dominant wild gene for **proportional** length feathers: the feathers in all parts, including the flight feathers, are proportioned just the same as they are in a Wild Budgerigar. They are also homozygous for the wild gene for **short** feathers all over. Modern Show Budgies are homozygous for the recessive mutant gene for **extra-short** tails and flights and also homozygous for the semi-dominant mutant hereditary mechanism for **long** feathers all over.

All of the hybrids from a first-cross hybrid are heterozygous for everything:

Long feather mechanism + short feather gene = medium-long feather appearance (phenotype).

Long tail and flights gene + extra short tail and flights recessive gene = long tail and flights phenotype.

That is, the hybrids should be fairly coarse (compared to the original Clearwings) with rather long tails and flights. This is exactly what you get.

Right: Is this really what we want? Messy tails and messy flight feathers? Needless to say, these birds with long and messy flight feathers do not fly very well either.

The proof

If the theory is correct, when you mate two of the F1 hybrids from the mating above together, you should get (roughly):

1 in 16 birds with long feathers and short tails and flights

3 in 16 birds with long feathers and long tails and flights

2 in 16 birds with medium-length feathers and short tails and flights

6 in 16 birds with medium-length feathers and tails

1 in 16 birds with short feathers and disproportionately short tails and flights

3 in 16 birds with short feathers and short (Normal) tails and flights.

It is the second-last of these results that will prove or disprove the theory. I went back over my detailed records to see if the results confirmed all of the predictions of the theory. Did I get roughly one bird in 16 that had short feathers in general and tails and flights so short that it looked silly? Yes I did. Some had very short tails and flights indeed. Did the rest of the predictions pan out? Yes they did, but as usual, some of the numbers were a bit out. Since the original proposal of this two hereditary mechanisms theory, I have raised hundreds more babies from the same crosses and all of the results support the theory.

What does it mean?

What it means is this… To breed short tails and flights you can't just select for parents with short tails and flights. You need to select for birds **with long feathers overall** but with short tails and flights as well. Equally, hybrid long tailed and flighted birds which have one parent with both long feathers all over AND short tail and flights are very useful to breed from – much like any birds split for a desirable gene. So, within strains of Modern Show Budgies, short tails and flights behave like a simple recessive gene.

To breed the desirable birds with long masks and short tails, you simply must train yourself to easily distinguish birds with the long mask and head feathers plus **short** tail and flights **from** birds with long mask and head feathers plus **long** tail and flights.

To upgrade **Heritage** varieties, choose Modern Showbirds with very long feathers but very short tails and flights. Don't expect short tails and flights in the first generation, but you should get about three birds in 16 in the F2 (two hybrids mated together) with reasonable length of feather but short tails and flights. These birds should breed true for short tails and flights if crossed together since the short flight and tail feather gene is recessive.

You must avoid back-crossing your new modernised Heritage Budgies to the original Heritage stock. For Heritage variety (e.g. Clearwing) breeders PLEASE NOTE: If you breed a modernised Clearwing with coarse feather and short flight and tail feathers to a Heritage fine-feathered bird you will bring back the awful issue of messy flight and tail feathers **all over again**. Stick to breeding your modernised Heritage birds to each other…. And be patient while you attend to juggling varietal characteristics and feather types together.

I would be interested in other breeders' views on this new theory. So far, it works for me. Obviously, some smaller gene modifiers (e.g. for length of mask) may be discovered to help finesse the perfect feathering in Modern Showbirds, but the main game is outlined above.

One last bit… This is a way-out guess, but there could be a link between tailless wonders (circovirus) and the disproportionately short tail and flight feather gene. This newly-discovered recessive mutation reduces the length of flight and tail feathers: it could also reduce the vigour of the flight and tail feathers. This fits in with my observation that I have never had a tailless wonder (i.e. circovirus victim with missing flight and tail feathers) among my old-fashioned short-feathers-all-over birds. This is surprising since I breed them both side by side and I have experimented with cross-fostering their babies. One supporting observation is that none of my Heritage birds get wing- or tail-feather cysts either.

If the disproportionately short tail and wing feather gene is **not** related to flightless and tailless wonders, it then certainly must be related to the basic long and coarse feather all over gene(s). **No long/coarse feathers = no circovirus and no wing feather cysts**.

So, as I said at the start – there is no specific gene for long tails or flight feathers. We are merely failing to notice that the long feather hereditary mechanism gives us long feathers all over the bird. But there is a gene mutation for **disproportionately short tails and flights** … and it is recessive.

Below are two photos of a Modern European Exhibition Budgerigar with wing-feather cysts. I have bred more than 3,000 Heritage and Bush Budgies over 60 years, and none of them have ever had wing-feather cysts.

This is a Modern European Exhibition Budgie with the feather-loss virus circovirus, which causes wingless or tailless wonders. Again, I have never had either a Bush Budgie or an Australian Heritage Budgerigar with this disease. However, both Bush and Heritage Budgies do get French moult, which is a different viral disease.

- Semi-dominant means partially dominant. That is, it behaves a bit like Spangle – cross a Double Factor Spangle to a Normal and the Single Factor Spangles produced are roughly halfway between the two parents in appearance. In feather length, cross long to short and you tend to get **medium**. New research indicates that most if not all genes have both on/off switches and volume control mechanisms as well. These can produce 'blending inheritance' rather like semi-dominant genes do and these are probably the major cause of the typical blending inheritance that we see in most highly variable exhibition characteristics. So, on top of the basic mutations here, we also have gene volume controls adding a bit more of refinement to feather length and width, etc. These switches and volume controls were once thought to be 'modifier genes' – this concept now seems rather obsolete in most cases – the newer discoveries have revealed a far more functional and sophisticated system.

This is a very nice Modern Darkwing ruined by long flights and tail, which are caused by outcrossing a Heritage Exhibition Budgie to a Modern Showbird.

Below is a point form list of the basics of my theory. It may help people a lot, but please don't publish this box without the full article. As I have mentioned elsewhere, I still haven't recovered from the then editor dropping the details of my crest theory article in 1963. Looking back, that editor's decision to drop the guts of my work set crest breeding back by about 50 years.

• Breeding ever-longer masks, and longer head and body feathers in show Budgies **causes** tails and flight feathers to also get ever-longer as well.
• But there is a way of fixing this problem. A mutant recessive gene exists that shortens only tail and flight feathers.
• Short tails and flights in Modern Showbirds are created by one single recessive mutant gene. This gene leaves mask, head and body feathers long, but shortens the tail and flight feathers.
• In the mad scramble for ever-longer mask feathers, breeders have unconsciously overlooked the fact that they have gone back to breeding from long-tailed and long-flighted birds when they are selecting for stupendously long masks. This is a very serious mistake. There are obviously trade-offs here, but we all must return to breeding **only** from birds with overall long feathering **combined** with short tails and flights, **or from birds who carry** the recessive gene for short tails and flights (i.e. birds which have one parent with overall long feathering but with short tail and flights).
• This will slow down the progress towards the perfect loooong mask, but it is an essential step to take. Patience is more than a virtue, it is **the** technique used by **all** great breeders.

True Crested Budgies

The Modern Exhibition Budgerigar is a spectacular example of the first truly Crested Budgerigar. A true bird crest consists of longer head feathers in a certain area, which can be erected for display or communication (think of a Sulphur-crested Cockatoo). This is exactly what the Modern Exhibition Budgie has; a magnificent arrangement of frontal head feathers that the bird expands upwards, outwards and forward. The best specimens maintain this display for most of the day. This modern crest is a development of the much more subtle forehead 'blow' that all male Budgies (even Wild Budgies) have – it is a sort of 'Hey, look at me' signal that males use to attract the females. Both male and female Bush Budgerigars also erect their facial feathers as a sign of aggression.

What we have previously called 'crests' are in fact feather **whorls**. Whorls exist all over birds and mammals: you have one on the back of your head. Whorls exist

Right: This is a Modern European Exhibition Budgerigar showing the extreme true crest of very long and wide facial feathering fully erected. You could well argue that the mask is part of the crest since Modern Showbirds erect their long mask feathers to embrace the beak.

mainly for streamlining; they arrange the growth of feathers or hair so that the hair or feathers complement the contours of the bird or mammal. Whorls cause the feathers to grow out radially to hug the tightest contours on birds and mammals: to permit smooth airflow and to shed rain. The most critically important feather whorl is on the scapulars – see the scapular whorl below.

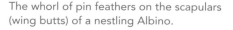

The whorl of pin feathers on the scapulars (wing butts) of a nestling Albino.

Close-up of the scapular whorl.

All birds have a whorl on the point of each of their scapulars. This allows the wing coverts to exquisitely tightly hug the three-dimensional aerodynamic challenge of the wing's 'shoulder'. The feathers have to hug the topside and underside of the wing and to bend around the edges as well. This creates the streamlining necessary for efficient flight.

There are many other whorls all over the Budgie, and us as well (for example, they are visible on the chest and back of hairy men). My theory is that all birds also have a whorl right in the middle of their faces to make all face feathers grow radially outwards and curved backwards away from the wind. The central 'dot' of the whorl is probably under the beak or near the top of the cere. This is evident in the Modern Showbird below left.

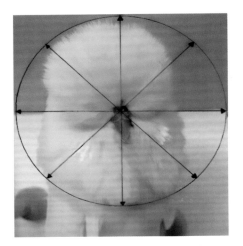

If you look carefully at this pin-feather stage baby Albino Budgie (above right), you can see that all the facial feathering appears to grow outwards radially from a spot in the central notch in the top of the cere. To test this theory, I guessed that some birds just might have a higher, visible dot just above the cere.

After poring over hundreds of photos of parrots, I did find some photos of normal wild-type Monk (Quaker) Parakeets which clearly show the visible central whorl dot (see below). These are not crested birds – this is how most or all wild Monk (Quaker) Parakeets are: it is just that their wild-type facial whorl dot is about 3mm higher than it is in other species. Which makes the magical dot visible.

Monk (Quaker) Parakeets. Photo: Christopher DeNatale.

You might notice that the short feathers below the central whorl dot on the Monk (Quaker) Parakeets grow down over the cere, possibly providing some protection. Presumably, this need for cere protection was the cause of the higher than usual, visible central whorl dot.

The more that you look at Modern Exhibition Budgies, the more it becomes apparent that this is indeed the first true crest in the Budgerigar. Earlier birds referred to as 'Crests' were in fact Budgies with an extra feather whorl on the top of their heads.

From all of this, the most important issue in breeding crests is the location of the centre of the whorl. Birds with off-centre whorls are never worth breeding from.

Advanced variety information

Golden Budgies

Would you like to breed Golden Lutinos or Golden Double Factor Spangles or Golden Black Eyed Yellows or even Golden Dark Eyed Clears? It appears that all over the world, particularly among the Rainbow Budgie breeders, there are many variants on the golden-yellow mutations. Look at the Pied below …

This is the best yellow colour that I have seen on a Budgerigar since Dave Pogson's Lutinos way back in the 1960s. It was given to me by Connie Kuitert, who is a very savvy pet Budgerigar breeder. She knows exactly what colours people want. She is also very generous in giving me such an amazing bird. In the photo, the bird is not fully moulted out, hence the immature blue area near its vent.

Connie also gave me his sister, so I bred them together to see what would happen. They bred Dark Greens and Double Factor Australian Golden Faced Blues(!), as well as more rich Golden babies. Here, I am ignoring the Pied effects.

What I have worked out is that both parents are Greens split for Australian Golden Faced Blue. Why this should create a rich golden overall colouration, including the body, is still a bit of a mystery, but it does. However, I realise that Single Factor Australian Golden Faced Blues do have a greenish body colour.

Opposite is a pair of Australian Golden Top Mauve Rainbows for comparison. Note that very little yellow colour appears on the wings and the body. But the rich golden face is similar to the above hybrid Australian Golden Faced Blue x Green birds.

So, if you want to breed all-over golden-coloured Lutinos, Black Eyed Yellows, Double Factor Spangles, etc, cross some Australian Golden Faced Blue into these yellow lines. Maybe use a male Lutino mated to a female Golden Faced Blue. If the male is Double Factor for the Yellow gene and the female is Single Factor for the Australian Golden Faced Blue gene you should get roughly half of the young females that are Golden Lutinos.

Let us know what you get!

The colour yellow

There are only two pigments in Budgies: the Golden-Yellow-Red-UV group and the Black-Brown group. All come in many shades, but in this section we will look at the Golden-Yellow.

Yellow is very variable, and often poorly observed. For instance, no one noticed that Double Factor Greens carry a different shade of yellow from Greens split for Blue. Below are two young Red Violet Dark Green Clearwings. The one on the left is split for Blue and the one on the right is a homozygous Green. They are both from the same line of Clearwings, but the one on the right is from homozygous Greens and is a much brighter and deeper shade of Yellow.

Back in the 1960s, Dave Pogson in Sydney bred amazing Lutinos: they were almost orange, and their primary flight feathers were a deeper yellow than the body colour of today's best Lutinos. He gave me a pair of incredibly-coloured Lutinos, which I line bred for even greater depth of colour. After three more generations, they were orange. No one wanted them, or my crests either. So they were sold off to junior novice breeders.

319

Lutino with typical silvery-yellow forehead.

All Green Budgies have a silvery light yellow cap (i.e. forehead), which is a much lighter shade of yellow than elsewhere on the bird's body. It is easiest to see in Lutinos such as the bird on the left. The forehead is, however, awash with UV yellow, which we mere humans struggle to see at all. Somehow, deep down, I guess this all relates to White Caps (note the very pale ghost mask spots too!).

In Golden Tops, the forehead is very yellow indeed. The bird below is a classic example of a Double Factor Golden Top (it is also a Double Factor Spangle).

In their heyday (between 1930 and 1960), all Black Eyed Yellows were Double Factor Yellows. So far as I know, no Black Eyed Whites ever appeared from good-quality Black Eyed Yellows back then. The reason is simple – Double Factor Black Eyed Yellows are much richer golden yellow colour. Yellows split for White are a pale lemon yellow, usually with green showing through.

In their 1961 book *Genetics for Budgerigar Breeders*, Taylor and Warner imply that Greens split for Blue are indistinguishable from Double Factor Greens. They were mistaken. The new unnamed birds with the richly golden faces that I have bred recently are the brightest gold of the lot. As yet I know little about them except that they came from a cross between a White Cap and a Golden Faced Blue. Nor can I think of a name – maybe Golden Headed? I have investigated their UV colours and they are spectacular. BUT, unlike Australian Golden Faced Blues, they are of a superb exhibition quality whether they are Double Factor or not.

Golden Top showing rich yellow forehead.

On the left is a male Golden Headed Sky Normal. On the right is the same bird Normal under black UV ('Disco') lighting in a pitch-black room. His whole head glows with a rich golden UV colour. Other Parblue varieties under UV lighting glow a lemon colour. Note the golden striping on the back of his head in line with his mask, and also that his yellow wing markings are a pale purple-white under UV lighting.

On pages 85 and onwards I will go over the breeding of the traditional Yellow Faced Blues and Golden Faced Blues, White Caps, etc.

Heredity of patterns in Australian Dominant Pieds

I began a project to try to unravel the heritability of patterns in Dominant Pieds in 2010. To cut to the chase, it is now quite clear to me that most if not all seemingly random Dominant Pied patterns are hereditary, and what's more they are quite easy to breed.

It seems that there has been no previous systematic attempt to get to the bottom of Pied patterns in Budgerigars. Straight away my initial studies into many patterns collectively grouped under the vague term of 'Variegated Pied' or 'Reverse Pied' showed that there were indeed many strikingly different patterns that were both different **and** hereditary. Some of the truly lovely hereditary patterns discovered were:

1. 'Rumped Pied', which is a Reverse Pied (i.e. predominantly white or yellow) with a small area of stripes on the head and a spectacular splash of body colour on the rump – see below.

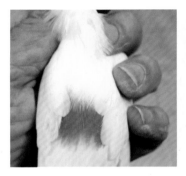

2. 'Collared Pied', which has a white band around the back of the head joining mask to mask around the back. Collared Pieds can be Reverse Pieds or even Banded Pieds. The collar pattern is part of the STRAIGHT LINE Pied pattern that I have discovered (see right and below). This pattern is massively important in Pied breeding, but until now has never been recorded. It forms the essential ruler-straight line seen in Banded Pieds and it tidies up most general Pied patterns. It also appears to assist with the bilateral symmetry seen in many Pieds.

3. There are many more pied patterns that are quite stable within families. Reverse Pieds with small flecks of body colour could easily be stabilised if breeders liked the look of them. Perhaps they could be called 'Starburst Pieds'?

Collared Dominant Pieds.

The Straight Line Pied pattern

This is a huge breakthrough in Pied breeding. The Straight Line pattern is without doubt what early Australian Pied breeders used to create the stunning ruler-straight 'Australian Banded Pieds' of yesteryear. There was a culture of secrecy with the breeders of the 1930s, 1940s and 1950s. For instance, Clearwings, Yellows and Whites were all mysteries to most Australian Budgie breeders. Articles on Clearwings were published in the Budgerigar magazines of the day, but they only dealt with the basic heredity of the variety – and the theory they put forward happened to be incorrect. The initial breeders kept their techniques and methods for **perfecting** Clearwings, Yellows and Whites to themselves. For example, Harold Peir, the creator of the Clearwing and probably of the creator of clear and bright Black Eyed Yellows and Whites, was very secretive about his methods according to his grandson Richard Henry Peir. He took them to his grave.

Variations on Banded Pieds.

Harold Peir was also exhibiting Banded Pieds in the 1930s and it seems likely that he may have developed the Banded Pied as well. There is evidence that the earliest Australian Dominant Pieds that appeared were Banded.

The Banded Pied breeders who followed on from Harold Peir also appear to have left no record of how they bred these lovely birds – maybe they bred them by sheer luck! This lack of information presumably led Ken Yorke to write in his *Budgerigar Variety Bible*, in reference to Banded Pieds, Clearflighted Pieds and Variegated Pieds: "These types are ideals only, the actual pattern is virtually impossible to control, being probably subject to modifiers and random development patterns during growth." My research disproves this statement. I can now pump out large numbers of precisely-patterned Pied Budgies quite reliably. It should also be noted that 40–50 years ago, some Pied breeders had aviaries full of nothing but Banded Pieds.

Please bear with me as I recount my experiences with other animals. I have bred pied cattle (Belted Galloways and Holstein-Friesians), pied horses (Tobianos, Overos, Sabinos and Splashed Whites), pied mice, pied finches and pied parrots: believe it or not, the hereditary patterns that control the shape and extent of white (or yellow) areas in all of them are reasonably similar.

Belted Galloway cattle. These are pied cattle with pattern modifiers.

Just as it is easy to breed beautifully marked Belted Galloway cattle (above), it is easy to breed beautiful belted Budgies (i.e. Banded Pieds). In both there are two basic mechanism groups at play. One controls the overall amounts of white (or yellow) and the other group of mechanisms controls the position, straightness and symmetry of the pied areas.

The real problem for Pied breeders is to teach yourself how to accurately observe your birds. Bands in Budgies and Belted Galloway cattle are caused by one major shaping mechanism. The basic pattern is based on a straight-line mechanism that controls the top line where pied meets body colour under the mask or neck. Once you set up this neat straight line, the rest is dead easy: just raise the bottom line of the band to an aesthetically pleasing result by selective breeding. Significant numbers of Straight Line Pieds (a form of Banded Pieds) are unfortunately discarded every year since breeders fail to realise their value. For my breeding experiments, I found my initial Straight Line Pieds in pet shops.

If you think that breeding Banded Pieds is difficult, Collared Pieds must be even worse: a finer line requiring far more precision. Yet it is also really easy. Then why has no-one ever developed a line of Collared Pieds?

The answer lies in how observant and disciplined you are. If you teach yourself how to pick partial collars, establishing a line of Collared Pieds is fast and easy. Look for bits of collar near the cheek patch or on the mask itself (see photo below) while the babies still have pinfeathers in the nest: pink skin and white or yellow pinfeathers. Look for wider head spots. Look at Rumped Pieds to see if the area at the back of the head, where the collar would be, are free of markings, maybe a few head stripes remain to define the edges of the collar. A partial collar is VERY useful.

Now for the messy bit – BUT YOU MUST MASTER THIS IF YOU ARE TO BE SUCCESS-FUL IN BREEDING BANDED OR COLLARED PIEDS. The hereditary mechanisms that control pied areas are separate from the Pied gene itself. To go further, Normal non-Pied birds from Banded or Collared Pied parents (i.e. Band-Bred Normals) are still likely to carry the shaping mechanisms. So, non-Pieds from nests of, say, Banded Pieds are VERY useful for breeding to Banded Pieds to produce more Banded Pieds. To repeat, it is best to call them Band-bred Normals.

This bird has a partial collar. If you look closely, you will see a partial collar coming from under the cheek patch towards the pied spot on the back of its head. When they join up, you have a collar.

Equally, breeding Pied to Pied is a really excellent way of honing your Pied markings. Presumably, if you breed Banded Pieds together, within a few generations they should be as perfect as Belted Galloway cattle or Boer goat's heads. Breeding NON-RELATED, NON-PIED NORMALS to Banded or Collared Pieds is a mistake. This will usually significantly damage the distribution and shape of the Pied markings in the young. And this practice is possibly what has given rise to all of the myths about Pied breeding.

It may seem crazy but all Budgies carry mechanisms that shape pied areas, EVEN IF THESE BUDGIES ARE NOT PIEDS AND HAVE NEVER HAD ANY PIED ANCESTORY. They carry unknown shaping mechanisms that may ruin the quality of your Banded Pieds, or occasionally they may perfect the bands.

After doing extensive research into Rumped Pieds, I have now established that they are either Single Factor or Double Factor (homozygous) Pieds which are Double Factor for the Band pattern mutation. When you mate two Banded Pieds together, approximately 25% of the Pied young will be Rumped Pieds. Mating a Banded Pied to a Rumped Pied will produce around 50% of the Pied young showing the Rumped Pied pattern. Rumped to Rumped produces 100% of the Pied young showing the Rumped Pied pattern. If at least one of the parents in any of these matings is a homozygous Dominant Pied, then 100% of all young will be Pieds. If not, only 50% of the young will be Pieds.

I have also discovered that Straight Line Pieds, Banded Pieds, and Winged Pieds are all various expressions of the Banded Pied dominant major modifier gene. Many, many other modifier elements combine together to thin, widen, bend or even partially obliterate the band. But with persistence, you can create a heritable ruler-straight band in most progeny like the belt in Galloway cattle.

These are Straight Line Pieds. The lines are not dead straight as these are aviary-bred mixed-breed pet-shop Budgies. Straight Line Pieds are just Pieds with very wide bands. Winged Pieds are Banded Pieds with the band broken in the middle. There are almost always bits of broken band underneath the wings (if you lift them up).

I test mated some Double Factor Pied, Rumped Pieds to Band-Bred Normals and all produced 100% Pied young. All of these young were more or less Banded Pieds. That is, all had bits of a band if you looked closely enough. A huge part of the problem with Pied breeding lies in the fact that most Pied breeders do not accurately record Pied patterns in their young. When you look for and record Pied patterns **and name them**, as I have done, the hereditary nature of the patterns is able to be worked out. You might note that ALL of my Rumped Pieds are also Collared Pieds (see various photos in this section).

To repeat, breeding Banded to Banded is the best mating of all, but it does often produce 25% Rumped Pieds and 25% Normals. The second best is mating a Banded Pied to Band-Bred Normal, i.e. one bred from Banded parents. This mating produces up to 50% Banded Pieds, even if some of the bands are a bit wonky. Equally, you could cross a Rumped Pied to a Band-bred Normal, and produce 100% Banded Pieds, even if some of the bands are barely visible. The overall percentage of Pied young depends on whether or not at least one of the parents is a Double Factor Pied.

It is SO much fun checking your nests of baby Pieds to see if any bands or collars are appearing. I am now getting 50% or more bands or collars in many nests. Not all bands or collars are perfect, but give me a few more generations …

Double and Triple Banded Pieds

In one of my earlier matings, I had a brood of eight young: the mating was of a Rumped Pied English Yellow Faced Violet to a Normal Double Factor Australian Yellow Faced Violet. Out of eight young, four are Normals and the other four are all Double Banded Pieds (see photos below). You might note that the lower band almost always forms a crescent shape, embracing the legs (which I think is very pretty). The Rumped Pied (dad) was bred from Straight Line Pieds (he is yet another Reverse Pied that is a Single Factor Pied). The Australian Yellow Faced Blue (mum) has no background in Pied breeding at all, however, I am reasonably sure that she is a BIG PART of the heredity of the Pied pattern here. This mating suggests that not all Rumped Pieds are Double Factor for the Banded modifier gene. That is, that Rumped Pieds are caused by a doubling up of the dominant pattern mechanism, rather than doubling up of the Pied gene itself.

Please allow me to explain. I have bred Dominant Pied (Overo) horses for more than 35 years and I have consistently found that the Quarter horse stallions that we breed to our Overo mares tend to dominate the patterns on our foals even though they are not Pieds themselves. Some stallions regularly reduce the Pied markings on the foals to just one blue eye, yet others

This is a Violet Australian/English Yellow Faced Double Banded Pied.

regularly produce nearly all-white foals. In all cases of Pied mutations that I have studied, the pattern genes (or gene modifiers) are totally separate from the Pied gene itself and are also carried by **all** animals of that species, including non-Pieds.

So, I believe that these Double Banded Pieds got a significant part of their pattern from mum (the Normal parent). Put another way, mum would be a future great producer of Double Banded Pieds, when mated to Pieds (especially Straight Line Pieds).

I predicted that it should be possible to breed a Straight Line-based Pied pattern with THREE BANDS: a double band as above, and a collar. Well, when I looked at these four Double Banded Pieds, the first three had partially developed collars and the fourth, a female Opaline, HAS A COLLAR AS WELL AS DOUBLE BANDS (see pics below). She is a TRIPLE BANDED PIED, the last photo of her shows the band around the back of her head. Sadly, when she is mature, we may struggle to see the collar due to the Opaline head colour.

Triple Banded Pieds can be bred

Below is the TRIPLE Banded Yellow Faced Violet Opaline Pied – the sibling of the bird in the photo above. The last photo shows her collar, making her the first recorded TRIPLE BANDED PIED: i.e. a Double Banded Pied WITH a collar.

It is hardly a new revelation, but all female Pieds, probably in all Pied mutations, have 20–30% less white or yellow than males do. Thus, you must make allowances for this when choosing birds that are compatible with each other for breeding purposes. As an example, all of the Rumped Pieds shown in this section are males: the female equivalents have rather larger areas of colour and markings. That is, female Rumped Pieds have less white or yellow.

Opaline – magnificently variable

The Opaline mutation is the most flexible and fascinating of all Budgie mutations. It can almost be whatever you want it to be. This sex-linked mutation has just been waiting, since its discovery in 1933, for creative breeders to make better use of it.

Opaline is therefore a much misunderstood variety of Budgerigar. The variety is surrounded by misinformation, which is a pity since this is potentially a revolutionary variety which could help create many amazing new sub-varieties. Just consider the Rainbow … This is an extraordinarily beautiful Budgerigar, arguably mostly due to the artistic use of the Opaline mutation. Rainbows are usually Opaline Golden Faced Blue Clearwings.

The Opaline mutation allows the blue or green body colour to replace the white or yellow wing markings, but it can also replace the black, brown or grey wing markings as well. In addition, it changes the black, brown or grey head and wing markings so that they are barely visible.

The amount of body colour on the wings is up to the breeder. It is possible to breed an Opaline where the body colour also replaces the black, grey or brown wing markings, as well as the yellow or white, thus covering all of the wings (except for the flight feathers). A Normal Opaline of this type would be green or blue over the entire wing, with black flight feathers. In effect, an all-blue or all-green Budgie with a faintly striped yellow or white head. Curiously, the mechanisms

The amazing colours of a baby Double Factor White Cap Rainbow Violet Sky.

that replace the black wing markings do not remove the black markings from the 'V' between the wings, which are removed by other independent mechanisms. The better Rainbow breeders already breed Rainbows with amazing amounts of body colour on their wings. Rainbow breeders in North Africa, the Middle East and the Indian subcontinent excel at this.

Opaline does varied and wonderful things, but from its appearance in 1933 in a group of wild-trapped Budgies, unimaginative Budgie clubs have sought to rigidly control its expression via the variety Standard. This is such a pity. It has been an imprisoned and undesirable work of art, not unlike Vincent van Gogh's paintings during his own lifespan. Remember that Rainbow Budgies originated in Australia – 85 years later, they remain a renegade pet shop colour that kids love, but which

This Opaline Clearwing Light Green has mostly greenish wings. Most Opaline Clearwings have pale grey-white or grey-yellow ghost wing markings where the black wing markings would occur in Normal Opalines. This bird, however, has 90% body colour on its wings with very little grey-yellow wing markings at all: he is nearly green all over – a so-called 'Self Green'.

Budgie clubs in general pretty much ignore. However, perhaps this most beautiful of Budgie varieties owes its artistry to the fact that the mainstream Budgie clubs left it alone. Free from the Budgie bureaucracy, breeders were free to become creative and have fun.

To return to Rainbows, they are Opaline Golden Faced Blue Clearwings. Opalines turned up in 1933 (from a wild-caught female), Clearwings were created by Harold Peir around 1930 and Australian Golden Faced Blues originated around 1935. There appears to be no precise record as to exactly when and by whom Australian Golden Faced Blues were first bred. Rainbows were first recorded in 1939. When I began breeding Golden Faced Blues in about 1960, I could find no details as to how the gene for Golden Faced Blue worked, so I did experiments and in 1963 I published my results in the Budgerigar Society of Australasia's magazine. Double Factor Golden Faced Blues were blue birds with deep yellow faces, and Single Factor birds were greenish-blue with yellow faces. This may well have been the first publication on this variety, as in the 1961 book *Genetics for Budgerigar Breeders* the authors dismiss the Australian Golden Faced Blue, saying on page 100, under the header 'Golden-faces': "The evidence suggests that Golden-faces are homozygous (Double Factor) Mutant II Yellow-face birds." They were wrong, as it is a separate mutation. Sadly, this serious mistake was repeated in the 1986 second (revised) edition of *GFBB* on page 101, also under the heading: 'Golden-faces'.

In many Opaline Clearwings or Rainbows, there are faint 'ghost' wing markings visible. That is white, grey or cream ghost wing markings. Smart breeders select for all blue or all green wings; without the ghost markings.

For that matter, what would the Rainbow be without the Opaline mutation? It would be very dull indeed.

This is a young White Cap Seafoam Rainbow. It has greyish wing markings. These markings may moult out, exposing a blue/green wing. You can also select in favour of more Seafoam colour on the wings as well. Having said that, the markings are a beautiful colour as is.

The left Cobalt Opaline Clearwing has grey ghost wing markings.

This Greywing Opaline has less wing markings and more areas of body colour.

So, advanced breeders can remove most or all of the wing markings, and they can also select for extra body colour where the markings used to be. Or they can just follow the usual Standard of Perfection Opaline wing pattern, which features a mixture of markings and body colour.

This Cinnamonwing Opaline has very few cinnamon wing markings left.

Opaline also affects the face and forehead markings, offering the possibility of creating an all-black face and mask. Some Opalines also have white cheeks/ears.

All of these aspects of the Opaline are hereditary. All offer the opportunity to develop even more varieties – the only limiting factor is your own imagination.

It is my theory that the Opaline green-all-over bird with no wing markings at all is the original Budgerigar. That is, the Opaline gene was carried by all ancestral Budgies – in this sense, Opaline may be the TRUE NORMAL. Thousands of years ago when Australia was a land of lush green forests and grasslands, Budgies probably looked much like Red-fronted Parakeet of New Zealand and Norfolk Island – green all over, with black flight feathers (minus the red cap and ear).

This female Opaline White Cap Normal has very heavily marked, mostly black wings. It is much closer to a common Opaline on the show bench. Compare this with the Cinnamon Green on the previous page. Opaline certainly is happy to be whatever you want it to be!

This Normal Opaline has beautiful white cheeks/ears and the (outlawed) contrasting forehead flecking which some could consider attractive in this case. White cheeks/ears are hereditary as are the blue areas on the back of his head. Maybe, in certain varieties, flecking could be very pretty?

Right: This is a Red-fronted Parakeet, or Kākāriki. Note the black flight feathers – this is exactly what the original, ancestral forest-dwelling Budgerigar might have looked like. It is also what a self-green Opaline Budgie would look like (except for the flash of red).

As Australia dried out, forming deserts around 45,000 years ago, mutations evolved to camouflage the backs of the Budgies while they were feeding on the ground in open, dry areas. The mix of black and yellow stripes provided the Budgies with a neutral, ground-like camouflage colour.

To repeat, the true 'normal' Budgie, the ancestral Budgie, is probably an all-

This young White Cap Rainbow is developing a good percentage of body colour on its wings as it is moulting out. Note that the grey wing markings have been largely replaced by body colour.

green bird: at base, an Opaline. The black and yellow striping came much later.

But the main point of this section is that we have hardly even begun to explore the possibilities of the Opaline Budgerigar.

But how would you actually breed all-blue or all-green Opalines? There do not appear to be any genes for the absence of markings on the wings. But there are modifiers that will bit-by-bit remove more and more markings. Other modifiers will replace the areas where the dark markings (black, brown or grey) used to be on the wings, with pure body colour.

All that you need to do is to look through your Opalines and select for birds with less wing markings and more body colour on the wings and the 'V' between them. If you have none of these, check out Opalines that your friends have, or go to a bird sale or auction and buy a few Opalines with lots of body colour in their wings and/or the 'V' area. Equally you should seek out Normals with greenish or bluish suffused wings. Many Modern Normals which do not carry Opaline still have body colour suffusion on their wings: these are pure gold in your quest for the all-blue or all-green Budgies. At this stage, I have no theory as to how to remove the lighter head, neck and mask colours on Opalines, by the way. At a guess, just select for more body colour on the head.

This is a Normal Violet Budgerigar which is not split for Opaline. It is a very valuable bird for a creative colour breeder. It has an amazing amount of violet in its wings. This bird would improve Rainbow wing colour enormously.

Since there are no genes for these effects, you get blending inheritance. The harder and longer you select for body colour on the wings, the more you will get in their progeny.

Progress will be slow at first, but in a few years you will have transformed your Opalines, Rainbows and Opaline Clearwings. If you are already doing it, send in some photos of your birds to the Australian Heritage Budgerigar Association on Facebook.

Opaline is a sex-linked mutation, so:

- Opaline male to non-Opaline female produces females that are all Opalines and males that are all split for Opaline.
- Opaline male to Opaline female produces 100% Opalines.
- Opaline female to a non-Opaline male produces all males split for Opaline and all females carrying no Opaline genes at all.
- Split Opaline male to an Opaline female produces half of the males Opaline and half split Opaline, plus half of the females Opaline and half non-Opaline.

Opaline will link tenaciously to Cinnamonwing. That is, if you cross Cinnamons to Opalines, many young will be Cinnamonwing Opalines which breed many more Cinnamonwing Opalines. Both mutations are sex-linked and they get glued to each other. Don't cross them together as this limits the flexibility of your breeding.

Some misunderstandings

Contrary to what is generally believed, Normal males with body colour on their wings are not necessarily split for Opaline, as you saw in the photo on the previous page.

Opalines do have more and larger spots, but they can't pass this on to non-Opaline babies.

Opaline-bred babies are not different in exhibition qualities either; i.e. Opalines do not improve or change your non-Opaline babies other than what any non-Opaline bird usually does.

Opaline does change body colour a bit (i.e. opalescence), but any Normal-looking non-Opaline babies will not have their body colour affected. But it is true that the Opaline body colour change is at its best in White Cap Rainbows.

This is a painting of 'Ideal Normal Opalines' from circa 1950. This is how the original mutation looked and it is more or less still today's ideal pattern. This is fine, but we could have bred so many other variants!

Lastly, it is important to note that Opaline intensifies the colour of the black markings on the wings of all varieties (except 'Inos', etc). For

| type 1 | type 2 | type 2 |

Drawing of wing covert feathers showing type 1 and type 2 wing patterns.

It is the recessive type 2 wing mutation that underpins most REALLY CLEAR WINGS. Both wing mutations can still produce the PERFECTLY CLEAR wings, but even if you do get fairly clear wing colour with the type 1 wing pattern, the flight feathers often seem to remain grey.

Above: This is a spectacularly beautiful Opaline Violet Texas Clearbody Spangle Greywing Pastel. It might even be a Clearwing rather than a Greywing. Pastel Budgies are beginning to take off around the world. This variety might soon be named a Glacier Pastel. If interested, contact Naomi Watts on the Australian Heritage Budgerigar Association Pastel Facebook page.

instance, Opaline Fallows usually have blackish wing markings as against the brown wing markings of Normal Fallows.

Thus Opaline Clearwings and Rainbows have frustratingly dark wing markings. I have found that about 50% of all of the Opaline Clearwings that I have bred have 'dirty wings' (i.e. visible greyish wing markings) and 50% very clear wing colour. Thus it seems that type 1 wing pattern combined with Opaline creates greyish wing markings in Clearwings, and type 2 wing markings in Opaline Clearwings leave the wings quite clear – all you see is the body colour on the wings.

Opalines can easily get confused with Saddlebacks. They are similar, but Saddlebacks have no body colour on their wings. Saddlebacks can produce hazy grey wing markings on the shoulder of the wings through to dark, near-normal wing markings below. It also produces a pale back of the head and neck similar to Opalines. Below is the comparison between Opaline and Saddleback.

On the left is a Saddleback, on the right is an Opaline. Note that the Saddleback has NO body colour on its wings.

Opaline genetics

Opaline mated to Opaline always produces 100% Opalines.

Opaline is a sex-linked recessive mutation and Saddleback is an ordinary recessive mutation. So, males can carry one gene for Opaline (i.e. Single Factor) yet still look non-Opaline. If a male carries two genes for Opaline (Double Factor), he is a visual Opaline. Females can only ever carry one gene for Opaline and if they carry it they are visual Opalines.

An Opaline male crossed to a non-Opaline female produces males that are all visually non-Opaline but split for Opaline; all females are Opalines.

A non-Opaline male mated to an Opaline female produces 100% visual non-Opaline babies. All the males are, however, Single Factor Opalines; this are called 'split for Opaline'.

A male split for Opaline mated to an Opaline female produces 25% non-Opaline male split for Opaline, 25% Opaline male, 25% non-Opaline females and 25% Opaline females.

A male split for Opaline mated to a non-Opaline female produces 25% pure non-Opaline males, 25% non-Opaline males split for Opaline, 25% Opaline females and 25% non-Opaline females.

Horrible as it is, this is the standard way that sex-linked genes work.

These percentages will work for any sex-linked matings. Just substitute Cinnamonwing (or whatever) for Opaline.

Advanced genetics

Genetic archaeology of Budgerigars

The Budgerigar has been bred in captivity for more than 150 years and over that time it has changed quite enormously. So perhaps it is time to take a look back to what the origins of colours, varieties and other mutations actually were – for this, the answer lies in the genes themselves … and in modifier elements in the Budgerigar's DNA.

Hence, what I call 'genetic archaeology' – using old or remnant genes to trace the history of domestication of the Budgerigar. The key to all of this for me is the Wild (a.k.a. Bush) Budgie. In the pure Wild Budgie lies the unadulterated blueprint for everything that we have today. I have several strains of Wild Budgies which I have kept meticulously pure – that is, free from contamination caused by Modern crosses to the domesticated Budgie.

As mutations gradually pop up in the Wild Budgies (mostly from inbreeding producing birds homozygous for hidden recessive genes), I get a snapshot in time of what the original mutation of that colour or variety actually looked like.

One of my first 'pop-ups' was a Blue Budgie, followed by Australian Yellow Faced Blues. Both of these varieties are recessive to the Wild Green colour. Perhaps the most interesting discovery that I have made is that the Dilutes that subsequently popped up in my Australian Yellow Faced Blue Wild Budgies all have the recessive type 2 wing pattern that I discovered in Heritage Clearwings. So the type 1 wing pattern (see diagram) is highly likely to be a mutation that occurred in captivity and presumably serves some purpose in exhibition breeding. Possibly it causes more areas of pure black on the wings of Normals.

Wild Budgies have tricoloured wing feathers: a yellow crescent at the tip, then a black crescent, with the rest of the feather being a swirling yellow-grey colour mixture (see photos at the end of this section). Black melanin pigment is expensive for a Budgie to produce, so they produce as little as possible. Evolution does not tolerate wastage of difficult to produce pigments. But in captivity we aesthetically prefer to have a wing with lots of PURE black pigment with no swirling greyish areas, so perhaps we selected for type 1 wing pattern to create the crisp black and yellow wing markings (again, see photos at the end of the section). I am still doing research to

type 1   type 2   type 2

337

confirm if the crisp black wing markings are caused by the type 1 wing pattern gene seen in Dilutes, Clearwings and Greywings. This is very difficult and could take five to ten years to complete. I had previously stated that the type 1 and type 2 wing patterns in Clearwings, etc, did not affect Normals, but it appears now that I might have not looked closely enough. This is a classic example of how frustratingly subtle and easy to miss the effects of modifier elements are.

The most interesting aspect is that most Clearwings, Greywings and Dilutes have been significantly affected by the type 1 wing pattern which appears not to occur in Wild Budgies. This seems to be the DEVIL that we created to darken the wings in Normals, Cinnamons, etc, that we now have to remove from Clearwings and Dilutes in particular.

This is a Sky Dilute 100% pure Bush Budgie – note the classic type 2 wing pattern.

This is a close-up of the Sky Blue Dilute Bush Budgie's Type 2 wing pattern.

Far left: This is a Single Factor Australian Yellow Faced Blue Dilute 100% pure Bush Budgie. It clearly has the type 2 wing pattern. Note that this young male has a central area in its wing which has not yet moulted out.

Left: This is a close-up of the Australian Yellow Faced Dilute Bush Budgie's type 2 wing pattern.

From left to right: Dilute Sky Bush Budgie's type 2 wing feathers, Dilute Australian Yellow Faced Blue Bush Budgie's type 2 wing feathers and two groups of type 1 wing pattern feathers from the Clearwing Violet (right). Note the even grey shade right throughout these type 1 wing feathers.

This female Violet Clearwing has a classic type 1 wing pattern. Curiously, when the wing feathers are looked at separately (see the feather pictures above), they do not seem so dark.

Above left: This male Normal Sky appears to have the wild-type, type 2 wing pattern – note the thin black line next to the white crescent tip of each wing feather. The rest of the wing feather is greyish. With birds like this, there is quite a lot of visible grey colour in their wings. This has always been seen as bad wing colour on Exhibition birds.

Above right: This Exhibition female has the type 1 wing pattern, producing a totally black and white wing colour. She has virtually no visible grey areas.

Right: This is a Heritage Budgerigar also with type 1 wing pattern – just black and white.

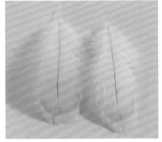

Above left: 2 wing feathers, Modern Exhibition bird's type 1 wing feathers and lastly, a Heritage Budgie's type 1 wing feathers. Note the thin black line on the type 2 Normal wing feathers on the left, but the much greater area of black on the type 1 wings, middle and right.

Above right: Above are close-ups of the wing feathers from the two Dilute Bush Budgies featured in this section. These are classic type 2 wing pattern feathers.

Above left: Bush Budgie showing the TRICOLOUR wing pattern. Note the yellow crescent on the feather tip, below that a thin, dense black crescent then the greyish-yellow area, i.e. type 2 wing pattern.

Above right: Close-up of the wing pattern of a Bush (a.k.a. Wild) Budgie. Note how thin the true black area is. Greyish-yellow areas are very widespread. This is the type 2 wing pattern.

Gene linkage – huh?

When I read Taylor and Warner's book *Genetics for Budgerigar Breeders* as a teenager in the 1960s, I was very much unimpressed by 'Chapter 4: Linkage'. To cut to the chase, it predicted that, when mating a Sky Blue to a Dark Green Split Blue together, sometimes you get less Cobalts and Light Greens than Dark Greens and Skys … So what?

The fact that the gene for a dark shade of colour is loosely linked to the Green gene is not all that important. But the linkage between the Cinnamon and Opaline sex-linked genes is a bit of a worry if you want to breed Rainbows, for example. You need Opaline in Rainbows, but Cinnamon dilutes the body colour, making the

Rainbow less attractive. Once Cinnamon and Opaline come together in one bird, they stick together like two magnets. Separating them is very difficult: thus, a male split for Cinnamon and Opaline will only rarely produce an Opaline daughter that isn't a Cinnamon as well. Both Cinnamon and Opaline lie on the Z* sex chromosome (yes, Z* – see the end of this section on page 185). Unless you want the Cinnamon Opaline combination, avoid crossing Opaline to Cinnamon at all costs. According to C. Warner, they only break apart about 36% of the time. My experiments indicate that the recombination rate is much less than that, maybe less than 10%. My new Golden Tops are mostly Golden Top Cinnamon Opaline Clearwings and it is proving very difficult to produce them without the Cinnamon element (however, Cinnamon Rainbows are permitted in our new Rainbow Standard of Perfection).

At a Glance

Gene linkage means that because some genes are located close together, they basically get 'stuck' together, rarely come apart, and therefore are passed from parent to offspring as a combined unit. So, if you are trying to create a special Budgie with special features, linkage might just muck things up. All of the sex-linked genes like Albino, Lutino, Lacewing, Texas Clearbody, Slate, Cinnamon and Opaline can get stuck together (all being located on the same chromosome). This can be disastrous. To make matters worse, bad feathering and small size are linked to: Australian Golden Faced, Recessive Pied, Fallows, clear wing colour in Clearwings and Black Eyed Yellows and Black Eyed Whites, as well as to good colour in Darkwings. Some solutions to these problems are provided below.

Other sex-linked genes like Albino and Lutino, Lacewings, Texas Clearbodies and Slates also link to each other, and to Cinnamon and Opaline as well. So, do not cross them together.

Thus, gene linkage DOES matter, and it matters a lot. From my experimental crosses, the following colours and varieties are all very tightly linked to small size, tiny heads and awful feathering:

This female White Cap Grey is a classic example of the linkage between Cinnamon and Opaline. Often you don't want these two genes together and this means that you have, in effect, lost another female. Females are precious and easily lost to egg-binding, etc.

- Recessive Pied
- Very clear wings in Clearwings
- Clear colour in Black Eyed Yellows and Whites
- Darkwings
- Australian Golden Faced
- Australian Fallow

But: the following are not linked to size and feather:
- Clearwing (the variety)
- Dilute

You can get Recessive Pieds, etc, with great size and feather, but it is extremely difficult.

So, if you mate an awful, ugly and small Recessive Pied to a big, bold and beautiful Normal, then back cross to get Recessive Pieds – they will usually still be awful, yet the splits will be OK.

The same applies to Australian Fallows. What gives? The gene or genes for small size and awful feather (e.g. small heads and short masks) are welded onto the gene for Fallow and the gene for Recessive Pied. They are nearly impossible to break apart. The split Fallows and split Pieds look lovely, but their Fallow siblings or children usually look awful.

With Clearwings, Darkwings and Black Eyed Yellows, the gene(s) for size and feather are not linked to the Clearwing or the basic Dilute gene, but rather to the very clear wing colour DNA. So it is very difficult to breed a big, bold and beautiful Clearwing or Black Eyed Yellow or White **with great clarity of colour**.

The worst of the Lot

In Australian Golden Faced Blues, you can easily breed a big, bold and beautiful Single Factor Golden Faced Blues (the greenish coloured ones) but the Double Factor birds (the Golden-Faced true blues) are little runts. This is due to a recessive gene for bad feathering being attached (linked) to the Aussie Golden Faced Blue genes. Reputedly this led the world's greatest Budgie breeder, Jo Mannes from Germany, to finally get rid of all of his Golden Faced Blues after breeding and exhibiting them for over 30 years. He reputedly admitted that he could never breed a good Double Factor Golden Faced Blue – only his greenish Single Factor birds were any good.

On page 345 is an article by myself from the Budgerigar Society's magazine of December 1963, regarding the problem of bad feathering in Double Factor Golden Faced Blues. Even with the tiny, tight-feathered birds of that era, poor feathering in Double Factor Golden Faced Blues was a noticeable problem.

The Single Factor Aussie Golden Faced Blues are lovely due to the dominant gene(s) for good feather and size being welded to the hidden gene* for Blue (Single

---

* This linkage is so unavoidable that it may be the Golden Faced Blue gene itself that causes poor feathering in the Double Factor form. This is called a pleiotropic effect of a gene.

This is a Golden Faced/Yellow Faced hybrid. Any judge or breeder would accept this as a Double Factor Golden Faced. He is a very useful Violet Clearwing.

Factor Golden Faced Blues are split for Blue). Once you get Double Factor Aussie Golden Faced Blues (which can never have any genes for Blue), you get little runts. If you cross Aussie Golden Faced Blues to English Yellow Faced Blues, the hybrid Yellow Faced Blues you get will look virtually identical to Double Factor Aussie Golden Faced Blues **BUT** they will have the feather quality of an English Yellow Faced Blue – **problem solved!**

However, in general, your job as breeders is to keep tossing the dice until you break the weld (linkage). That is, you must constantly outcross to good Normals (or Cinnamons in the case of Black Eyed Whites and Yellows, but definitely not a Cinnamon Opaline) until you get ONE bird with great colour and great size and feather. The odds of success are small, however YOU ONLY NEED ONE GREAT BIRD TO REINVENT YOUR BREEDING. The basic idea though is to break the weld to bad size and feather and to re-weld to good size and feather.

Then sell all of the rest of your birds of that variety – the whole lot! If you backcross your poor quality Fallows, Clearwings, Black Eyed Whites and Yellows, Recessive Pieds or Aussie Golden Faced Blues, to other members of that variety, you will totally destroy all of your good luck in producing the good one. Use the good one to produce a new line of birds by crossing it to Normals or other birds of great quality.

Better still, buy a pair of great birds of your chosen variety from a great breeder who has already re-welded the variety to good size and feather. Pay a lot for them too, if necessary. This will save you heaps of money in the long run.

There can be little doubt that lots of other varieties are linked to genes for good size and good feather. Thus, you will never know about the linkage since they almost always produce reasonably good young.

The wonderful news is that, once you re-weld the genes for Fallow, Aussie Golden Faced Blues, clear Clearwings, clear Black Eyed Whites and Yellows, clear-bodied Darkwings and Recessive Pieds to great size and feather, your problems are over. It will become very difficult to breed rubbish birds of these varieties ever again if you follow my advice.

So linkage does matter. For the boffins among you, linkage often occurs when a gene (e.g. Fallow) is close to another gene (feather and size) on the same chromosome. The closer the genes are together, the tighter the linkage and the higher the chance of them being inherited together. Although chromosomes do snap apart through a process called crossing-over, which shuffles genes during the formation of an embryo, the number of breaks is small, so the shuffling is minimal. Hence the chances of linkages breaking is fairly small; thus the genes are more or less welded together. Linkage also occurs when two or more chromosomes are touching when the chromosomes are folded up.

New research also indicates that linkage might be caused by genes lying close together when folded. They can actually be on different chromosomes yet be neighbours when folded up, and therefore many genes could be controlled by the same nearby gene modifier. That is, one modifier can affect many different genes on different chromosomes. Where this is the case, it may prove impossible to break apart this weird form of gene linkage, since the chromosomes fold exactly the same away every time. Thus, the proximity of the two genes never varies and obviously crossing-over does not affect this arrangement. This could easily be the case with Golden Faced Blues being linked to poor feathering, etc.

The usual 'double sausage' picture of chromosomes (below) that you see, is a momentary pose taken by chromosomes in preparation for sexual reproduction (called meiosis). For more than 99.999% of a chromosome's life, it is tightly folded up like cut leaves in a cabbage-head (see lower picture).

Bird sex chromosomes used to be called X and Y the same as ours are. For those who remember high-school science, in humans they are XY in males and XX in females.

But birds are different, so their sex chromosomes are called W and Z. Surprisingly, Male birds are ZZ and females are ZW.

On the next page is a scan of my 1963 BSA magazine article on Yellow Faced Blues, which are now known as Golden Faced Blues. I was grappling with what was

This is an Australian or German Fallow bred by Ian Hannington in Australia in 2007. Ian had broken the linkage to bad feathering by crossing to Normals and then ONLY breeding from the split Fallows produced. This is Budgie breeding at its very best.

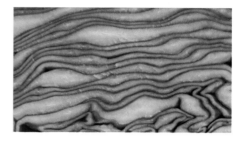

Above is how chromosomes look just prior to meiosis, when the chromosomes divide up for the re-combination with the DNA of the sexual partner. This is a momentary stage, but it is the stage that almost all illustrations show.

Above is how tightly folded chromosomes look for 99.999% of their lives. This is actually a photo of a purple cabbage growth-bud (i.e. a cabbage head). But you get the idea (I hope): lots of loops. And they always fold exactly the same way every time!

going on with Double Factor Golden Faced Blues being such poor quality birds. Sixty years ago, linkage of bad feathering to Double Factor Golden Faced Blues was a real problem – the same as it is today. This is a frustrating example of unbreakable linkage.

Time and tide wait for no man, and the passing of yet another year brings us to the festive season when thoughts turn to peace on earth and goodwill to all upon it.

It is my honoured pleasure at this time to send greetings and good wishes to all our members wherever they may be. 1963 has seen changes in the B.S.A., particularly in its administration. The control and management is now equally shared between all branches, who have instituted a number of favourable and beneficial suggestions which when in full operation will undoubtedly bring together the somewhat dividing views so obviously creeping into our ranks. Let us all work to this end, the goal of such effort, bringing back the united high reputation enjoyed by the B.S.A. in former years-- We need more members, more enthusiasm, more loyalty. An important step in this direction is the hope of staging during May 1964, the greatest combined budgerigar exhibition ever attempted in the Southern Hemisphere. Meantime, we all look forward to continued advancement, which can only be achieved by your support in any activity undertaken by your elected office bearers.

In wishing you all a very Happy Christmas and prosperous New Year, may I also express the hope of bigger and brighter things to come for the B.S.A.

H. K. Nott.
President.

May Christmas bring Joy

and

the New Year Health

and Happiness

from

THE BUDGERIGAR SOCIETY OF AUSTRALASIA

Members Write

Don Burke.
Sydney.

ABOUT YELLOWFACES

For many years numerous theories have been put forward about the factor of the yellowface. As they all conflict they are only confusing.

WHY SHOULD YELLOWFACES GO GREEN?

Do yellowfaces go green because of having too much yellowface in them? In my opinion it is the single factor yellowface that is greenish.

Many breeders have produced good coloured yellowfaced blues from greenish ones by pairing them together. This proves the theory. The greenish ones were single factor and produced the double factor young.

This year I purchased some excellent coloured yellowface, and as few yellowfaces are good show birds, I crossed them to my normals; although the yellowfaced parents were excellent the young were all greenish, coming from the normals. They were single factor, but they were all yellowfaces proving that the good Yellowfaced parent was a double factor, the "true blue" bird

Yellowfaces, today are a poor bird in type and size, a good one rarely being seen. My belief is, that if you cross yellowface to normal to improve type and size, the young are all greenish and thus are discarded when they moult out. The yellowfaced blues of good colour almost never get good fresh normal blood into them, which would improve them in type and size after a few seasons.

If you breed yellowfaces and wish to improve them, I would suggest that :-
YEAR 1.   Cross yellowface to normal and select only the youngsters with the best type to breed the following season, forgetting about colour.
YEAR 2.   Mate either two of the single factor yellowfaces together or one single factor to a double factor and thus show yellowfaces will be obtained.

Remember never discard the greenish yellowface, if he is basically a good bird because in all probability he is a single factor yellowfaced blue.

Sometimes the greenish tint in the single factor bird doesn't show through till after its 1st. moult, but eventually the single factor bird will go greenish.

You may have noticed that most successful breeders of good blue yellowfaces breed only yellowface blue to yellowfaced blue and never outcrosses to normals at all. This proves the theory because the tendency would be to cull towards the double factor because it looks better and thus a strain of double factor birds is established.

Whether this green tinge in the single factor bird is "hybrid vigour" or merely incompletion of the factor I don't know but the proof of the greenish bird being single factor is abundant.

2

December, 1963

December, 1963

3

Gene modifiers: the key to breeding winners

Tandem repeats are the best known of gene modifiers. They modify the function of the genes. For example, it is Tandem Repeats that control the length of dog's snout: large numbers of them combine to gradually turn greyhound snouts into bulldog snouts.

They also control spot size, length of mask, overall size, shoulder width, length and coarseness of feather, amount of directional feather, etc.

Tandem repeats are just a number of short DNA base pairs, for example adenine adenine guanine thymine – AAGT. They can vary from one to hundreds of these groups of letters repeated again and again: AAGT AAGT AAGT AAGT, etc.

Tandem repeats of DNA occur within the length of a gene's DNA, but they are not actually part of the gene itself. They control aspects of what and how much the gene does. The more of the individual bits such as AAGT, the more that this tiny group achieves. Sort of like the more grains of sugar you add to your coffee, the sweeter it tastes.

Tandem repeats mutate up to 100,000 times more often than genes do. They can rapidly increase their numbers of repeats too, and remember the greater the number, the more they achieve. While one AAGT might achieve little, 100 AAGTs all lined up in a row, may achieve a lot.

So, in cleaning up a Clearwing's wings, you are probably building up more and more tandem repeats that clean up the wings. Since tandem repeats are somewhat unstable, this explains why mating a perfectly clear-winged Clearwing to another perfectly clear-winged Clearwing sometimes produces some dirty-winged young.

But in a nutshell, simply selecting for ever-clearer wings will, over time, produce birds with perfectly clear wings. Bit by bit.

This also explains why crossing a beautifully clear Clearwing to an average Normal will, upon backcrossing, produce Clearwing babies with scrambled modifiers. That is, they will look like Greywings because that is what they really are genetically. All Clearwings are heavily-modified Greywings.

Mistakes and myths

There are many mistakes and myths surrounding the genetics of Budgie breeding. The book *Genetics For Budgerigar Breeders* by T.G. Taylor and Cyril Warner has been the **go to** book for dedicated Budgerigar breeders since it was first published in 1961. It has been a powerhouse of the best genetic advice on Budgies for more 60 years. But science keeps advancing and changing ever more rapidly, so there are obviously things in the book that are now out of date and need correcting. What we will look at here are the important bits that need changing. The most important changes relate to Clearwings, gene linkage and gene modifiers, but we will look at anything that is useful which needs changing.

Variations of Banded Pieds. Third from the right is a true Banded, and the others are Straight Line Pieds, which in essence have much wider bands. These birds are all Single Factor for the Banded modifier gene.

Myth 1: Most Dominant Pied breeders believe that Double Factor Australian Dominant Pieds have much more white or yellow on them than Single Factor Pieds. Not so. Even way back in 1961, *Genetics for Budgerigar Breeders* (GFBB) said of Australian Dominant Pieds: "Homozygous and Heterozygous individuals do not differ in appearance" (GFBB, page 92 – all page number references in this article are from the 1961 edition of GFBB). This one they got right, but they didn't research the pied patterns which even back in 1961 were obviously hereditary. One gene which is now called the Banded gene, in the Single Factor form, causes Banded, Straight Line and Winged Pied patterns. In the Double Factor form you get a Rumped Pied pattern. So the pattern is strongly hereditary. GFBB noted (on page 90) that female Recessive Pieds have more colour and markings on them than males, and the same applies to Dominant Pieds – i.e. males have more white or yellow. GFBB opined that this meant sex-linked genes. No, these are sex-limited genes that affect female Pied patterns. Sex-limited genes only affect one sex or the other, never both. For example, the genes for blue versus brown ceres, or the genes responsible for the development of ovaries versus testes.

A group of Rumped Pieds, the right-hand Yellow Faced Sky is showing his coloured rump. These are all Double Factor for the Banded modifier gene.

347

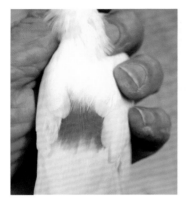

This is the rump of a male Rumped Pied. Very few female Rumped Pieds have this much white or yellow on them.

This is a pair of Recessive Pied Bush Budgies. Note that the Blue male has a much greater area of pied markings than the female on the right.

Myth 2: The one serious weak link in *GFBB* is their information on Clearwings. Clearwings were developed in Australia, and, although many were sent to the UK, they failed to get a genetic handle on them. Ahead are a few of their errors. *GFBB* said about Clearwings that: "It seems probable that there is a degree of linkage between the genes for depth of wing markings and depth of body colour … If this is so, all attempts to breed Clearwings with pure white or yellow wings and Normal body colour by selection from existing genetic material are doomed to failure" (*GFBB*, pages 62–63). This turned out to be incorrect. The best Australian Clearwings today have perfectly clear wings combined with **much better and darker body colour** than the corresponding Normals.

According to *GFBB*, attempts to breed Clearwings with this deep body colour and totally clear wings, are "doomed to failure".

Doomed to failure? These Violet Clearwings, all four different birds, each have better than Normal Violet body colour, plus perfectly white wings.

Myth 3: This next mistake has made well-coloured Clearwings almost impossible to breed. And it made many, many breeders frustrated and miserable. *GFBB* said that Clearwings were a separate mutation in the Dil series (Dil is short for Dilute), which they said was composed of four alleles – Normal, Greywing, Clearwing and Dilute. This wasn't well researched because the correct answer was already published 28 years earlier in Neville Cayley's 1933 book *Budgerigars in Bush and Aviary*, which was widely available in the UK. To make matters worse, *GFBB* also **named** the colour of the Normal Budgie: "Full Body Colour" and stated that it was "completely dominant to all three of its alleles" (pages 58–59). Astonishingly, they then called the cross between a Greywing and a Clearwing, a "Full Bodied Greywing" (see *GFBB*, page 60), even though there is no Normal gene in such a bird. No wonder generations of Budgie breeders were totally confused from thereon in. If their theory about Clearwings was correct, about full body colour being dominant to all three of its alleles, the words 'full body colour' could only be used to describe visual Normals (including Normals split for Greywing, Clearwing or Dilute). The correct science here is that there are only three alleles at the Dil locus, not four: Normal, Greywing and Dilute. There is only one mutation for Greywing, but it occurs in two types, a full body coloured one and a half-strength body coloured one. The darker bodied one is caused by a dominant body colour modifier gene. This is a mobile, dominant modifier gene that darkens the body colour in Greywings to near that of a Normal. Some of these Full Body Coloured Greywings were later turned into Clearwings by careful selective breeding using modifiers. In Dilutes you also get two types: light and a bit darker. Here, the differences are only slight, but they are visible. There is abundant evidence that Clearwings were developed from full body colour Greywings which were in existence about 10 years **before** Clearwings were produced in Harold Peir's aviaries (so how could full body coloured Greywings be the result of a Clearwing crossed to an ordinary Greywing when full body colour Greywings existed about 10 years before Clearwings even existed?). Harold used subtle gene modifiers from Yellows of light suffusion to remove the wing markings, while retaining the full body colour modifier gene (this disproves comments on page 66 of *GFBB*). Curiously, most if not all Normal domestic Budgies do not carry this dominant full body colour modifier gene. It appears that they don't need it for their Normal body colour intensity, although some of my pure Bush Budgies do seem to have the full body colour gene. The proof that the full body colour gene is absent from most Normals is that when you cross Clearwings carrying the full body colour gene to Normals, then backcross the splits together, you get around 25% of **NON full body coloured Clearwings** among the Clearwing progeny (see below). This proof is abundant: **Clearwings without the full body colour modifier are common in the UK, elsewhere in Europe and even in Australia. These are rather pale body coloured birds that cannot possibly exist under the muddled theory put forward in GFBB. In their theory, pale Clearwings simply can't exist because the Clearwing mutation itself creates full body colour, i.e. they postulate that full body colour is not an independent gene, but rather it is part of the Clearwing 'mutation' itself. This is clearly incorrect.**

Left: According to the book *Genetics For Budgerigar Breeders*, the bird on the right above cannot possibly exist. He is a Cobalt Clearwing lacking the full body colour gene. The bird on the left is a full body colour Clearwing Cobalt. The non full body colour bird on the right has no Dilute, Greywing or Cinnamon in him at all. He is bred from a pure Heritage Clearwing mated to Normal, then backcrossed, split to split. Pale, non full body coloured Clearwings are common throughout the UK and continental Europe, yet again proving that the full body colour gene is a free agent, rather than part of the Clearwing gene itself. This discovery totally disproves the theory that Clearwing is a multiple allele at the Dil locus. Yet no UK or continental European breeder seems to realise this.

It might help if we retained the 'full body coloured' description for intensely body coloured Greywings and Clearwings, and possibly for the deeper body coloured Dilutes, but we need to come up with a new name for body colour in Normals such as: Normal Body Colour. Thus retaining the original identifying letter of 'C'. Although there is no mutation for Clearwing, the variety and the name of the (modifier-based) Clearwing will obviously be retained. They will then be considerably easier to breed.

Right: Another bird that can't possibly exist according to the *GFBB* theory. The bird on the right is a non full body coloured Sky Clearwing. The female on the left is a full body coloured Sky Clearwing. Again, there is no Dilute, Greywing or Cinnamon in the bird on the right (note his dark grey feet and deep purple cheek patch).

Myth 4: Half-siders (Mosaics, etc), according to *GFBB*, are caused when "one chromosome is lost from one of the daughter cells during the first division of the fertilised egg." Or, less likely, through "failure of chromosomes to separate during cell division …", and on it goes (*GFBB*, pages 104–107). I published the correct theory in about 1995. Halfsiders are two non-identical twins joined together into one body … like a much closer version of conjoined twins. The chromosomal theories were easily proven incorrect by the fact that more than one chromosome was often involved, often one of which was a sex chromosome and the other was a normal, autosomal, non-sex chromosome. Mosaics or, as they are known today, Chimeras, are two birds in one body. Sometimes a male on one side and a female on the other. This has been proven by DNA analyses in other species.

Myth 5: Recessive Pieds are "far inferior to Normals in size and shape, etc… The best way to improve them … is to mate the best Pieds to the best Normals" (*GFBB*, page 89). If only this were true. Even back in 1961 they were aware of gene linkage. While they wrote in *GFBB* about green/blue

Above: This is a Chimera Budgie.
Photo: Brett Martin

linkage to the dark gene (which was of no great importance), they missed the obvious point about linkage in other areas, particularly linkage of poor feathering, small head and size to certain varieties. Bad feathering and poor size are linked to Recessive Pieds, Australian Fallows and Australian Golden Faced Blues in particular. The linkage is variable. It is at its worst in Australian Golden Faced Blues and Fallows. Recessive Pieds and their love child, Dark Eyed Clears, are a close third. Virtually all Double Factor Australian Golden Faceds have relatively poor feather and head qualities. The only Golden Faced Blues that have great feathering are the hybrid Yellow Faced Blue x Golden Faced Blue birds. These look like Double Factor Golden Faced Blues, but they are hybrids.

Right: This is a two and a half year old hybrid English Yellow Faced x Australian Heritage Golden Faced Violet. It is also a hybrid Heritage x Modern Showbird. Note his unbelievable body colour, free from yellow suffusion. Note that he looks like a Double Factor Golden Faced Violet. Best of all, note his great size and feathering for a half Heritage bird. This sort of super head and feather quality is not possible with a Double Factor Golden Faced Blue (so far).

Legendary Budgie breeder Jo Mannes of Germany reputedly gave up breeding Golden Faced Blues after 30 years, because he couldn't ever breed a Double Factor Golden Faced Blue with a great head and feathering, yet his Single Factor Golden Faced Blues, with their greenish body colour, were very nice birds. Why? Genes can be very close to other genes on one chromosome or, when all folded up, they may be intimately close to genes on other chromosomes. This can mean that some varieties can be all but impossible to improve. Curiously, on page 100 *GFBB* dismisses the Australian Golden Faced Blue as follows: "The evidence suggests that Golden Faced Blues are homozygous (Double Factor) Mutant II Yellow Faced Blue birds". This embarrassing mistake is repeated in the 1986 version of *GFBB*, on page 101. The Golden Faced Blue linkage is linkage at its worst. Fallows in Australia are much the same, the split Fallows look great, the Double Factor Fallows are almost always puny and small headed. The genius who broke the linkage to bad quality in Fallows to produce the world's best Fallows is Ian Hannington of Australia. He did it by crossing his Fallows to Normals, then only using the splits to produce their 25% of Fallow progeny. Sooner or later, you will get a baby Fallow which has the linkage to bad head and feathering broken. Ian's genius was that he NEVER crossed this freakish Fallow with great head and feathering back to any other Fallows. Instead he mated it to top quality Normals to maintain the correct linkage to good head and feathering. Later on, other Fallow breeders mated Ian's elite birds to other lesser quality Fallows and thus destroyed the Fallows by re-establishing the linkage to bad feathering. Thus the information on page 86 of GFBB is counter-productive; it says: "Pairing split Fallows together is not very satisfactory". This is tragically wrong as it is the only way to eventually break the bad linkages. Mating top quality split Fallows to poorer quality Fallows destroys the chance of ever creating modern head, feathering and overall size. Some well-feathered and large-headed Recessive Pieds and Dark Eyed Clears are beginning to appear. Why GFBB bogged down on the dark gene linkage to blue or green I will never know; see GFBB 'Chapter 4: Linkage'.

Myth 6: Double Factor Green Budgies and Greens split for Blue look the same.

Not so. Page 20 of GFBB states that: "The important difference is that gene b (the recessive Blue gene) has little or no effect when present with gene B (the dominant Green gene)". The observable fact is that pure Greens that are not split for Blue are an altogether richer and deeper shade of yellow. Lutinos, Black Eyed Yellows and Double Factor Green Spangles all look much richer yellow colour if they are not split for Blue.

Myth 7: GFBB said: "Double Factor Violet Skys and Double Factor Violet Mauves are extremely scarce. It has indeed been doubted whether they exist at all" (GFBB, page 75). I breed Double Factor Violet Skys to Double Factor Violet Cobalts to produce 100%

These are both baby Dark Green Clearwings from the same line of Budgies. The bird on the right with the brighter and richer yellow colour is a Double Factor Green and the left hand one is split for Blue.

visual Violets every time, and have done so for over 25 years. I also breed quite a few Double Factor Violet Mauves each year. What GFBB said was incorrect. What is apparent is that the authors couldn't readily identify many of the various types of Violet combinations with Sky, Cobalt and Mauve".

The male on the right is a Double Factor Violet Sky Clearwing. The female on the left is a Double Factor Violet Red Cobalt Clearwing. Both are visual Violets, and paired together they will breed 100% Violets – half Double Factor Violet Sky and half Double Factor Violet Cobalt.

Myth 8: Exhibition qualities. Chapter 15 of GFBB is best deleted from the book. So many advances have occurred over the years from 1961 to today, that this chapter is best ignored and a totally new one put in its place. It is now recognised that most exhibition features are controlled by hereditary factors such as tandem repeats, micro RNAs, methylation of genes and even environmentally-caused DNA changes, all of which are relatively new scientific discoveries. I have done quite a bit of research into non-gene heredity and now can understand a lot of the heredity of exhibition aspects such as feather density and length, etc. The heritability of long flight feathers was particularly difficult to crack. It turned out that long flights is a side issue created by longer feathering all over. There is one recessive gene that creates shorter flights and tails in long-feathered birds, plus a heap of modifiers which tidy other things up.

This female has ugly, disproportionately long flight feathers. When you try to 'modernise' old-fashioned Budgie varieties with fine and short feathering all over, you will usually run into this sort of trouble. Mating them to Modern Budgies with coarse and long feathering, will produce young with long flights and tails even though neither parent has them. I have a research article on the genetics of solving this problem.

354

This pair has perfect-length flight and tail feathers.

Despite the caveats above, *Genetics for Budgerigar Breeders* is still a very good book on Budgerigar genetics. However, maybe a third edition incorporating these changes, plus a few more, is needed.

More useless genetics

For more than 80 years Budgie breeders have ensured that almost every colour or variety of Budgerigar is based on a separate gene mutation. Breeders of the vast majority of other animals, however, did not do this – they just selected bit-by-bit improvements, to create ever-prettier animals without trying to work out the

At a Glance

How the science of genetics has prevented many wonderful Budgerigar varieties from being developed, and how I hope to develop the world's first PINK Budgie.

underlying genetic mechanisms. You can strongly argue that the results for this bit-by-bit system have far exceeded the results from the separate gene mutation system that we Budgie people use. Just look at ornamental chicken varieties alone.

Chickens, ducks, cattle, goldfish, dogs, canaries, pigeons and so on were developed by selecting for ever-prettier or more precise patterns and colours. In general this happened before Mendel's laws of heredity were rediscovered and used. Mendel's systems have helped Budgie breeders enormously, but they have also very significantly hindered the creation of more beautiful varieties and colours.

The very few non-gene Budgerigar varieties are: Clearwings, Black Eyed Yellows and Black Eyed Whites, all of which were developed by one renegade, Harold Peir from Peakhurst in Sydney. One could also argue that the Darkwing, being a modified Black Eyed, is also a non-gene variety (a Darkwing Dilute looks like a Greywing – it only takes on the Clearbody appearance when combined with a Black Eyed White or Black Eyed Yellow, both of which are gene modifier based colours. My guess is that the Darkwing mutation hung around undiscovered for many years, producing messy Greywing-like birds (when combined with Dilutes, Greywings, etc) until one day, Darkwing and Black Eyed Yellow were unintentionally combined to produce the world's first Clearbody.

Think about it, the bit-by-bit system was used in Budgies to breed ever-bigger spots, ever-longer masks and so on. Just selecting for slightly better birds each generation produces huge gains over time. But, in general we did not use this technique to develop new colours and varieties. Only Harold Peir, the inventor of the Clearwing, Black Eyed Yellow and Black Eyed White, was brave and creative enough to use this method in developing varieties and colours.

Clearwing Budgerigars are modified Greywings, not a separate mutation. This is a man-made variety created by Harold Peir selecting for ever-clearer wing colour and ever-darker body colour in Australian Greywings.

You may well ask does it really matter if we just use the 'gene-only' system for creating new colours and varieties? Well, I believe that this system has severely limited our range of Budgerigar patterns and colours.

Recent research on the Budgerigar genome by Ganapathy *et al.* points to Budgies having about 16,000 genes (as against our human quota of about 19,000 genes). If genes determine every detail, then these are hopelessly inadequate numbers of genes to enable us to create the fabulous Budgerigar varieties and colours of the future. They are also hopelessly inadequate to produce a human being.

For instance, my new work on Dominant Pied patterns has helped me to estimate that there are probably many more than a thousand different hereditary micro-patterns at work: little variations on the major patterns like Banded, Winged and Rumped Pieds. In Banded Pieds alone there are thin bands and dozens of increasingly thicker bands until you get almost a full white or yellow front. Then there are chevron bands that look like army stripes (i.e. a v-shaped band) or a diamond-shaped band. There are crooked bands in hundreds of shapes too. And there are double bands in hundreds of configurations as well as a hundred types of Winged Pieds, and probably a thousand types of Rumped Pieds. There are dozens and dozens of Collared Pied types and the newer ones of cheek-patch Pieds and spot-free masked Pieds. And many, many more. All appear to have a solid hereditary basis, even if they do not segregate as neatly as Mendel's genes did.

This row of Banded Pied variants shows the huge range of heritable band types: from wide band to one with a diamond shape in the middle (third from left).

All of these above patterns and micro-patterns are hereditary.
I can confirm that no two Pieds have identical markings, so if separate genes are involved in each detail of each micro-pattern, then we could have thousands genes for Pied patterns alone ... yet there are supposed to be only a total of 16,000 Budgerigar genes all up?

There are probably hundreds of hereditary micro patterns and marking colours on the wings of Clearwings, Black Eyed Yellows and Black Eyed Whites. Similar numbers apply to spangle markings and crest types. Hereditary patterns which control feather length and width would also number in the hundreds. Then there are hundreds of spot shapes and sizes. Feet colours come in scores of hues. Beak shape and length varies enormously, as does the overall size of each bird ... and on and on it goes.

Internally, birds differ even more. Bones and joints, internal chemistry and musculature differ from bird to bird, as does width of shoulders, etc, etc. In feathering, there are birds with floppy, useless alulas, fluffy, obstructed vents, long tails and flights, plus messy secondaries – again all of these are hereditary and all vary slightly from bird to bird. Disease resistance and susceptibility genes number in their hundreds too.

Right: This baby has floppy alulas. These are the droopy black feathers hanging at the front of the wings immediately above its feet. Hereditary mechanisms control this. These feathers act like the bent-up wing tips on aeroplanes: they reduce wind turbulence.

Physical co-ordination varies from bird to bird and these micro-variations too are all hereditary.

Surely by now it must be clear that genes are not the main game in either evolution or the domestication of animals.

So what is? What on Earth can produce the hundreds of thousands of subtle variations in each animal? Yes, gene mutations play a part, but they are clearly not the main game.

Genes are rather rigid, inflexible controls that normally produce major, uniform results: e.g. they change a Green Budgie to a Blue Budgie. They also change a Normal Budgie to a Dilute or a Cinnamonwing, and so on. Mostly, genes make big, precise and predictable changes.

But in nature and with exhibition breeding, most desirable or undesirable effects involve continuous, microscopically small changes. Sort of like winding the sound up or down on the car radio. So maybe something winds the genes up or down. Something that creates smooth acceleration of change.

Contrary to what Mendel discovered, this would produce blending inheritance. Big mated to little would produce medium-sized. Then, unlike Mendel's genes, in subsequent generations the sizes would not segregate back into big or little again at all. What would happen is that a vast range of new intermediate sizes would appear. This is exactly what happens in real life.

So, in evolution, as the Earth gradually changes, the animals gradually change as well. If a Brown Bear suddenly changed from brown to white, it would probably die, since it would stand out like a sore thumb against the forest. Cooling of the planet to produce permanent snow during natural climate evolution takes tens of thousands of years. Bears that gradually produce a slightly lighter coat each generation would do very well indeed during these glacially slow processes. This is the method of origin of the Polar Bear, rather than one immediate catastrophic white mutation.

Gene volume controls

Only gene volume controls can do this sort of thing. And gene volume controls do exist and they are very common indeed. These are often bits of DNA that are not themselves genes, but they do control genes, turning them on or off, up or down. Think about it: something turns your growth on at conception and turns it off around the age of 18 or so. And almost every human is a slightly different height to anyone else.

This Black Eyed White has near-perfect colour, but he is at base a Dilute – his exquisite colour is caused by many many gene modifiers.

The difference in the face and snout of dogs, from pointy-nosed borzois and greyhounds to the bony, melon-shaped face of an English Bull Terrier, to the squashed-in face of a British Bulldog are **not** due to gene mutations. These huge changes are created by the gene volume controls acting on one basic face shape gene. In this case, the bits of DNA that control face shape are called tandem repeats. These are repeated bits of 'nonsense' DNA: AAGT, AAGT, AAGT, AAGT, AAGT repeated again and again. The more or less of these repeated elements, the shorter or longer the snout: you get almost limitless variation, without any new gene mutations at all.

These tandem repeats are what is often used to determine parentage in humans and animals since each animal has its own unique signature of repeated bits of DNA. These repeats are also used to identify and convict criminals.

Genes can also be turned off by a process called methylation, which involves the tacking of a CH_3 group onto one of the gene's bases (either cytosine or adenine).

Sometimes animals have extra copies of different forms of one gene. These un-natural, extra genes can even come from hybridising with other species. Many humans have extra Neanderthal genes from hybridising with this archaic species thousands of years ago, and science has shown that the two groups of genes act in concert to produce good or bad results.

There are other gene regulators such as micro RNAs which are neither genes nor part of the DNA. These are RNA molecules that also regulate gene expression.

Gene regulators of one sort or another are the basis of breeding winners in any competition animal (or plant). They drive variation and allow for exquisitely precise control of progeny while permitting enormous flexibility as well. Tandem repeats mutate at about 100,000 times the rate of the genes and can be rapidly assembled for fast, radical changes of any animal when needed. Although each tiny regulator only makes a very small change, you have hundreds or even thousands of them acting together on each gene. If enough of the regulators change, massive changes occur quite rapidly.

Genes occupy only about 1% of the DNA, but 80% of the DNA is **active** (search online for 'ENCODE project'), presumably mostly regulating or otherwise altering the effects of the genes.

The first gene modifier insights

The evolution and the domestication of animals and plants is overwhelmingly due to hereditary modifier elements, not genes themselves. Only in recent years did I chance on the following brilliant discoveries.

The first person to discover gene modifiers was Nobel Prize-winning scientist Barbara McClintock, who is arguably the greatest mind ever to study heredity. She is probably best known for discovering jumping genes (a.k.a. transposons). Between 1948 and 1950 she developed a theory that mobile elements regulated genes by inhibiting or modulating their actions. Her work on gene-controlling elements and gene regulation was not accepted by her contemporary scientists, and from 1953 onwards she stopped publishing her research on these controllers to avoid alienation among the scientific mainstream.

To this day, her brilliant theories on gene control are not at all well understood, even by many leading geneticists. But since the publication of the ENCODE project's discovery that while genes only make up about 1% of our DNA, an amazing 80% of our DNA is active, Barbara has been totally vindicated. Barbara McClintock was right, way beyond her wildest dreams.

Genes are the factories, and modifiers are the staff and management which run each factory. They bend genes to their will. Using a knowledge of these modifiers empowers you create tomorrow's truly great Budgerigars.

Barbara McClintock BS PhD (16 June 1902–2 September 1992) is one of my heroes. She did receive a Nobel Prize after she retired in 1983, for her work in discovering 'jumping genes', but most of her life, her work on gene 'controlling elements' was considered too radical and it was ignored. She was very disappointed in her colleagues and stopped publishing her brilliant work on how heredity really works in 1953. Her ideas have since been proven correct, and are still cutting edge today. One wonders whether her work might have been better accepted had she not been a woman. Photo: Nik Kleinberg.

The electrome

As mentioned in the section on Chimera Budgies, the electrome also plays a large part on the creation of Budgies, yet it is not a part of an animal's DNA. This is the HUGE breakthrough that many of us have awaited for decades. It finally explains the basic structure and nature of animal and plant development. All plants and animals are electrical beings where every cell is electrically active, acting as tiny batteries. They lay down the framework of all living things, from skeletons, repairs, and organs in animals, to the framework of plants.

The electrome uses the tiniest of electrical currents, around 0–90 millivolts, to make the template of our bodies, which genes are unable to do by themselves – e.g. two eyes, one nose, plus a backbone, etc. After laying down the structural plan, the electrome dictates which bit goes where – 90 millivolts creates skeletal muscle, 70 millivolts creates nerve cells, etc.

So how does this relate to breeding Budgies? The voltage changes form the blueprint of our bodies, organs, etc. These voltage changes do more than just form a blueprint, however: they actually instruct the genes when to go to work, what to do and where to do it, even though the electrome is not part of the DNA itself.

Classic electrome effects in Budgies would be Crest and Hagoromo structures. The bilateral symmetry and placement of the whorls in Hagoromos will be controlled by the electrome. The placement and shape of the crests/whorls will be electrome controlled, which fits in very well with my crest theory. Obviously, the electrome is the mechanism behind Chimeras (see 'You are electric' by Sally Adee in *New Scientist* magazine on 25 February 2023).

Thus, the ancient, humble dog, horse and goldfish breeders of Europe and Asia who worked out the bit-by-bit system of animal and plant selection over the last few thousand years were arguably more on the right track than Gregor Mendel was. Constantly selecting for slight improvements each generation produced most of the varieties and improvements in our dogs, cats, Budgies, horses, cattle, goldfish, wheat, rice, apples, pears, mangoes, cherries, lettuce, carrots, corn, tomatoes and most man-made plants or animal types.

One can argue that, useful as the science of genetics has been for Budgie breeders, it has also limited the success and creative reach of Budgie breeding considerably.

So many of the breathtakingly beautiful varieties of animals are modifier-based, not gene-based.

Consider this ... almost all pigeon, chicken, dog, cat, goldfish and koi carp colours and varieties are made mostly from gene modifiers. Many different chicken varieties are made from the **same** genes: Spangled, Pencilled and Lacewing chicken varieties are made from the same basic set of genes. It is the gene modifiers that have made the key differences between these varieties. These modifiers are sadly absent from the chicken genetics books.

Right: This is an intense reddish Violet Clearwing Budgerigar fledgling, just out of the nest. His breathtakingly perfect colour is ALL due to gene modifiers. He has perfectly clear wings, no spots on his mask, and darker body colour than a Normal Violet.

The Clearwing Budgerigar is arguably the most beautiful Budgerigar variety of all. Both the exquisite wing colour and the deep body colour are the product of modifiers; modifiers that were bent to serve a vision that Harold Peir had of a royal blue and white Budgie. Clearwings are the product of the human mind, not of a particular gene mutation.

Similarly, the Black Eyed Yellow and Black Eyed White are creations of the human mind (so much so that Black Eyed Whites and Yellows are shown in a different ANBC class to Dilutes at Australia's national show, even though Dilute is the base mutation for all Black Eyed Whites and Yellows).

Recent work by Budgie breeders in Australia has seen the Spangle modified into Melanistic and Cleartail sub-varieties. Even the 'straight' Spangle is a human-manipulated appearance of this basic mutation.

The Red Cap Oranda Goldfish is the result of an unknown breeding genius (or perhaps a group of people) somewhere in China. It is not caused by one single gene mutation. Somehow a white-spotted red goldfish was turned into a reproducible red-capped one, AND a warty head crest was added in **exactly** the same area for emphasis. Now, this fish has a 3D red hat on its head! On top of that, the Oranda has a fully divided double veil tail, plus a severe hunch back to make

This is a Red Cap Oranda goldfish. Perhaps this is mankind's greatest-ever breeding triumph – mostly accomplished by using gene modifiers over some hundreds of years by very gifted Chinese breeders.

the fish look more chunky. Mendel's theories could never produce this, nor can they produce winning Budgies on the show bench. They just produce a basic mutation.

How many other dreams are waiting for the vision of a great breeder to create? I believe that it would be relatively easy to create a White Faced Green from selecting from existing White Cap Greens. Most White Caps have areas of white around their cheek patches and spots. Surely someone can select for ever more white on the mask, until the whole face: mask, cap, the lot, is white. Whoever does that will become a legend in the Budgie world: Budgie breeders have long dreamed of producing a White Faced Green. **And it can be done.**

If you look closely at the White Cap Green below, you will notice that it has white feather tips around its cheek patches and spots. Surely a talented and dedicated breeder could select for more and more white on the mask until a White Faced Green is achieved.

I am working on another dream. I want to produce the world's first Pink Budgie. I might fail, but it might just work. And I will do it without any new mutation whatsoever. I found some very reddish-purple Heritage Violet Budgies and diluted their colour with various genes: Texas Clearbody, Fallow, Clearwing, Dilute, Cinnamonwing, Opaline and Spangle, to see if any of them left me with a pinkish colour. Some did.

Interestingly none other than Cyril Rogers, in his 1981 book *The World of Budgerigars*, said:

"Among the early exhibitors of the Visual Violets … was F. Garvey. It was this exhibitor who possessed the most brilliant and richly coloured strain of Violets in the country (UK). Garvey's birds were well known for their beautiful **pinkish tone of violet** and no-one else seemed to be able to produce this colour unless they had birds that came actually from the Garvey strain. It is now a considerable time since any bird of this **particularly rosy violet colour** have been seen on view at the shows as **the birds seen at the present time are of a more bluish violet shade.** This could mean that birds of the Garvey strain have faded out, or there may still exist remnants of the strain in some decorative aviaries where birds are not exhibited … All varieties of visual Violet birds are undoubtedly very handsome and exceedingly colourful, two of the most striking forms I have seen are the Cinnamon Violet Cobalt and the Opaline Cinnamon Violet Cobalt. In both instances, the addition of the Cinnamon character gives the birds a **beautiful, soft,**

warm, rose-tinted, violet shade, which is set off to perfection by their rich cinnamon markings."

It is clear that the potential for Amethyst and eventually **Pink** Budgies had been noticed long ago. Violets first appeared in Europe in the 1920s, so presumably by the use of the phrase 'early exhibitors' Cyril means around the 1930s and 1940s, perhaps the 1950s at the latest. The Amethyst has lain dormant for perhaps 60 years or so. It is long overdue to carry on the work of the early pioneers of reddish or pinkish Violets and their cinnamon derivatives.

This is a pinkish-lavender Budgerigar male: it is genetically a Cinnamonwing Clearwing intense, reddish violet Budgie. The Australian Heritage Budgerigar Association has decided to call this colour Amethyst since it is identical to the colour of this precious stone. Surely most breeders can see the pink in this beautiful bird. Over the years ahead, we will try to select for ever-pinker birds. One day, we hope to develop a Pink Budgie from these birds.

I am quite confident that bit-by-bit selection for ever-deeper yellow colour in Lutinos could produce an orange-coloured Lutino over time. Back in the 1960s, Sydney breeder Dave Pogson produced very intensely coloured Lutinos that were actually a light orange. I purchased his deepest-coloured pair and line bred from them for ever-deeper colour. The end result was clear orange Lutinos, but breeders of that time said: "But, Lutinos are supposed to be yellow!" So orange Lutinos sadly died out.

Nonetheless, I suspect that the science behind my scheme to create the world's first Pink Budgie might be good. I have now begun a journey: only time will tell whether or not I will join Harold Peir as another dreamer who developed a beautiful new Budgerigar variety. If I fail to achieve a clearly pink colour, at least I will have tried …

… and I haven't had so much fun in years.

Index

Published in 2024 by Reed New Holland Publishers
Sydney

Level 1, 178 Fox Valley Road, Wahroonga, NSW 2076, Australia

newhollandpublishers.com

A record of this book is held at the National Library of Australia.

ISBN 978 1 76079 610 5

Managing Director: Fiona Schultz
Publisher and Project Editor: Simon Papps
Designer: Andrew Davies
Production Director: Arlene Gippert

Printed in China

10 9 8 7 6 5 4 3

OTHER TITLES BY REED NEW HOLLAND INCLUDE:

Slater Field Guide to Australian Birds. Third Edition
Peter Slater, Pat Slater and Raoul Slater
ISBN 978 1 92107 316 8

Field Guide to Birds of North Queensland. Second Edition
Phil Gregory and Jun Matsui
ISBN 978 1 92554 625 5

Australian Birds In Pictures
Matthew Jones and Duade Paton
ISBN 978 1 92554 634 7

Parrot Conservation
Rosemary Low
ISBN 978 1 92554 646 0

Encounters With Australian Birds
Stephanie Jackson
ISBN 978 1 92554 695 8

A First Book of Beautiful Bird Songs (book with speaker)
Fred van Gessel
ISBN 978 1 92554 677 4

For details of these books and hundreds of other Natural History titles see
newhollandpublishers.com and follow ReedNewHolland on Facebook

 ReedNewHolland
 @NewHollandPublishers and @ReedNewHolland